Love Never Fails

Ron Johnson

2st Edition

Copyright © 2015 by Ron Johnson

Published by: Freedom House.

All rights reserved.

Please contact the author at ronandjennyjohnson@yahoo.com if you would like to reproduce this book or sections of the book for your own purposes. All personal correspondence will receive a reply.

Printed in the United States of America

ISBN 1511489642

EAN 978-1511489645

Contents

Introduction	1
Who Is Jenny Lynn Johnson?	3
The Wedding	13
The Honeymoon	21
The Early Years	34
That Was Unusual	44
Something's Not Right	49
The Diagnosis	56
I Love You	67
Be In Health	79
The Motor Home	88
New Adventures	97
Finding the Missing Link	107
Miracles Across America	125
The Joy of the Lord	140
On The Road	154
The Spider Bite	166
Caring For My Baby	171
In Love with Jesus	181
Time With Jenny	190
Your Inheritance	194
Freedom from Fear	203
Hope for the Future	217
Doctor Jesus	231
Sickness and Faith	239
Return to Carrabelle Beach	253
Hospice	261
Jenny is With Me Now	275
After She Left	281

Jenny's First Love 287
Ron's First Love 294
When Father God Took Lazarus Home 298
A Closing Thought 304

Introduction

I tell everyone Jenny and I are the most blessed couple in the world and we are! I tell everyone we have the most blessed marriage of anyone I know and I believe we do! So why are we so blessed? Let me back up a couple years to show you why I believe we are so blessed.

I have been extremely blessed by God to be on this Journey! I am going to share the blessings with you but I want to preface this book by saying I do not want to bring any guilt or shame to anyone that might be on a similar journey. The decisions you make depend on your circumstances.

I know we would be on a completely different walk of life if I were the one sick and Jenny had to decide what course to take in our life. I know Jenny would want to take care of me if she could but some of the care would be humanly impossible for her.

You will see the circumstances I'm in and how God has given me strength to overcome them. Jenny literally would not be able to pick me up and carry me around. So the choices she would make in being a caregiver for me would be completely different then I made, and would not reflect any lack of love for me. So if you had to put your loved one in a home for care, I believe God will bless your decisions also. I know if you ask God into your decisions, you will know you are making the right ones and you will know God is blessing them!!!

On November 11, 1972, Jenny chose me and I chose her to live with forever. One of our wedding presents from my parents was a little prayer book. In that prayer book was a special prayer Jenny prayed all our married life. The prayer was titled, FOR A HAPPY MARRIED LIFE, and it went like this:

> Lord bless and preserve my cherished husband; whom you have given me. Let his life be long and blessed, comfortable and holy; let me forever be a blessing and a comfort to him, a sharer in all his sorrows,

a consolation in all the accidents and trials of life. Make me forever loveable in his eyes, and forever dear to him. Unite his heart to mind in the fondest love and holiness, and mine to him in sweetness and charity. Keep me from all ungentleness; make me humble, yet strong and helpful that we may delight in each other according to your blessed word. May both of us rejoice in you Father God, having our portion in the love and service of God forever. In the name of Jesus I pray.

I believe Jenny's prayer is the reason we have such a blessed marriage. It proves to me beyond any doubt that God rewards us with what we ask for when the request lines up with His will. I know Jesus heard Jenny's prayers and we have been blessed forever! Thank you Jesus, I love you forever too!!!!

Who Is Jenny Lynn Johnson?

Was Jenny just a cute little girl born on May 23, 1954? Here is Jenny's story. You decide.

I met my Jenny in April of 1972. Jenny was a foster child all her youth and lived in many different foster homes around the Cincinnati area. Actually very little is known about the first 17 years of Jenny's life because Jenny would not talk about it. She really didn't want people to know she was in foster homes because Jenny did not want people feeling sorry for her. She used to say, "I just want to be normal." The following is what I do know about her youth and is as complete and accurate as possible.

Jenny lived with her mother, Rosemary, in downtown Cincinnati and was the fifth of seven children, we think. Jenny's mother went from apartment to apartment whenever the rent was due. As best as I can remember, when Jenny was about 3 or 4 years old she thought of her sister Florence as her provider. Florence, who was about 2 years older then Jenny, seemed to be very street smart.

Florence who preferred to be called Flo, played together with Jenny and looked after Jenny and provided their meals. Flo told me how they worked as a team. She would have Jenny go into the same little neighborhood grocery store every morning and ask the storeowner, "What time is it?" Then the storeowner would walk all the way to the back of the store to check the time. While he was back there, Flo would run in, grab some candy bars, and run back out. When the storeowner returned to the front of the store, he would tell Jenny what time it was and Jenny would thank him. Jenny then went out to meet Flo and the two of them would have breakfast on his front steps. Can you imagine two little girls, Jenny and Flo, just 3 and 5 years old wearing nothing but their dirty underwear, barefoot, eating the candy bars they had just stolen while sitting on the store owner's front step?

Jenny and her sister Florence had a source of income too. They would beg for money from drunks as they came out of the bars at two o'clock in the morning. Some drunks would reach in their pocket and give them change. Others would act like they were reaching into their pocket and instead unzip their pants and try to pee on them. Flo talked about how they slept in hallways and on steps when their mother was on a binge. Jenny remembers having a little brother they called Bugs because he played with the bugs in the apartment. She also recalled seeing Bugs trying to smoke a cigar, only to find out it was human waste that had dried on the floor.

Thank God someone called Children's Services and as Jenny remembers, one day a car pulled up and some nuns asked Jenny and Flo if they wanted a pretty dress. They were excited and accepted the dress. The nuns then asked Jenny and Flo to get in the car. I'm not sure of the details but that is how Jenny remembered going to Allen House in Cincinnati. Allen House must have been a place to house foster children until the children were placed in foster homes.

They went to Allen House and were put into the foster care system. Jenny told me they hated it there. Her whole life, Jenny bore a scar on her leg from trying to escape. Flo devised the escape plan. It was quite simple really. They got on the swing set and would swing as high as possible and use the momentum from the swing to jump over the barbed wire fence. Flo cleared the barbed wire fence but Jenny did not, thus the scar on her leg. On a later attempt they cleared the fence, ran away, and went to a relative in Kentucky. Their aunt however turned them back into the authorities.

In the foster system Jenny and Flo were placed together most of the time. Their life in the system was quite an experience. I believe Jenny was around 5 years old when Florence and Jenny were placed in a two-story home. In this home the two of them lived on the second floor, which was only accessible through what is called a hide-a-stairs. That is a stair system that folds up like a ladder and retracts into the ceiling. The stairs needed to be closed during the night so the hallway on the first floor was open and accessible to walk through. When Jenny and Flo went to bed they were literally closed in the upstairs bedroom all night.

Jenny recalled one afternoon while living in that home, she saw what she thought was a box of chocolates on the kitchen table. She ate some, only to find out that night the chocolate was Ex-Lax, a laxative. Jenny was locked upstairs like usual because the hide-a-stairs was closed for the night, she soiled herself and the closet where she tried to hide the mess. The next day was not a pleasant one for her, to say the least. Sometime after that they were removed from that house and went back to Allen House again.

Florence told me that whenever they were back in Allen House, their mother Rosemary would usually come to see them. Someone from Allen House would tell Jenny and Florence that their mother had come to see them and Jenny would ask, "Is Rosemary drunk?" If she was, Jenny would not go visit her. Florence, however, would visit with Rosemary drunk, and usually came back crying.

Jenny did tell me about one night while in Allen House; when some children started beating her up. She managed to scream out for help and, as Jenny recalls, a huge black lady came to rescue her. This lady put the "fear of God into the bad kids," and put the love of God into my Jenny! Jenny said she slept well that night because she knew that lady was looking out for her. Jenny never talked much about her childhood but she talked often about how nice that lady was. If you have ever wondered if children remember those special acts of kindness—the ones adults do and then wonder if children even remember when they get older, I can tell Jenny did.

Yes Jenny remembered the protection of that nice black lady, Jenny always had such a soft spot in her heart for black people, especially women with children. Even 40 years later, while stricken with Pick's Decease, Jenny will go out of her way to be nice to black people. I guess it is safe to say God's love poured out of that lady and into Jenny, and God's love passed through Jenny to everyone else Jenny met. The good deed Jenny received as a child turned in to a lifetime of good deeds. Thank you Jesus for putting your love and your protection into the heart of this black lady and then allowing your love and protection to flow through her into my Jenny.

Jenny recalled one day her mother came to Allen House to pick her and Flo up. Her mother had met a man who was rich and had an apartment. This man told the girls they didn't have to go back to Allen House any more. They could live with Rosemary and him. That night her mother fixed a spaghetti dinner. They had a table with real dishes. Jenny was really impressed with the table and the dishes. And she was really hungry. When they sat down to eat, the man was at the head of the table, and as he took his first bite of spaghetti he found a hair in it. He became so angry he flipped the whole table over and started fighting with Rosemary. Jenny and Florence hid in another room until her mom and the man went storming out to a bar. Jenny remembers watching her little brother licking the food off the floor and off the broken dishes. Just two days later Jenny and Flo were back at Allen House; Jenny said she never saw that man again.

Jenny told me one other story about another foster home. Her foster parents there had a natural born son. He would do bad things, like break something of his mom's, and then blame Florence. When asked Florence denied breaking the thing, her denial resulted in Florence receiving a whipping for lying. Sometime later the boy broke something again but this time he blamed Jenny for it. Jenny was asked by her foster parents if she had broken the thing, Jenny would just say, "I did it, but I won't do it again." Jenny would get praised for telling the truth. So the boy only blamed Florence for bad things he did. Eventually the family asked the social worker to take Flo out of the home. Jenny had the option to stay with those people but she chose to go with Flo back to Allen House.

At one point Jenny and Flo went into another foster home in Reading, Ohio. They lived there for about 4 years. Jenny really liked her foster father, whom I'll call Frank. Frank worked out of town all week and was only home on weekends. He had a pilot's license and loved to fly a small single engine plane. Jenny was afraid of flying and afraid of heights, but went with him because it made him happy. Every time they flew, Jenny would get sick and throw up. Frank told Jenny she would get used to flying and I think at some point Jenny did stop throwing up. Frank was a very good influence on Jenny, and Jenny loved him. She referred to him as "Dad."

Frank's family went to a Baptist church and Jenny sung in the choir. She loved the minister and his wife. The church had a lot of activities and children's events for Jenny to participate in. Jenny and the other children had a nickname for the pastor. They called him "Rev". Jenny really liked going to church there because she had made friends and had a lot of fun at that church. She loved Rev and his wife who was the youth leader.

In school Jenny was taking home-making classes and learning to sew and cook. Jenny already knew what she wanted in life and was laying the foundation for a good life. Jenny chose her friends wisely and had the respect of her peers at school and church. She had a good support system, and some of Jenny's friends' parents stood up for Jenny when they saw the unjustness going on in the foster home.

That is all I know about the first 16 years of Jenny's life. Jenny put her younger years. Jenny did not want anyone to know her past because she did not want people to feel sorry for her.

At age 17, Jenny was suddenly removed from Frank's home. Living conditions there had gotten so bad. One Friday night Jenny ran away from home. She spent the night at her girlfriend's house. The girlfriend's mother covered for Jenny when the police came looking for Jenny. The next day Jenny went home, but her foster mother was so mad she took Jenny to a juvenile detention center. There her foster mother told the officer, Jenny was out of control. She told the officer Jenny was on drugs, alcohol, and she said Jenny was a whore.

This all happened on a Saturday morning so the juvenile system had to keep Jenny there until Monday morning for a hearing. Jenny reveled to me how afraid she was there. They have to do a search and it was very intimidating and embarrassing.

When her foster mother came into the courtroom Monday morning, the judge was going to release Jenny back to her but her foster mother started screaming about the same charges she told the officer. The judge said we will see about this and ordered tests to be done and the hearing to reconvene on Wednesday.

On Wednesday afternoon when court reconvened, her foster mother again started screaming about what a whore Jenny was and how Jenny was on drugs and out of control. The judge quieted her mother and told her the tests were completed and Jenny had no drugs in her system, not even in her hair. The test also proved Jenny was not sexually active. The judge declared her foster mother an unfit parent and had her foster parenting license taken away by the State of Ohio.

Jenny had to go back to Allen House again and she knew the chances of someone wanting a 17 year old girl was pretty slim. It turned out she was not there too long when Jenny was placed in another home. Later she told me about her first day in that home. Naturally she didn't know her new foster parents and they didn't know Jenny. When they sat down to eat dinner, Jenny put her napkin on her lap. That night the new foster parents told her she stay because she had good table manners. This family had two little boys they we fostering also.

Her foster father in this new home was my boss, Don. He ran a plumbing business out of his house. Jenny lived there for a while before I started working for Don. I was 23 years old and had just returned home from a 4-year hitch in the navy. The moment I met Jenny I was attracted to her. I mean she was beautiful and had the prettiest smile I had ever seen.

The routine at Don's house was for all the plumbers to meet in Don's kitchen every morning and there we received our work orders for the day. In the evening we all came back to Don's house and would have a cup of coffee while filling out our time sheet. Usually Jenny would make the coffee and then sit down and have a cup with us plumbers. I was always amazed with her. She would speak her mind and was very opinionated for a 17-year old. Almost everyday I would end up laughing about some comment she would make.

I was immediately attracted to Jenny but didn't want to let on because Jenny was already going steady, and I didn't want to cause a break up if she was really happy with her boy friend. Also, I didn't want to date someone so young. I was six years older than her. I didn't want to date a teeny-bopper with a curfew! As the weeks went by I realized I really would like to date Jenny.

One Friday night I came in from work late and started filling out my time sheet in the kitchen like usual. Except this night Jenny was doing the dishes and her foster parents where out for the evening. Jenny asked me if I would like a cup of coffee, to which I said yes. As we talked, Jenny continued doing the dishes. Jenny's history had made her personality very hardened. She tried to act tough like nothing could get to her. She had no one to back her up, so she looked out for herself by hiding her emotions behind her hard personality.

While I was filling out my time sheet, I watched Jenny doing the dishes. I told her, "Jenny you act so hard but I believe under your hard façade there is a special, sweet little Jenny just aching to come out." Jenny turned around and, with a dish in one hand and a cigarette in her mouth, she flipped me the bird with her other hand! I guess Jenny was really saying, I like you but you can't see through me; I am tough, and I'm hard, and I'm surely not sweet.

The next weekend Jenny broke up with her boyfriend. A couple weeks later we started dating. We fought so much on our dates, you might say every date we went on, we were at war. I didn't realize then but Jenny was establishing the ground rules for a long term relationship. Jenny had a great relationship with Jesus and He had given Jenny an inner strength I had never witnessed before. Jenny fought for her own rights and let me know in no uncertain terms that this is the way it would be if you want to date me! God's strength was so strong in Jenny; I couldn't help but admire her courage, her morals, and especially her love of God. I had never witnessed such conviction before.

I was six years older than Jenny, so I thought I was her senior and had the right to tell her the way things should be. For example I remember telling Jenny, "Next week we are going to go to (where ever), so Friday night I will pick you up at six." Jenny responded with, "I'll think about it." Even though I would see her every day at my boss's house as we plumbers filled out our time sheets and had coffee in his kitchen, Jenny never let on. I never knew if she really liked me or not.

I loved her feistiness and the way she stood up to me. She had no place to go, no one to back her up, and the home she was living in was not the greatest. But she would not even think of backing down. Fear never entered her thinking. She trusted God to look after her and He was her security.

I was already in love with her and just hoped it didn't show too much. I remember the first time we went to Coney Island on a date to the world's largest swimming pool; I couldn't wait to see Jenny in her swimming suit. When Jenny came out of the water her long brown hair was all pulled back. I looked at her pretty face and said, "I hope you never have a hairdo with bangs." Jenny was puzzled and asked why. I said, "You have the prettiest face and it would be a shame to cover any of it. Even your ears are cute." Jenny looked away (to hide a tear I think).

A few months went by and things were not going well in that foster home. The circumstances were less than tolerable. Her foster parents were really good people but they were trying to adopt two young boys. The boys were 3 and 5 years old and had been abused by their biological parents. The adoption was not going good and the pressure on Cathy, the foster mother, was taking a toll on her.

This is what I believe was happening to Cathy because the adoption was not going well for the boys. Cathy became overbearing and was taking discipline too far. If either one of the boys did anything wrong, Cathy overreacted big time. So the boys started gravitating toward Jenny for comfort and love. The boys would run to Jenny when she came home from high school. At night they wanted to sleep in Jenny's room. This really upset Cathy, so she started making Jenny's life miserable.

Sometimes when I would show up to take Jenny on a date, Cathy would come to the front door and tell me that Jenny had stormed out of the house. She had a certain glee about the fact I was there for a date and Jenny was not there. What her foster mother didn't understand was that Jenny's security was in God. When Jenny needed help she turned to God, and therefore I knew Jenny was in church.

Just two blocks from her house was an old church with big stained glass windows. I knew that is where I would find Jenny. Sometimes she just wanted to be left alone, so I would go to the back of church and wait and listen. Jenny told me she could hear God talking to her out loud. After Jenny talked to God for awhile we would go on our date. When I inquired as to what happened at home, Jenny said that God took care of it. I truly loved the way Jenny went directly to God for guidance. I was so in love with her and I wanted to make things right between her and her foster parents but I didn't know how. I simply didn't know what to do. Now looking back I am sure glad Jenny had Jesus in her life.

Jenny turned 18 and a couple of weeks later I took her out of that house. We had no place to go because I had only been home from the Navy five months and I was living at my parent's home trying to save money. My parents let Jenny stay at their house for a while because they had a whole second floor that was not being used. Jenny was going to high school and I had found a new job working nights. We rarely saw each other except on weekends.

Two weeks later, on a nice Saturday afternoon, I took Jenny to see an apartment that needed a lot of work. The landlord and I had worked out a plan: if I did the work, he would pay for the paint and materials to fix up the apartment. I ask Jenny if she would like her own apartment. She was excited but reserved. I told Jenny, "Jenny I have the money to rent you an apartment and I want you to know there is no obligation on your part." Even if you want to date other guys you can. I just want to provide a nice place for you to live in as long as you want. If you decide to date other people you can and I will still pay the rent. I assured her I would get her furniture and help her in any way possible.

She looked at me like I had two heads. Then she said, "I don't want to live alone." Jenny really surprised me with her comment. I mean I had never met someone with such high moral standards. I didn't know what she meant, so I asked if she wanted me to live with her. Jenny said NO WAY; I would never shack up with someone! She said I will not live with anyone!

Just then I realized my dream of marring Jenny might come true. The girl I loved was practically asking me to marry her. With all my heart I wanted to marry Jenny, almost from the day I met her. So I asked, "Jenny are you asking me to marry you?" Jenny gave me a great big BIG hug and said, "I thought you would never ask." Tears came down both our eyes and life actually stood still for a while. Later Jenny told me, "You know, Ron that had to be the world's worst proposal!"

We told the landlord we wanted the apartment. We then went to a park and sat and held each other on a blanket in the grass until the stars came out, and for the first time I told Jenny, "I love you".

You see before I went into the Navy I had fallen in love with a girl; I'll call her Diane. We dated for months and I thought we would marry. I freely told her I loved her on every date. Then for some reason I fell out of love for her and I didn't know why. I prayed to God to let me fall back in love with her because she was still in love with me. I tried to fake it for awhile because I just did not want to hurt her. She was sweet and loving, and I couldn't figure why I was not in love with her anymore, but I just wasn't.

Finally I told Diane that I was sorry I did not love her and she cried, we both cried, and I dropped her off at her house and actually thought about suicide. I swore to myself that I would never tell a girl I loved her until I was totally sure I was going to marry her. I saw the hurt in Diane's eyes and I knew I could never tell anyone I loved them unless I was totally sure. I will never hurt anyone again. I had shared this story with Jenny the first time she told me she loved me because I knew she was waiting for me to tell her I love you back. I told her I will never tell you I love you unless I am absolutely 100% sure I will marry you.

Now the truth was out of the bag. We were going to get married for sure. Now I couldn't stop telling Jenny, I LOVE YOU. I knew we were going to get married and Jenny was telling me how the wedding would be. I thought to myself, "This is your big day, girl," and so I told her I would do everything in my power to make it special for her.

Jenny saying yes to me was the greatest gift God could give anyone! We talked about family, church, and children. We talked about God's timing for children. We had never been sexually active and we decided we would not use any kind of birth control after we were married. It was our belief that children are a gift from God, so it takes three to make a baby, Jenny and I, and God. Children are a blessing and therefore God determines when you get blessed.

We didn't want this day to ever end. God sure does work in mysterious ways. All I started out to do was ask Jenny if she wanted her own apartment. That simple question ended up giving me the nerve to ask Jenny to marry me. The answer was a lifelong commitment to love and life together forever. Jenny's "yes" was the right answer to all my prayers, hopes, and dreams. Thank you Jesus!

So is Jenny just a cute little girl born May 23, 1954? No, Jenny is more—a lot more, as you will see. God had a plan for my Jenny and He will see it through.

The Wedding

The day after our engagement, Jenny and I went to church. We then went back to my Mom and Dad's house to tell them about our engagement. We wanted to see their reaction. I'll never forget my Moms response. She told Jenny, "I hope you can do something with Ron's temper." Dad wanted to know, "How big a wedding do you want?"

Their reaction meant a lot to me because I was so in love with Jenny but somewhere down deep inside of me I was afraid my love was infatuation. Truthfully I think I was afraid my love for Jenny might die like it did for Diane and I might hurt Jenny somehow. I still didn't know how or why I fell out of love with Diane, so I prayed to God, please God I never want to hurt anyone with my love and please God never let me fall out of love for Jenny. Jesus definitely answers prayers!

Mom and Dad's reaction to our engagement was a great big green light. They weren't afraid of Jenny's age or the fact Jenny was just starting her senior year in high school. I don't know this for a fact but I think they were impressed with how mature Jenny was; I know I was. Finally I felt released to tell Jenny I love you and I could tell everyone we are in love. Just being able to tell everyone how much I loved my Jenny was a blessing in my spirit.

I remember years before when I was in the Navy hospital in Charleston, S.C for a few months. I prayed for God to mend Diane's heart and bless her with someone else to love. As I prayed, I remember feeling a release from God about Diane, and so I started praying for someone to love myself, and someone I would never hurt like I did Diane. The answer to my prayer came years later when Jesus sent Jenny into my life for me to love. I am so blessed to know Jesus answers prayers.

We left Mom and Dad's house and started wedding planning. We planned for hours and Jenny told me she wanted Frank, her former foster father, to walk her down the aisle. So we went to his house to announce our engagement to him. Jenny asked Frank to walk her down the aisle. Frank was excited, but his wife saw an opportunity to wield her power. She said Frank could walk Jenny down the aisle only if her daughter Jane was the maid of honor. Jenny had already picked her maid of honor so Jane couldn't be the maid of honor.

Frank was the only father figure Jenny had ever had, and she really wanted him to walk her down the aisle. This was a big disappointment for Jenny. I tried to comfort her, but with little success. Jenny just wanted to go back to the church with the big windows and sit alone with God for a while. I knew God would comfort Jenny, and He did. Thank you God for looking out for Jenny and I.

The next step was securing a church and setting a date. While dating, we went to a Catholic Church and Jenny started taking conversion lessons just because she had so many questions about Catholics. After talking to the priest and setting a date, Jenny wanted to share the big news about her wedding with her friends Rev. and his wife. We went to her old church but everyone had left for the day so we decided to come back next Sunday.

The following Sunday we went to her church only to find out that Rev. and his wife were divorced. Without Rev's wife, the youth ministry had fallen apart. The church was fractured and most of Jenny's friends were gone. This was very hard on Jenny and she was sad all Sunday afternoon. We spent the rest of the day talking about our wedding but not making any definite decisions.

One day Mom told us we needed to go register for wedding gifts. I had no idea that this is how people pick gifts for your wedding. So off we went. Jenny and I started filling out the registry and picking out gifts. When we were only part way finished with our list Jenny started looking at china. I thought to myself, "How stupid. We need all the basics, not china." But when I told Jenny my thoughts, she simply said, "China is very important to me."

So I went back over to where the toasters were and started watching Jenny from a distance. I watched as she carefully looked at every design. How some designs really lit her little face up! I realized this was important to her and if it was that important to her, I wanted to be part of her joy. I think Jenny was already visualizing a big Thanksgiving Day meal in the dining room with the whole family there.

Now here it is, 35 years later, and we still have the wedding china. Thank you so much Jesus.

For our first 24 years of marriage, every time Jenny set the dining room table with her china, she really enjoyed it. We still have some of our other wedding presents too but I thank God Jenny picked out the china, because of how special it really is. Jenny was so young then and yet had so much wisdom; I loved her more and more every day. If there is really such a thing as a cup running over with love, our cups were truly overflowing. Jenny was teaching me the importance of things I had never thought about. All I knew was, if I could somehow put Jenny inside my skin, we would still not be close enough.

The next week we went to pick out her wedding dress. I had seen in movies when the bride picks out her dress her mother always helped her. This was supposed to be a special time between the mother and the bride. I felt a little sorrow in my heart for Jenny, not having a mother to help her pick the dress, but Jenny's happiness removed my sadness immediately.

As I sat outside the dressing room I thought how this could take days and a lot of trips to a lot of stores—after all, the dress is very important. Wrong. Jenny was out of the dressing room and ready to go in a half-hour. I asked where to now? Jenny said, "We are done." I was pleasantly surprised and asked if she was sure. Jenny assured me she had the dress she wanted.

As it turned out Jenny had dreamed about her wedding day for years, and knew from looking at wedding dress books, which dress she wanted. She even knew which store carried it. I'm sure glad she found it and it was affordable. Having the dress of her dreams made Jenny so happy and made her even more excited for our wedding day.

Anyone who has planned a wedding knows how stressful it can be. We received a nice reprieve from the hustle and bustle when we went to Grandma's house. My grandma is a very special lady. Years ago, Grandma's husband died quite suddenly, leaving Grandma to raise seven young children on her own. For an income, Grandma took up sowing and baking. She totally mastered both skills. She sewed aprons that were sold at stores and she could not keep up with the demand.

I liked Grandma's baking the most. Grandma made the best bread on earth. She is one of the reasons I'm looking forward to going to heaven. Grandma's house was built by her two sons and five son-in-laws. It was a small concrete block house that was very hard to heat. But even with the heating problems of Grandma's house, I never remember being cold there; I think Grandma's house was warm because even on the coldest days of winter, Grandma's house was filled with her love. Also if Grandma knew you were coming, her house was filled with the smell of warm fresh baked bread.

Jenny and I were excited to see Grandma and tell her about our wedding. I think Grandma knew I had an alternative reason for coming and so she asked, "Jenny, would you like to learn how to make bread?" We set a date for Jenny and I to go to Grandma's house and spend the day with her.

When the day finally came, Jenny and Grandma hit it off really well and I'm proud to say Jenny carried on Grandma's bread baking skills forever. The slow pace at Grandma's house was such a nice reprieve from planning the wedding. Grandma had a way about putting things into perspective without saying a word.

Jenny and I had to design our wedding invitations. Most invitations read formally: "The parents of the bride wish to invite you…" etc. Our invitation simply stated, "Jenny and Ron request the pleasure of your company at our marriage on Saturday November 11, 1972, with the reception at Mom and Dad's house 2000 Hunt Rd. Reading, Ohio." Jenny took on the responsibility of sending out the invitations. My mom gave Jenny a list of all the relatives to invite. I remember a couple days after Jenny had mailed them all out, Mom asked her, "Did you send one to Aunt Dorothy?" Jenny had only met a few of my relatives, so I was amazed when she said, "You mean Busmeyer's on East Mill Street?" Mom nodded and Jenny said, "Yes, I did."

Our wedding would not be complete without mentioning our friends Tom and Lori. I babysat their children when I was in high school. Tom owned his own jewelry store so I naturally bought our wedding rings from him. Lori was very much involved in the planing and the traditions of the wedding. She taught us about "Something old and something new, something borrowed and something blue." They bought our toasting glasses and the wedding cake decoration, a cross with a double ring. We are very grateful and very blessed to have their wonderful friendship all these years. Their friendship has truly been a big blessing and more than that, a guiding light in time of need.

When we went to pick out a wedding cake, I thought Jenny picked the prettiest cake I had ever seen. I didn't know Jenny's wedding dress was white with light blue ribbons. The cake Jenny picked was light blue and had white ribbons and white flowers on it. I guess that isn't such a big deal but I thought Jenny was amazing.

My mom was amazing too. She made all the bridesmaids dresses, and they were perfect in every detail. When she realized I was running out of money she suggested we have the reception in their basement. It would be crowded and there was no room to dance or have music but it was finished off real nice and we had a great reception there. Mom and her sister made all the finger sandwiches and snacks ahead of time. Our wedding and reception went great because Mom's attention to detail was unbelievable. She had managed two of my sister's weddings already and her experience was on display. She organized everything, she had neighbors help with serving, and Dad ran the bar and managed the drinks. They had the house spotless and everything went great. Mom and Dad were so instrumental in making our wedding day extraordinary.

Jenny had set some personal goals for our wedding. One was to lose 10 pounds; the other was to grow her fingernails. She was succeeding in both. She was down about 7 pounds and that put her weight at 99 pounds. And her nails were long and trimmed. There was just one more thing to make her wedding complete.

Jenny wanted to talk to Frank one more time about being in the wedding. She had prepared her argument to try to win over Frank's wife. She wanted to go alone because she knew Frank's wife disliked Catholics. Jenny was determined and I knew better than to try to stop her. So I dropped her off at Frank's house by herself and parked down the street like she wished.

When Jenny came to the car she was crying and her finger nails were completely bitten off. I ask Jenny what happened? Jenny just wanted to leave. Jenny said she was upset mostly because Frank looked so bad. She said he just looked so tired and worn out. His face looked drawn and old but Frank was always so strong and healthy. Jenny had had enough rejection to last a lifetime. (Frank died of Leukemia about 13 months later).

As our wedding day came closer everything was falling into place. Jenny asked my dad to walk her down the aisle and Dad said he would be extremely honored. Jenny completed her conversion lessons and was baptized Catholic. A couple weeks later she made her First Communion. We both went to Pre-Cana lessons but didn't see any benefit so we figured a way around them. Jenny picked out the songs for our wedding and they were beautiful. Mom and Dad had the house in order for the reception and it looked great.

Dad let us use their Winnebago motor home for our honeymoon camper. It was literally a box on wheels, no bigger than a pick-up truck but it was ours to use and we felt great in it. I had fixed the furnace and serviced a couple of other things. The love box was ready to go!

We had also rented the apartment I talked about earlier. It needed a lot of work. The last tenant had stayed for 15 years, so Jenny and I had our work cut out for us. We washed the walls and painted them. We stripped the hard floors and refinished them. While painting the bedroom, I painted the words I LOVE YOU JENNY on the wall with a roller. The letters were about four-foot high and across the entire wall. Even with three or four coats of new paint, you could still read I LOVE YOU JENNY on that wall. We added a chair rail in the kitchen and a two-tone paint job. Jenny stripped the light fixtures and outlet covers, and scrubbed the basement walls and floor. When the landlord came in for the inspection he was impressed.

My Mom found a 10-dollar stove in the paper and I went and bought it. We bought our bedroom furniture new. I told Jenny I wanted her to have a nice set of furniture because it would last us forever. She picked a nice set and 35 years later we still have it in our bedroom. Our apartment was now clean, Jenny had a stove and nice bedroom furniture, and now we had a place to come home to after our honeymoon. Also I had fixed an old Crosley shelf-a-door refrigerator so we were set.

Jenny and I really couldn't wait to get married. We were both virgins and trying real hard to stay that way. I think God knew a four month engagement was all we could handle, so God kept us real busy and out of trouble. Thank you Jesus.

Joe, my best friend ever was stationed in Mobile, Alabama. Joe and I met in the Navy. He was still on active duty and we would kid each other saying our friendship is the only good thing we got out of the Navy. When Joe got married a year earlier, I was his best man. Now he was going to be my best man, so that made us the best men! Joe and his wife Renee arrived the day before the wedding and helped us with the last minute details.

On the wedding day Joe and I left Dad's house to go to the apartment and get dressed in the tuxedos. We had plenty of time so I showed Joe the furniture Jenny picked out and our stove. Then we started getting our tuxedos on for the wedding. I got upset because my tux didn't fit. Joe's tux didn't fit him either. I must have been nervous. Thank God Joe wasn't because it turned out I had mixed up the boxes when I handed Joe his tux. He had mine and I had his. By the time we got to church everyone was wondering, are they coming?

I remember looking at Mom and seeing her big sigh of relief. It was really great to see Joe and Renee again, and have them meet my Jenny. Our friendship has lasted all these years and Jenny and I both cherish their friendship.

Finally the big day had arrived. Jenny looked gloriously beautiful in her wedding gown. She cried as Dad walked her up the aisle and then started smiling when our eyes met. As we stood before God and all our friends and relatives, I thought how awesome, all these people took time out of their busy schedule to come and see Jenny and I get married.

I knew in my heart how special Jenny was to me, but it seemed as though everyone there could see her specialness too, her love and our joy. I remember Jenny saying, "I do" with no hesitation and as she put the ring on my finger I thought, "I'll never take it off." My ring has not been off my finger for even one second in over 42 years and I will keep it on my finger forever. Jenny's green eyes looked so radiant when I put her ring on her finger. Her eyes told me beyond any doubt, this was forever. In just a heartbeat we were walking down the aisle, everyone was smiling and joy was in the air. We had to take some pictures and then off to Mom and Dad's house.

The reception was very crowded but warm with happiness. One of my uncles reached into his pocket and gave me a 5-dollar bill. He said, "Buy a nice meal on your honeymoon." Jenny and I did all the normal things a bride and groom do. We cut the cake and Joe gave our toast. All too quickly the wedding and the reception was over. As we headed for the Carousel Inn to spend the night, I thought, "Someone pinch me and tell me this isn't a dream."

We were like on the top of a wave, riding the crest, for we knew we were starting a new life together. Phase one was the wedding and reception, and phase two was our honeymoon.

We had made reservations at the Carousel Inn. As we headed to our room some people saw Jenny in her wedding gown and started shouting, "Newlyweds! Let's get them!" We ran to our room and locked the door. They politely knocked and we politely did not answer. The bed in our room was the biggest bed I have ever slept in. We did, well, you know what people can't wait to do on their wedding night, and then fell asleep. Around 2am, I awoke and wanted to kiss Jenny, but the bed was so big I spent the rest of the night looking for her.

The next morning we overslept and almost missed the 12:30 mass, so we hurried up and ran off to church. Reality had not set in yet, but it was waiting around the bend. It almost felt weird going back to the church we were just married in. Less than 20 hours ago the church was full of our friends, relatives, and love, but now it was just full of people. After church we were off to Mom and Dad's to pick up the love box, and we finally took off on our honeymoon. YEE-HAW!!

The Honeymoon

DAY 1

We were so happy to be on our honeymoon! We started north on I-71 heading towards Niagara Falls. I think we were both still exhausted because we stopped at the first rest area, about 40 miles from Mom and Dad's house. We converted the table into the bed and we both slept for four hours.

The first night we camped near Cleveland, we arrived late so the campground office was closed. I checked and the water was still on in the bathhouse. We were the only ones in the campground, and I wanted to take a shower with my wife. Jenny was afraid someone would come in and see us because there was no lock on the door to the bathroom and Jenny would not agree to going into the men's room to take a shower with me, so I had to improvise. I carried a wooden picnic table into the bathhouse to block the door. We had our first shower together and argued about the temperature of the water. I found out I still had a lot to learn. Jenny and I had a great time even though we could not agree on the water temperature.

DAY 2

Still on our way to Niagara Falls, so much for an early start. Jenny's cooking was surprisingly good. The first meal Jenny ever cooked for me was back when she still lived in the last foster home. She made pork chops. Her foster brother Billy summed up the meal when he asked for some more burnt toast.

Knowing we were going to be camping in cold weather, I didn't put water in the camper for fear the water lines would freeze. So we had to do dishes in the campground bathhouse. This turned out to be quite a job. Although Jenny didn't complain, cleaning the dishes was a hard job because we had to carry the dishes to and from the bathhouse in the cold. Most of the time Jenny had to clean the sink before starting the dishes and there was no place for her to set them as she cleaned them. I helped as much as possible.

We finally made it to Niagara Falls. It was just turning dark and we could see the colored lights that shine on the falls at night. We decided to go on the Canadian side for the best view. At the motel I requested a room overlooking the falls, the motel clerk looked at me funny when I said I wanted a room overlooking the falls. What I didn't know, and he didn't explain, was in the winter they turn off the lights at 9 o'clock. It was already 8:55pm when we were checking in. The clerk only explained this to me when I called from our room to complain that we couldn't see the lights on the falls. I also made him refund the extra money we paid for a room overlooking the falls which we couldn't see.

The good news is the room was warm and comfortable. Jenny was having fun kidding me. While planning our honeymoon I had promised her snow when we got up north. "We are up north aren't we," she said. "Where is the snow? You promised me snow didn't you?" We wanted to play in the snow, get cold and then have to snuggle up to get warm. The "snuggle up" part sounded like the best part and it definitely was!

Day 3

What a wake-up call! I opened the heavy drapes by our sliding glass door to find snow on the balcony. The first snow of the season, so Jenny and I were excited. We went out, turned on the heat in the Winnebago and then had some fun playing in the snow. I took a picture of Jenny on a park bench all bundled up, hat, scarf and coat.

When we got back home and had the pictures developed, while showing them to my new boss, he looked at the one of Jenny sitting on the park bench and said, "Ron this looks more like a little girl waiting for the school bus, then a wife on her honeymoon." I liked the picture so much I had it blown up into an 8x10 and still have it in my camper to this day. I started calling Jenny "little Jenny" from then on. Jenny was not real fond of my new title for her so I only used it in our own company. I told her when I say "Little Jenny" it is like saying, "You are so cute, I want to hug you real tight." But Jenny was still teaching me the rules. At least we weren't fighting like we did while we were dating. Learning the do's and don'ts was getting a little easier for me, yet just when I thought I was doing better, I usually found out I had a lot more to learn.

When we were running and playing in the snow, we ended up by a wall that separated the safe area we were in from the raging river that supplied the water for the falls. I decided to be smart and show off how brave I am. I climbed up on the wall and started walking on icy snow covered wall. If I had slipped and fell on the river side I would be dead. We were only feet from the falls and there would have been no chance to recover from a fall.

Jenny started screaming for me to get down and I responded with acting even stupider. Then Jenny started crying so I jumped off the wall and wrapped my arms around her, picked her up, and assured her I would not do anything stupid again. "Please don't cry Jenny!" I said. Jenny was still crying and said, "I love you and I don't want to lose you." This really struck me; Jenny didn't want to lose me. I had done stupid and dangerous things all my life and no one had ever stopped me and no one had ever cried for me.

Jenny settled down, and I was still holding her, and I think I could feel her heart beating through all the winter clothes. I knew how much Jenny meant to me, but I had not thought about how much I meant to her. What I had done had nothing to do with bravery and everything to do with stupidity. The only good thing to come from this was a new awareness of how much Jenny loves me.

We saw the falls and had hot chocolate in the camper. Then we headed back to the United States. The security guard was funny. He entered the camper, looked around and evidently thought I was the only one in the camper. Jenny was in the back of the camper taking a nap on the bed. I guess to the security guard it just looked like the covers were piled up on the bed. He was quite tall and his head was only a few inches from the ceiling. It was obvious he took his job seriously and he commanded a certain respect. He wore his uniform smartly. I knew right away he was there to inspect the camper and he was going to do a thorough job. He started asking me some questions about buying things in Canada. Our talking startled Jenny awake and when she moved, the covers moved. Then she started talking from the back of the camper. The movement and the talking startled the security guard so bad he jumped and hit his head on the ceiling. Embarrassed by his own reaction he said, "Everything is okay, just go on through."

That night we went to Grand Island to camp. Although the office was closed, the gate was open and the water was on in the shower house so we were all set. We had all we needed. Jenny and I showered at the same time but not in the same shower stall. Jenny likes the water so hot I thought it would bring blisters on my skin.

Day 4

We had spent the night on Grand Island. Upon arising we realized we had a lot more snow on top of the slushy rain that was falling when we went to bed. The snow and slush from the day before was topped off with more rain that came after the snow, and was followed by more snow during the night. This winter mix of snow, rain, and more snow along with 30 mph winds and near-zero temperatures had turned the mix into four inches of ice. The camper was literally frozen in place. I put the camper in gear could not even spin the tires because the tires were frozen to the ground. There was absolutely no one else in the campground; no one was even in the campground office. I found a five-gallon bucket in the shower house and kept filling it with hot water to pour on our tires, until the hot water melted the ice from around the tires. Once I got the tires unfrozen, the camper wheels popped up on the ice and we were off for Fort Niagara.

We toured Fort Niagara and went into a gift shop. To our surprise, they carried Jenny's china there. They had pieces we never saw at the store in Cincinnati. Jenny wanted to buy some, but I was afraid we would run out of money, so I told her when we got home we could order those special pieces. Jenny was okay with that and so we went on. But looking back I believe we should have bought the pieces there. The store in Cincinnati said the pieces Jenny wanted were not available from the manufacturer. We never found them again.

We started for Vermont. We had a campground directory that was a year old but we figured not too much would change in a year. As we headed across New York State we decided to camp the night at a place we found in the book. We took the exit and drove down this country road to where we thought the campground was located, but we could not find it. We drove way past where we thought it was according to the directory.

After searching for it and not finding it, we finally stopped at a farmhouse and asked. They said this was the campground last year, but they had closed it for the winter this year. They were very nice and let us camp alongside their barn. They also ran an extension cord to us so we would have electric. One thing about farmers, besides being nice, they get up very early. We woke up to the sound of chain saws cutting firewood and a tracker dragging more logs up from somewhere. I went outside to see them and pay for the night. They were so nice they would not even let us pay for the electric we used. As Jenny and I were leaving I mentioned to Jenny how nice those people were. Jenny looked at me laughingly and said, "You love 'free' don't you?"

I think back on that night and think, "We were on our honeymoon and sleeping alongside a barn? Gee, I need to write a book on how to have the perfect honey moon!"

Day 5

The drive through upstate New York was totally awesome. The scenery was as beautiful as any place we have ever been. The snow-covered mountains, and the beautiful lakes looked like they were frozen in time. Jenny said this place is so beautiful it takes your breath away. I know we were both having the time of our life. Having Jenny with me was truly the neatest thing. I wish we could relive every second. I know Jenny brought more joy into my life then I could have ever dreamed. I felt like we were in our own little world. Actually I guess we were in our own world. Our love for each other, the way Jenny would look at me, the pictures we took, our hearts were bonding and I just could not get close enough to her, I couldn't love her enough to prove the way I felt in my heart.

Our only problem for us was our honeymoon was going by so fast. I prayed and ask God to slow down time so we could have more time together.

Around noon we were traveling on a country road when we stopped in a rest area to eat. From the rest area we saw a house under construction across the way. We decided to go for a walk and take a look at this big log house. The owner was working on the inside of his house when he saw us and invited us in. He showed us around, and I had never seen a house with a blacktop floor before. I asked if this was normal up here in New York. He started laughing and said no. Then he explained that he'd just run out of money and there was so much moisture coming out of the ground that he'd put down blacktop to help keep the place dry. It was a very large log home and moisture would have been a big problem if he did not control it somehow.

We took off again for Vermont and made it. Even though the campground directory we had said the campgrounds were open all year, we found out that the ones where we wanted to spend the night were closed. We were looking for another campground when Jenny saw a sign nailed to a tree in the form of an arrow that said "camp." I turned around and went in the direction the arrow pointed.

The road we were on was very narrow—more like a driveway than a road. We started down a big hill, a hill of no return, and the camper started sliding out of control. It turned sideways to the road we were on, and as we got closer to the bottom you could see a house with a big picture window. There were two men eating their dinner by the window. Their eyes went as big as golf balls when they saw the camper sliding sideways toward the house.

They jumped away from the window, and luckily as the camper was sliding sideways I was able to give the camper some gas, so we missed the house and slid into a field instead. When the camper stopped in the field, I looked over at Jenny and she was just staring straight ahead. Finally after a minute or two, Jenny looked at me and started breathing again. Looking back it's funny, but I think we both could have had heart attacks at the same time. This had to go into the honeymoon book of firsts things to do (check your heart).

The angry men came out of the house to ask us, "What the hell are you doing down here?" I said the sign out front said CAMP. He told me this was a Boy Scout camp in the summer. As it turned out, he was a dump truck driver and said he thought he could get the camper back up the hill. I said I thought I could drive it up there but Jenny wanted to let him drive camper. I didn't understand, Jenny was willing to let a stranger drive the camper almost like she had no confidence in me. I mean I did miss the house, didn't I? After a couple of attempts he did make it up the hill. THANK YOU GOD.

By now, new snow was coming down pretty heavy again and the wind was blowing hard. We were both hungry and wanted to eat, but where? I think we both needed a rest after that little episode with those men and that hill of no return. With the new snow falling fast, just finding a place to pull over was hard to do. We drove for a while and found a do-it-yourself carwash. We pulled into a bay, and Jenny said at least we were level and out of the wind.

Jenny fixed our dinner, and I must say for only having a two-burner stove, she was cooking some awesome meals. This night Jenny had decided to cook something brand new on the market called Hamburger Helper. I am not sure what happened to it, but it stayed like lead in our belles for what seemed like forever. I must report that Jenny's cooking was really good except Jenny liked to put hot sauce on everything and I mean everything. I think we even had hot sauce in our coffee. I told Jenny that was a little over the top for me.

After eating and resting in the car wash, I checked the campground book, looking for a place to camp. We decided to spend the night at a motel because we had so many dirty dishes to do, and we hadn't had water for a couple days.

We drove to a motel. While checking in the motel the manager saw the Winnebago camper out front and said he would like to see the inside of it. I immediately said okay, not thinking about all the dirty dishes we had piled up or all the wet clothes we had hanging everywhere, from us playing in the snow. He walked out with me to the camper. I opened the door for him to go in, and he took one look and said, "I'll come back later." When I looked in the camper after he walked away, I thought his first impression must have been, "They are a couple of crazy hillbillies!"

Our camper was equipped with two gas tanks. One has a gauge and the other does not. When you fill your tanks you are to run on the tank without a gauge until it runs dry, then you manually switch over to the tank with the gauge. This system usually works great if you're on the highway because you can feel the camper lose power and you know it's time to switch the tanks. The fuel pump is mechanical and the momentum of the engine will start sucking fuel from the full fuel tank if you are fast enough to switch the valve.

The problem was, this time the camper ran out of gas while I was in the motel office.

After switching the valve to the full fuel tank, the camper would not start. I had to ask the motel manager for a bottle of gas so I could prime the carburetor. If the manager thought we were hillbillies after looking into the camper, well I guess I proved we were when I had to ask for some gas to prime the carburetor. Luckily he had some gas in a can that was left over from the past summer for his lawnmower. The camper started, and we drove to our room.

Jenny and I did the dishes and hung our wet clothes in the motel room to help them dry out. While there I used the motel phone to call Mom and Dad and told them we were in Vermont. Jenny and I were so excited to be in Vermont. It was like our goal because I had been here while I was in the Navy. I had told Jenny how pretty Vermont was, and finally I could show Jenny the prettiness of Vermont in real life.

I didn't realize it then but we were just living on love. I mean nothing bothered us. We were so happy to have clean dishes and dry clothes. The warm room was so nice. Jenny and I thought we were in heaven and I believe we were.

Day 6

The Honeymoon adventure continues. We drove to some pretty areas of Vermont and decided we wanted to see Killington Mt. It is really a nice ski area and I wanted Jenny to see it. The snow from the night before had the roads pretty bad but the Winnebago was handling it almost like a four-wheel drive. We passed cars going up mountains that were sliding or stuck, I guess our camper was just balanced well and Dad had put really good tires on it.

As night came near we started looking for a campground I had found in the book. On the way there Jenny saw a sign for a campground that said it was open year round. We were happy because it was only six miles away. The next sign said "Turn Here," and we did. The road quickly narrowed, the tree branches were so loaded with snow and ice they were brushing both sides of the camper and the roof. All we could do was keep driving because there was no way to turn around. We continued for what seemed like forever, up and down hills. I was afraid the vents on top of the camper were being torn off. The tree branches had already pushed in the mirrors on the sides of the camper.

Finally as we came over the top of one hill and started down another hill, in our headlights we saw a little old man walking on the road with a real bad limp. I thought of a television show called The Twilight Zone, but when I started humming a few bars of the theme song, Jenny screamed, "Stop!" The man on the road waited until the camper was real close to him before he turned around and even acknowledged we were there. I asked him about the campground and he said he owned it. He told us to stay on the road until you get to the house, go on in, and my wife will get you something to eat if you are hungry. I'll be up directly, as soon as I finish my chores, he said.

To stay on the road I was just staying between the trees. There were no other tire tracks to follow. As we drove on we came to a large clearing, but there was no road because the snow had everything covered. I drove a little further and saw a bridge so I went for it.

After crossing the bridge we saw a fence, so I stayed on a relatively flat area to the right of the fence. Jenny asked, "Do you think you're still on the road?" I assured her we must be on the road because we were still moving. Around a couple bends and we saw the farmhouse in our headlights. It sure was a welcome sight. There was smoke from the wood burner inside, and as we got closer we could see the light from the windows which looked yellow in contrast to the whiteness of the snow.

We knocked on the front door. Finally a little voice said, "Come around the back. The front door will not open in the winter." The back door entered into the kitchen, which was a very large room, heated with a wood stove. The entrances to other rooms were blocked by drapes, I assumed this was to keep the heat in the kitchen.

The little lady asked us if we were hungry or at least had time for coffee. She poured our coffee and then started asking us questions like we were old friends, just catching up on the news. This amazed me because we only met her five minutes ago. Her husband came in to a warm cup of coffee she poured as quickly as he took off his coat. I asked, how do you get mail here? They both laughed and he said, "We don't get mail from the first snow to the spring thaw."

They went on to tell me to turn my running lights on the camper at four in the morning. When I questioned why, he told me about the New York city slickers that come up here during hunting season. "They sit around in cabins drinking all night and then, about four in the morning, they go hunting. They are so hung over from drinking and playing cards all night they will shoot anything brown, and your camper is brown, so turn on your running lights."

After talking for a while, he gave us directions to some camp sites up on the hill with the electric on. He also said, "If you slide off the path, just blow your horn and I'll come up with the Jeep to pull you back on the path." Sure enough, about five minutes later, I slid off the path with the Winnebago. His little Jeep looked like it was a World War II vintage jeep and although it was old, it got me on the path again and the little old man helped direct me to the camp site.

DAY 7

The alarm woke me up at 4:00am. I turned on the running lights and went back to bed. At 6:00am I woke up cold. The furnace was not working; we were out of propane gas. I started the camper and ran the in dash heater to warm us up. While outside checking the propane gas tank, I noticed all the deer print around the camper. In 1972, if you saw a deer in Ohio, it was in a cage. When we went to bed the snow was still falling, so the deer print in the snow had to be fresh. They were everywhere. The deer had even knocked some Tupperware containers off the picnic table. Jenny and I were so amazed with how many of them there must have been and how close they were to our camper.

Jenny and I walked around the camper ground for awhile because it was so pretty there. You could look down at the farmhouse and see the smoke from the chimney. This was truly a Norman Rockwell picture in real life. Jenny said the scene reminded her of the scene on the china she picked for our wedding. Each piece of china had a different winter scene. The plates looked like they were painted right here. Jenny's china is not elegant or really formal but when you look at the scene you think of a warm house with a friendly fire in the fireplace and the smell of good food in the kitchen.

Jenny and I were so happy, the peacefulness just overtook us. We wanted to find a place like this for ourselves. It would be the two of us, with a house in the woods, our twelve children, lots of snow and smoke to tell everyone passing by there is a warm friendly fire inside. Life would be perfect!

That's right, we wanted twelve children. That number wasn't etched in stone but it was the number of disciples Jesus had. It could have been thirteen. Jenny and I knew we wanted a big family and now we had the perfect setting to raise them in. All this dreaming and planning made us hungry.

We went down to the farmhouse to pay for the campsite. They would not let us pay the night. I think they just wanted to make sure we would visit them again. It must have been a little lonely for them since their children were grown and gone. Jenny and I went to the back door and it opened as we approached it. The little lady had hot coffee and a big hearty breakfast for us.

While sitting in the kitchen I noticed a new Sears stove off in the corner. I asked her if she ever used that stove. She said, "That stove was a gift from her children but it doesn't put off enough heat to warm a closet." She liked her huge wood burning stove with the warmer on top. Jenny and I could have stayed for two weeks or ten years or forever and not been bored with their conversation.

The two of them laughed as they talked about how almost every year the snow breaks the phone lines and they stay down all winter. For this old couple, broken phone lines was a good thing. You see, their son who lived about sixty miles away would come to check on them if he could not call them on the phone. They said they loved to see his big Suburban pull up because they got to see him and his family. They told us how the grandchildren made their day. Jenny and I didn't want to leave but we were out of propane and really needed to start back towards Cincinnati.

As we walked back up to the camper, a kind of sadness overtook us about leaving. We both wondered if we would ever see these two sweet people again. Their love for each other seemed to keep them warm and overflowed onto Jenny and I. They were in their late seventies when we met them, and that was 35 years ago.

We went from town to town, looking for propane and finding none. We decided to head toward home. We looked at the map and realized we had quite a distance to go. A little while later Jenny went to sleep in the back of the camper, so I just kept driving. I drove into the night and around midnight I stopped for gas and coffee at a rest area on the Pennsylvania turnpike. I went to the back of the camper to tell Jenny that I was getting coffee. I didn't want her to wake up and find herself in the camper alone. Jenny looked up at me and reached out her hands for a hug. I climbed in bed with her and fell asleep. Upon awakening I thought to myself, "We really have to get going." Now looking back I really can't figure out why I was in such a hurry to get going. Anyway, I went for the coffee and forgot to get the gas.

I drove for about thirty-five minutes before I thought about it. Just at daybreak, we ran out of gas. We only had three more miles to the next rest area. I was in the breakdown lane on my honeymoon and really didn't want to wake Jenny to tell her. I finished my coffee and then woke Jenny to see if she wanted to stay in the camper or go with me to get the gas. Jenny wanted to go with me. I started thumbing and we caught a ride in an eighteen-wheeler. The trucker saw us walking and figured we were the ones out of gas. He was so nice he even offered to take us back to our camper from the gas station. I told him we would just thumb back but thanks for the offer.

We walked across the highway and caught another ride from another trucker. I think he was a little disappointed because he had just started telling us a story when we saw the camper and he had to stop again. As we got out Jenny told the trucker how impressed she was with all the gears he had to shift. He gave her a big smile and said, "It is not like driving a car, is it?" We got the camper started and we went on our way. Here is another tip for the perfect honeymoon: you must run out of gas and thumb a ride in an eighteen-wheeler.

On the PA turnpike, they use coal cinders to give you traction in the snow. It works well but it sure makes a mess of the outside of a camper. When we arrived in Cincinnati at 2:00 in the morning, the camper was really a mess. So I went to car wash and cleaned it before we dropped it off at Mom and Dad's house. Jenny and I were both exhausted from the trip home so our apartment was a welcome sight. That day we slept in, and then at 3:00pm, I went to work.

Yes, all too soon our honeymoon was over. Recently I found a picture from our honeymoon of Jenny in her nightgown with insulated boots on as she was cooking breakfast one morning. You see the floor of the camper was ice cold. We had to convert the bed back into the table to eat and then convert the table into the bed again to sleep. We truly didn't care.

I believe we were so in love, nothing was a problem, and if we had our honeymoon to do over again we would not change a moment. I believe we were as happy to be together as any two people could possibly be. In forty years of marriage, we told each other we loved each other by our actions and our words every day. Jesus does answer prayers for sure! Thank you Jesus.

The Early Years

Home, sweet apartment. We were excited to spend our first night in our fixed-up apartment. You see, Jenny had never moved into that apartment before we married. So neither of us had ever stayed in it overnight. For us, it was a first of many firsts. Being back in Cincinnati meant going back to work for me, and for Jenny it meant going back to school.

Actually, I think Jenny was glad to be back because I had started teaching her to drive before we left on our honeymoon so she could get her driver's license. This was an exciting time in her life. Jenny did say school seemed different. Her friends were a little distant. I guess being married does change how your friends think about you. Jenny was having so much fun learning to drive on the weekends that I don't think she missed going to the high school games. Isn't it great how God filled the high school void with another fun thing to do? Jenny loved driving. Learning on a standard shift with no power steering didn't make it easy, but she handled our old 57 Chevy just great.

I loved to watch her as she drove. Her facial expressions were so cute, and she would look at me and say, "Stop looking at me, you make me nervous." Sometimes she would make a sudden turn just to get me to look at the road. Then she would laugh and make me laugh. Jenny was always a little unpredictable. I truly loved being with her, and it seemed I needed her more than she needed me. I think Jenny loved the Lord so much and she had her faith in Jesus. I knew Jenny loved me but I knew I was always "second place." I was fine with being second place to Jesus.

I worked nights at Procter & Gamble. My shift started at four in the afternoon and went until midnight. At midnight I would be the first one out the door and the first out of the parking lot. One night while at lunch, one of my coworkers asked, "Are you afraid your wife is having an affair?" I had no idea what he was talking about. He clarified his question with another question: "You are in such a hurry to get out of here every night, we think you are rushing home to see if someone was with your wife." I started laughing and said, "I just miss Jenny and can't wait to see her. She waits up for me." They laughed and said that would probably change real soon.

The nice thing about getting married in November is the holidays are right around the bend. Jenny wanted so bad to be part of a big family, and this was her first Thanksgiving with the Johnson's. Mom always made a great meal, but I also loved Thanksgiving because Grandma came to Mom's house. Mom made the holidays special, but having Grandma there was like icing on the cake.

Mom's dining room would not accommodate all of us, but the dining room was open to the living room, so as their family grew, Dad would just add more tables. After dinner we all went downstairs to play pool and complain about our bellies hurting from eating too much. Grandma and Mom listened to our complaining and knew their meal was a success. When we went to our apartment Jenny said we would have Thanksgiving dinner someday with our kids and my whole family. The anticipation of holidays with our own children was certainly a much-awaited event.

Christmas was coming faster than the disappearance of the Thanksgiving turkey. I had established one rule in our household: no debt. Looking back on our first Christmas, though, I wished I had gotten Jenny something. Our first Christmas together should have been special but we were flat broke after we paid our bills. Luckily our friend Lori gave us a small Christmas tree, made out of pine cones. It was decorated with lights and fake snow. We used this little tree for our first four Christmases.

We were excited to go to Mom and Dad's house for Christmas though because we had really big news! Jenny was pregnant! God was blessing us with a child, and He was blessing our marriage, and now we would be a family. The first of twelve! I would tease everyone saying I wanted a Corvette for Jenny and I, and a trailer for the children. We settled for our 57 Chevy. Everyone was happy but not quite as excited as we were. Mom and Dad had five grandchildren already, so they were a little more reserved than Jenny and I.

When we returned to our apartment, Jenny reminisced about Christmas past—the biggest Christmas she'd had was at Frank's house. She'd received a bracelet which she wore until the latch broke. Jenny was so proud of the bracelet she would lift her arm up and show it off every time she could. One year Frank bought her a transistor radio. It was the size of a pack of cigarettes, Jenny's first sound system. She had to hide it from her foster mother, because Frank never bought one for his daughter Jane.

After hearing about Jenny's Christmases, I really felt bad about being so tight that first Christmas. Jenny said we had so much to be thankful for, her being pregnant, our apartment and our furniture. I was thankful for all that too, but most of all I was thankful for my Jenny's love.

In January, Jenny's morning sickness got real bad. We went to the doctor, but the medicine did little to help. The sickness went from morning to all day. She would get stomach cramps just smelling food. Anyone who ever had dry heaves knows what Jenny was going through. School became impossible. She had to drop out. But Jenny wanted a high school diploma and said she would finish school after the baby came.

I started a new job that January. I went to work as a plumber for a company on the west side of town. I would be working days again, and Jenny and I were really happy about that. I also had weekends off so we had more time together. Before long, I was asked to work Saturdays again.

Our landlord had an unpleasant surprise for us. He so much liked the way we fixed up the apartment that he decided he wanted to sell it. The real-estate people would come in and show the apartment any time they wanted. Sometimes Jenny would be in bed trying to rest, and they would just walk in on her. I talked to the landlord and he said they had the right to do that. I asked if they could at least call first. He said they would try.

They never called. Sometimes there coming in scared Jenny real bad. They walked in on Jenny one Friday morning and Jenny was taking a shower. The real-estate lady told her to hurry up because she wanted to show her client the bathroom. When I came home from work Jenny was really upset. Luckily I had been complaining to my Mom about the situation, and that very day Mom called and said she saw another apartment for rent not too far away.

We went to look at that apartment and rented it. Our rent was due that Saturday on the old apartment, so we just moved out. The landlord was not happy when he came to collect the rent money and saw we were moving. I said now you can show the apartment any time you want and you don't have to call us; we're out of here! We had worked so hard on that apartment I couldn't believe we were moving already.

The new apartment, was really nice. We could move right in. The building was a two-family house and we had the whole first floor. The people on the second floor seemed real nice. Jenny was weak from not being able to eat but still wanted to help. I got our bedroom furniture moved in first and set up. Jenny fell asleep for about six hours. She was eating Tums like candy, and I was trying to eat outside so Jenny would not smell the food. If she smelled food she would get stomach cramps real bad. The doctor said the morning sickness would not last too long, and it did let up some but not the heartburn. We bought Tums in industrial size bottles.

We only lived there a short time when we realized the neighbors upstairs were not so great after all. They fought all the time. He worked at the GM plant in Norwood, putting screws in taillights as the cars came down the assembly line. He suspected his wife (or girlfriend—I'm not sure if they were married) was having an affair. So they fought all the time. Jenny and I tried real hard to stay out of their fighting but it was difficult because we were a witness to what was going on while he was at work. They would fight almost every night.

Jenny and I were still very happy even with the ongoing fights up stairs. Jenny was starting to eat again, and along with eating she was starting to get her strength back. It was great to see her feeling better. She even wanted to start driving again. So I was trying to teach her to parallel park the car—no easy task for a pregnant woman and a car with no power steering. My Jenny was up for the task, and on a very hot day in July, Jenny took her driving test.

I think the driving inspector gave her some headway on the parking because she was sweating and her belly was as big as a barn. He told her she did real good and passed her the first time. Jenny was so happy but so worn out she just wanted me to take her home. She did hold her driver's license in her hand all the way home, and continued looking at it while we had a cup of coffee together. I told her how proud I was of her. She finally put her license in her purse but not before staring at a little while longer.

Our apartment was not air-conditioned, and even with all the windows open, it was very hot and humid. I remember on a very hot day in late August coming home from work and finding Jenny lying in the middle of our bed with nothing on. She was 8 months pregnant and very big. She had arranged two fans to blow right on her. She was just trying to stay cool but I couldn't stop laughing at the sight. I found everything Jenny did to be fascinating to the point I could have watched a movie of her 24/7 and I would have never gotten tired of watching her. It seemed as though I could not wait to get home and see what Jenny did that day.

I remember one day coming home from work and Jenny was sitting by the kitchen table. On the table was a chocolate cake with chocolate icing. Jenny was so proud of herself and was waiting for me to come home so she could show off her cake. I said that cake is picture perfect and she looked at me and said, "I know, I already took some pictures of it!" Then I started laughing and Jenny could not figure out why that was so funny to me.

In September Jenny was looking like she needed to have the baby real soon. Dr. Keenly wanted to break Jenny's water to start her delivery because, by his calculations, the baby was a month overdue. By our calculations, though, Jenny was just due and maybe just a little early. We decided to go with the doctors' recommendations and let them start the delivery. Jenny was in labor pain for ten hours. I had the worst headache I have ever had. I just could not stand seeing Jenny in pain. I went to the nurse's station and asked for some aspirin. They said, "Why do you need pain medicine when your wife is the one in pain?"

Jenny had a beautiful baby girl. We named her Heidi. Heidi weighed 8 pounds and 3 ounces and everything worked—her fingers, toes, even the plumbing. She had pretty green eyes like her mom and the face of a beautiful angel. We praised Jesus and couldn't wait to bring her home. Back then, the doctors kept women in the hospital for a week after having a baby. It sure was a long week to sleep without Jenny in the bed beside me.

Heidi was only home about 9 or 10 weeks when one night around 10:30, we received a phone call from a guy named Robert. He said he was Jenny's brother. So I asked Jenny if she had a brother named Robert. Jenny asked what his nickname was, and he said "Bugs." She said, "Yes, I have a brother named Bugs." I don't know how he had gotten our phone number, but he had it. Robert had run away from his foster home and had no place to go. I drove the hour and a half to go pick him up and brought him to our house. The next day I called his probation officer to tell him Robert was with us.

The probation officer came over and started screaming at Robert, saying, "I had you in a good home and you blew it!" Robert was tiny and frail, and I could tell he was not listening to the probation officer. I ask the officer to step outside and we did. I told him I don't think Robert likes you screaming at him. We went to get coffee together.

He told me when Robert was a very young the system put him in a home and didn't check on him for two months. When they finally did check on him, they found him in bed naked with cigarette burns all over his body. He'd also had lead poison from being stabbed with pencils, was dehydrated and malnourished. No wonder he has a hard time listening.

So Robert stayed with us and we enrolled him in Reading High School. About four months later, we celebrated his 18th birthday. Not long after that I received a call from the principal saying Robert had not been to school for a couple days and wanted to know if he was sick. I asked Robert what was going on and he said he called the Navy recruiter and joined the Navy. A couple days later, he was gone.

We were being blessed again. Jenny was now pregnant with our second child. I guess whoever told us you cannot get pregnant while nursing didn't know what they were taking about.

Heidi was my girl but Jenny had to correct me all the time because I would refer to myself as "Uncle Ron" when talking to Heidi. Jenny is so patient with me. She had to tell me over and over, "I think you're her dad and not her uncle." You see, all my life I loved little children and to all of them I was "Uncle Ron." Having my own child was still new to me.

The fighting upstairs was escalating and Jenny was becoming afraid. I called a realtor and asked about the GI Bill and what do I need to do to use it. A couple weeks later we bought a three story five bedroom house in Oakley, a suburb of Cincinnati.

Jenny was so pleased to have a house and asked if we could stay there forever. It was not my dream home for sure but Jenny loved it. The kitchen was very small but it had a huge dining room. The realtor who sold us the house became good friends with us and called to tell us about an estate auction that had a dining room set for sale. We only bid $50 for the set and somehow that was enough to buy it.

Jenny was elated and we had our first dinner in our dining room with Jenny's china. I realized how much it meant to Jenny when I saw her little face glowing as she set the table.

Seven months into the pregnancy everything seemed fine. I came home from working late one night and Jenny had coffee waiting for me. We sat at the kitchen table talking when suddenly Jenny's body shook and I asked what that was about. Jenny said, "I think my water broke!" I looked under the table and there was blood everywhere. I called an ambulance and off we went to the hospital.

They checked everything and said Jenny needed complete bed rest for the rest of her pregnancy. Our five bedroom home had a bathroom on the second floor and the kitchen on the first floor. We chose to have Jenny near the bathroom. My mom came over and helped with cooking and laundry while I worked.

Almost a month to the day Jenny hemorrhaged again and we went off to the hospital again. This time the doctor said she needed a C-section because the baby was in distress and they were not sure Jenny would make it. I was in that waiting room for what seemed like forever. I don't think I ever prayed so hard in all my life.

I didn't know what was going on but it seemed like a really long time. Finally two men came into the waiting room and said they thought Jenny was going to be fine, and little Ronnie was in intensive care but doing good. They took me to a little office and explained what happened.

Our doctor had been in a car accident a couple months ago. He was in a coma for almost a week. When he came out of the coma everyone thought he was fine, and this was his first C-section since the coma. He had made some mistakes. He had cut Jenny from the top of her belly, down, and they were going to need to do some follow-up surgery to minimize the scar. They said Jenny would live and they were pretty sure Ronnie would be okay too, but that Jenny would never have children again.

I think Jenny was in the hospital two weeks before I could bring her and Ronnie, our precious little preemie, home. Ronnie was the prettiest baby—blonde hair, blue eyes, and a beautiful smile. Jenny was too weak to hold him at first but her strength came back pretty quickly.

The hospital did the follow-up stuff and Jenny never complained. Our friends told me to sue the hospital and the doctor but I just didn't have it in me. The hospital didn't realize the doctor's head injury was that bad. They did everything they could to save my Jenny and Ronnie, so how could I possibly sue them?

About a year later, the doctor said he thought Jenny could have one more child. We were so pleased and Jenny became pregnant in no time at all. The doctor said when they did this C-section, they would clean up the scar and do some internal things they wanted to do. When Jenny delivered Jason, the doctors came to the waiting room and told me Jenny could never have any more children, and that they wanted to tie her tubes while they were in there. I said NO! They said, "You know Jenny will die if she gets pregnant again?" I told them Jenny has been through enough, leave her perfect; I will get a vasectomy.

So we had our family of three. Jason had red hair like his Grandpa. He had green eyes like my Jenny, and a laugh that would make your day. It seemed like we had just brought him home when we had another surprise. Would you believe Robert's time in the Navy was up, and he was coming home? We fixed up a bedroom on the third floor of our home for him. We put air conditioning up there, along with wiring for plugs and more lights.

Robert came home from the Navy an alcoholic. He drank constantly. He lived with us for about two months before I had to tell him to leave. His drunkenness and foul language was horrible, and our children didn't understand. When he got a little abusive towards Jenny, I made him leave.

Jenny's sister Florence also lived with us numerous times during the first 23 years of our marriage. Some preacher had told Florence early on in life that if you get saved, you are saved forever. I think she took the "once saved, always saved" message seriously because she would profess it any time we tried to talk to her about the Lord. I sure hope and pray she is right.

There were times when Florence tried to straighten herself out and Jenny was right there to help her. Usually after being at our home awhile, her health would improve. But then she always seemed to go back to her own ways.

While all that was going on in our home, our neighbor across the street had won the lottery. She was a single woman and decided to move into a more upscale neighborhood. She gave the house across the street to her son, "Crazy Johnny," who was the leader of the Iron Horsemen motorcycle gang.

In two years, we had three shootings with two fatalities. No one was arrested and no one spent even a minute in jail. Our quiet neighborhood went to hell. The man next to Crazy Johnny was retired and couldn't handle his new neighbors, so in desperation he actually jumped out his third-story window headfirst to the concrete below. For some reason his suicide attempt didn't work. So his wife had to take care of him and deal with all the junk going on next door at Crazy Johnny's 24/7.

Finally Crazy Johnny and the gang went to a motorcycle rally in Texas. There, Johnny was beating up his girlfriend and someone shot him and killed him. The gang came back and things actually got worse if you can imagine. But all of a sudden, one day they decided to move out and just like that, they were gone. I believe their moving out was the answer to our prayers.

We had had our house for sale for two years and never had an offer, but right after the gang moved out of the house across the street, our house finally sold. We bought land in the countryside and built a two-story contemporary home on our land.

Eight years later we sold that home and built another home where I could have my woodworking shop alongside. Both homes were beautiful. Both were near streams and in the woods.

Jenny was in heaven with her flowers and big kitchen and big dining room. Life was pretty good. Our children were doing well in school. Jenny and I had our anniversaries, Thanksgiving dinners, and special occasions in our dining room with Jenny's pretty china.

I made her a dining room hutch and buffet out of solid oak. It had glass doors and glass shelves with a mirrored back and lighted interior. Jenny's china was so pretty. I loved to see her green eyes light up when the dining room table was set. I don't think Jenny was prideful about her china but she loved making people feel special when they came for dinner.

Jenny was a stay-at-home mom and took care of our children and all the children in the neighborhood. She loved them all and was always there for them. The neighborhood children called her "Miss J" for short and they all knew how impartial Jenny treated them. Jenny's love was on display 24/7.

Jenny and I enjoyed 23 years of life together that was pretty normal. Life started changing around our 24th anniversary, and for the next 16 years, our life together became extraordinary. Please read on and you will see what I mean. Thank you for reading about my special Jenny and our life together.

That Was Unusual

The next several years held some unusual moments for Jenny and I. I didn't realize what was going on. There seemed to be some kind of distance between Jenny and I but I could not figure out what.

1994

In 1994, our youngest son Jason graduated from high school and Jenny said it is now time for me to go back to high school. Jenny did, and received her diploma without any fanfare. She just wanted to have it! Upon graduating, she decided to go to school and be a medical assistant. Jenny graduated at the top of her class and could not wait to get a job working with people in a doctor's office.

She put off the job for awhile when she found out a girl in the neighborhood was pregnant and her parents had kicked her out. Jenny volunteered to watch the baby for her if the girl would choose to have it. The girl did have the baby and Jenny watched her for a couple months until her parents let her come back home. Her parents were really good people and were truly loving grandparents to the baby.

So now Jenny was able to start working. This was exciting for Jenny because she was now supplying our health insurance. Anyone in business for themselves will testify how hard it can be to pay for health insurance. Jenny was so pleased to provide our health insurance and it was a real blessing.

Jenny loved her job and made friends so fast. Jenny was so amazing; she would come home most nights and get on the phone, calling patients—sometimes four or five patients a night. She would tell them their test results and medicine changes along with what the doctor said and when their next office visit was. She did all this without any notes. She didn't even have their phone numbers written down. This was just normal for her. Jenny took all her patients to heart, mading sure they all felt loved and cared for. It was so easy for Jenny to give of herself.

November 11, 1994 was our first wedding anniversary with Jenny working a job. Our anniversaries were always celebrated with a dinner in the dining room served on Jenny's china. Jenny said dinner in the dining room shows the children how serious marriage is and how you should celebrate your wedding day—it is very special, you know. Now Jenny was working and I decided to make our anniversary special by cooking. I made spaghetti with Cincinnati chili. I read the recipe and it sounded pretty simple. I doubled it since I had also invited my parents. The recipe called for six cups of water, so I needed twelve. But I only put in six. No one ate much including me, and what I did eat was sitting in my belly for a week. Jenny still hugged me and said it was special. She said it was an anniversary to remember. I remember my belly hurting and it was not because I ate too much.

1995

Working outside the house seemed to be very good for Jenny. She was so happy and looked forward to working. Her job helped her fill the emptiness that we felt being empty nesters. We did have to make some adjustment, Jenny only had one week of vacation a year and that had to be scheduled ahead of time. This was different for us because being self-employed we were used to taking off spontaneously. The thought of taking a vacation by ourselves was strange. Our honeymoon 23 years ago was the last time we were on vacation alone.

On our first vacation by ourselves we went to Myrtle Beach. After arriving, we went to the amusement park and were watching families playing with their children. Jenny looked at me and said we don't have to do this anymore. So we went back to the tent and sat down and talked about what we wanted to do. It really seemed weird to think about what we wanted to do. We really had no clue.

We sat for a long time, we walked the beach. It was quiet that evening, and we started talking about Jenny's dream vacation of going to Maine. Ever since Jenny and I dated, Jenny wanted to go to the state of Maine. So we started planning a trip up to Maine for 1999. Then we both looked at each other and started laughing because we were on vacation, planning a vacation. How about right now? We have all week, so let's have some fun.

Also in 1995, Heidi our daughter had a baby boy, Taylor. Heidi was not married and was still going to college. Jenny was torn because she wanted to continue to work her job and she wanted to baby sit Taylor. Jenny was not worried about the loss of income because she had been handing her paycheck to Heidi for months. Heidi needed the money for her expenses in college. Jenny and I were really happy we were able to help Heidi some. Plus, my business was not doing too good at the time and I couldn't pay for health insurance. Looking back I believe I put undue pressure on Jenny to stay at her job.

1996

In 1996, Jenny started exhibiting some odd behavior. There was one doctor at her workplace that was known as "the Lion" for the way he treated his nurses. He was really rough on them. His own nurse usually only lasted a couple weeks with him and then would quit. One day Jenny's boss asked for a volunteer to work with the Lion, and Jenny volunteered. All her friends begged her not to because of his history.

Jenny said on her first day with him, she knocked on his office door and he said, "Come in!" Before she could even greet him, he asked, "Are you my new nurse?" Jenny said yes. He was standing with two patient charts in his hand, and he took them and threw them against the wall. Then he commanded Jenny to pick them up. Jenny looked at his desk and saw three more charts, so she picked them up and threw them against the opposite wall! Then she looked at the Lion right in the eye and said, "I will pick up yours when you pick up mine."

Then while still looking him right in the eye, Jenny pointed her finger right at him and said, "I don't take this crap from my husband, so I'm sure not going to take it from the doctor I work for." The Lion had met his match. Four weeks later, Jenny's nickname in the office was "Lion Tamer." Everyone was amazed because the Lion even had a smile.

The two of them became a source of laughter in the office. Turns out the Lion had a cool personality. Add Jenny's wit and her flip, and they had everyone laughing. Some of the things they did went beyond funny to almost crazy. Jenny loved going to work and I loved hearing the stories of what they did that day.

Everyone loved Jenny, the doctors loved her, and the patients loved her, but her boss developed an attitude and seemed to just want to make it hard on Jenny. Eventually her boss was put on report for how she was treating Jenny, but it didn't stop the abuse. So Jenny put in to work at a different office. When her request was okayed, the Lion actually cried on Jenny's last day. I believe this was a lot of stress for Jenny, so I attributed some of her little behavior oddities to stress.

1997

In 1997, there were a few small changes. We went on vacation to a beach in Florida, and Jenny seemed unusually quiet. She was a little distant even with Taylor to the point where Taylor asked, "Why you so quiet?" Jenny just smiled at Taylor and said, "Let's race to the water."

On our anniversary in 1997, we were married 25 years so I asked Jenny if she was ready for a big party. To my surprise, she said no. A couple years earlier we had a summer party and she had ten people bring baked beans. Everyone laughed and thought Jenny was just pulling one of her crazy stunts. She would do such things just for laughs. The summer party of 1994 was the last party that Jenny organized.

The night of our 25th anniversary Heidi's boyfriend Mike came to drop Taylor off for us to baby sit, and when he realized it was our 25th anniversary he was surprised we were not having a party. A couple weeks later Heidi, Mike, Ronnie, and Jason took Jenny and I to a really great steakhouse for dinner. We had a great time even though Jenny was unusually quiet.

1998

On August 6th, 1998, Ronnie's wife Jenny had a baby girl and they named her Ariel. She is the prettiest little girl and her parents and grandparents are all so proud. My Jenny was so excited to see her but at the same time seemed a little disconnected or distant with her. I justified this odd behavior to myself thinking it had something to do with work or the fact that Ariel had other grandparents and great grandparents. I don't know if it was real or imagined but Jenny was just not that connected with Ariel.

Thanksgiving came around, and Jenny needed help with some routine cooking and baking. I remember coming in the house one time and the timer was going off, but Jenny was not even in the kitchen. This was odd because Jenny never used a timer. She always kept track of everything in her head. When I asked what the timer was for she said, "Nothing. The bread has two more minutes before it comes out." She was right, but I remember thinking it was odd.

I believe it was the end of 1998 that I noticed Jenny did not make as many calls to patients as she used to. Jenny said she was able to make more calls from work so she did not have to make them at home anymore. When we were alone at home, Jenny just wanted to watch television, usually on the other end of the couch. She seemed the happiest when Taylor was there and I was busy with him.

In 1998, when our son Ronnie was building a house for his wife and family, Jenny showed signs of being irritated about the amount of time I spent helping Ronnie. I was totally shocked because Jenny always put our children's needs over ours. Jenny's motto had always been, "children first and nothing second."

Jenny's personality seemed to be changing, and in my mind I was blaming her job for the change. Other people were starting to notice though. I remember a friend stopping by and after talking awhile he said to me, "Jenny is working outside the home now, isn't she?" I said yes. He said he could tell and I agreed, Jenny had been working for several years already. It seemed to me something else had to be going on also.

Something's Not Right

The next few years were the beginning of a great test. But thank you Jesus your love would not fail us.

1999

A few months after our son Ronnie finished his house, he had a party for all the workers. While there we met Lee's wife, Diane. It was obvious Diane was suffering from something. So Jenny asked Lee what was up with Diane. Lee said Diane was just diagnosed with Alzheimer's. Jenny said, "I'm off on Wednesday's. I'll watch her if you would like." Lee said yes, and Jenny started watching Diane at our house every Wednesday. Jenny watched her for almost two years.

I think it was around this year Jenny asked me for a divorce. It was near Christmas and we were going to meet some of Jenny's friends from her work for dinner. We arrived at the restaurant first and got our name on the list. We waited a while and then called our friends who told us they could not make it. Jenny was acting weird or strange so I was not upset when they said they could not come.

Jenny said let's just go. So we left and as we drove away, Jenny said, "I want a divorce." I started laughing and asks her, what is the punchline? When it came to telling jokes Jenny would mess up a one-liner. Actually when Jenny tried to tell jokes, the funniest part of the joke was watching how she would mess it up. But this was no joke; Jenny was serious. She told me, "I want a divorce."

I stopped the van because I needed to find out what was going on. We talked for an hour or two and then went to Arby's for a roast beef sandwich. Arby's had their Christmas glass give away promotion going on. When Jenny saw the glasses she loved them and said these glasses will go great with our china perfectly. We talked the manager into giving us twelve glasses. Jenny seemed happy again and suddenly all was well.

Now, looking back on that night and talking with my friend Ann, we think Jenny knew what was coming and was trying to give me a release from our marriage. Jenny was actually trying to keep me from the pain of being an Alzheimer's caregiver. Jenny has the biggest most pure heart of anyone I ever met. I want to thank Ann for her helpful insight in this situation.

In 1999, Jenny was working at a new office. She liked her new doctor and her new boss. A lot seemed to be better. My business was picking up too and Jenny and I were planning that vacation to Maine. Jenny had talked about wanting to go to Maine even when we dated. We had saved our pocket change for over 19 years. But there was one problem. In 1990 when our daughter had gotten pregnant, she wanted to get married and we okayed the marriage. The sad thing was, a couple months after the wedding Heidi had a miscarriage. That was hard on us all but especially hard on Heidi. In order to pay for Heidi's wedding we had used up all the change we had saved for our vacation to Maine. I told Jenny we would still go, it would just take a few extra years to save the money again. Early in 1999 I told Jenny we had the money to go to Maine and she seemed excited. I hoped it would help pick her up out of the depression she seemed to be in.

Early in the spring we shopped around and bought a new pop-up camper. It was exciting to think about going to Maine after all these years, but in a new camper, wow! If that was not good enough, I had a wreck in my old work van and the insurance company paid for the damages. I bought aftermarket repair parts and put my van back together myself so I had an extra $1300. We were going to Maine with the biggest amount of money we had ever had for vacation. When I told Jenny we had this extra money she seemed okay, but not jumping for joy like I was. She would normally be real excited but not this time for some reason. Her lack of excitement was just not Jenny. I found myself trying harder to explain the changes. I could not wait to go and just have time to be alone with Jenny.

Our vacation to Maine was horrible. We stopped at the welcome center to Maine where Jenny picked up about 30 brochures and said I want to see all these places. Some of them were not even in Maine so I asked her to pick the top ten. Jenny said she had waited all her life to be here, so I pacified her by just saying okay. Jenny got mad at me for every little thing and seemed disconnected from the joy of going. We did and saw everything she had talked about for years and still she didn't seem happy. I had promised to take her to Maine on our 25th anniversary and here it was happening just two years later and with a new camper and 1300 dollars extra. I thought she would be on the moon with me but she was not. There was no reason for her disconnect that I could see.

Jenny was becoming a puzzle to me. At one point Jenny even asked, "When are we going home?" I said we just got here and what about all these places you want to see. Jenny said just kidding. I was thinking to myself, "I would like to go home too." I knew home was not the answer and vacation was not the answer, but what was the answer? I had started stuttering and having a hard time following directions on the brochures, I just could not figure out what would make Jenny happy.

When we got back home, Jenny seemed somewhat better. She was so happy to see Taylor and Ariel, our grandchildren. We were home and things got back to normal, almost.

Jenny asked me to help with Thanksgiving dinner prep this year. This was unusual but it was a big task for Jenny. She made all the holidays special and so they were also a huge amount of work. Jenny loved to bake everything homemade and great tasting baked goods were the norm in our house. I went shopping with her and it was very unusual to say the least. Jenny said if you don't like the way I do things then do them yourself. That too was a real unusual attitude for Jenny.

This year I decided to make a nativity scene for Jenny. She had always wanted a big one. I built one six feet wide, three feet deep, and two and a half feet high. We bought two-foot high Christmas trees to go around it. Taylor actually got in it to help stain it. After Jenny put all the statues in her nativity, Taylor and Ariel decided it needed more animals so our nativity had rabbits, mice, chickens, dogs, cats, ducks, and a fireplace with a wood pile, but Jenny drew the line on having the electric train go through her nativity scene. I don't know why Jenny would not want the electric train to go through her nativity scene; I thought that would be cool! The Jesus Express!

Christmas shopping was always a big job because Jenny had to have just the right present for everyone. This year Jenny still wanted to shop but Jenny was not as worried about everything being just right for everyone. In a way it made shopping easier and a lot faster, so I was happy. On Christmas Eve as we opened presents, we were all laughing because the presents were all labeled wrong. We all thought Jenny did it to make us laugh and Jenny said, "Blame Ron. He helped this year."

All our married life Jenny would take hot showers. I mean really hot showers. Jenny's showers were so hot that we could never shower together. Then in the middle of the winter Jenny changed to cold showers. I mean no hot water at all. Jenny said cold showers are good for you. Everything was changing and I could not figure what was causing the changes.

2000

In 2000, Jenny quit doing birthday cards and anniversary cards. This was unusual because she prided herself on sending them on time and writing something personal on each one. She said no one seems to appreciate them any more so why send them. Jenny also ran out of gas a couple times in the car. She said I just forgot, it's no big deal. She went shopping for hours one time and came home with nothing. It seemed as though I was missing something and Jenny couldn't tell me what it was. Our time together was being spent watching movies, not talking. Jenny still wanted to be held and to hold hands but other than that Jenny was very cold and insensitive. She seemed very distant especially at nighttime.

I think it was this year when Jenny started coming home from work with headaches. They were getting worse and more often. She said light hurt her eyes. She wanted darkness. I built our house in woods and we had so much privacy that we never had curtains. Our windows were huge like 6 feet wide and 5 feet high. They did not have dividers, they were just big open areas that let the sun in, and some people called our house a house of glass. We lived in the woods with pretty creeks and rolling hills. The view out our windows was just beautiful; you could not see another house from our house. We designed the house as one big room so there were almost no interior walls, just well lighted open area with big windows everywhere. So when Jenny said the light hurt her eyes I knew something was wrong.

I had to put thick cardboard in our windows. I had to tape the edges because even a crack in a seam was too much light. I look back now and realize I could have done more. For two weekends in a row she had to stay in bed all weekend. I fed her and made her comfortable but I knew she was working for doctors. I expected them to help or warn me if this was serious. The doctors started her on migraine headache medicine. Jenny started getting better and after a couple more weeks I could take down the cardboard. Eventually Jenny seemed totally better and quit taking the medicine.

2001

In 2001 things were changing more. One day Jenny called me in for coffee, we sat at the kitchen table as usual. Jenny had all the home bills out on the table, along with her adding machine. After I sat down she slid all the bills and the adding machine across the table and said I'm not doing this anymore. Again this was a very unusual behavior for Jenny! Jenny never liked math in school but she loved helping out anyway possible at home. Years ago she decided to do all the home bills and I did all the business bills. This was a big help to me not to do the home bills but if she didn't want to do them anymore it was not the end of the world.

Also in 2001 Jenny won a week's vacation in Myrtle Beach, South Carolina. Her work would raffle off this one week every year. So we went and Jenny exhibited some personality changes there also. There seemed to be a kind of sadness in Jenny and a quietness that just wasn't Jenny. We used to go to Myrtle Beach with our children and she said she was just missing them. Actually I was missing them too so I understood.

Remember Jenny was 18 years old when we were married. We had three children by the time Jenny was 22 years old. Jenny never had time to do the things a normal teenager usually did. So now our children were grown up and we suddenly had time to be a little crazy if we wanted to. She seemed to want to do something a little crazy, but I could not figure out just what it was. Upon arriving home from Myrtle Beach, Jenny got distant and seemed to be in deep thought, but she would not talk about it. This was very unusual because we talked about everything.

On Monday morning I woke her up in time for her to go to work. Jenny got ready for work and then said, "I'm not going in to work." I asked if she felt bad, and Jenny said No! I quit! Jenny just abruptly quit her job. This was such a shock because Jenny loved her job and she loved her patients. She said her work put in a new computer system and they just didn't pay her enough to learn the new system. I was shocked but I was happy about her quitting her job because she seemed so stressed for over a year, no actually a couple years.

I was happy to have her home fulltime and thought without the stress of the job Jenny would start being herself again. Actually I missed Jenny being home so much that I was glad she quit her job. Now we could have coffee time together again. I thought Jenny would be her old self real soon. Jenny started putting x's on the calendar every day. When I asked her why she simply replied, because I want to.

We went away in our little pop up camper for a long weekend. The first night, we had a couple beers and we both got so slaphappy it was funny. We were playing a card game and Jenny was winning, she was so happy. I remember telling her how good it sounded to hear her laugh and she stopped laughing and got real serious, then she belched out loud and we both started laughing uncontrollably. I loved hearing Jenny laugh, it sounded so good to hear her laugh so loud. You could not have made us happier, if someone gave us a check for a million dollars. Jenny's laughter was great medicine for me. I thought we were finally going to have Jenny be Jenny again. I didn't realize how long it had been since I heard Jenny laugh her special cackle laugh. If I would have known that night would be the last time to hear Jenny's special laugh; I would have stayed up all night and never let her out of my arms.

2002

2002 seemed to start out a little better. Jenny decided to start working again. I didn't want her to work, but she insisted. She started working at Anderson Mercy Hospital as a phlebotomist. She had a hard time remembering her way around the floors but seemed very happy to be working again. So in her off hours from work, we went to the hospital and I walked the floors with her to help her find her way around. That seemed to help her. She only worked a couple months and I could see the stress coming upon her. I asked her to quit but she said no. A couple weeks later one of the girls Jenny liked got fired and so Jenny decided to quit. I was glad Jenny stopped working because we were getting close to the holidays and I wanted Jenny home with me. I was still blaming her behavior on her work and the stress there.

Jenny loved Christmas and we had a nice one. Jenny seemed to need help with a lot of little things, and help with details she never needed help with before. Like starting things and then did not finishing them. Jenny didn't seem to want to take down the decorations until I helped. That was unusual. Then one day I was in my office and I heard the car start up. The driveway was right outside my office window. As I looked out I saw Jenny start the car, she put the car into reverse and as the car started to back up she slammed the car into drive and the car lunged forward and hit a tree in the front yard. I ran out to check Jenny; she was ok just shook up.

We went into the house and just sat down for awhile. I just held her in my arms and tried to talk about what happened. She insisted she was ok and then she went shopping.

But clearly something wasn't right.

The Diagnosis

2003 started off with more unusual behavior. Just little things and odd conversations, and odd words in her vocabulary. Jenny was becoming quieter. She wanted to watch television and if I tried to talk even during a commercial Jenny would seem bothered. Everything I tried to talk to her about, she just put me off; like we can talk about that later.

A couple months later Jenny got lost on a routine trip to pick up Taylor. She tried to hide the fact she was lost by saying the car broke down. Jenny and I never lied to each other so this was a major shift in her personality. None of this made any sense to me, it seemed as though I was losing Jenny a little at a time. She was quiet, cool, or indifferent. She was marking an X on the calendar every day, and even her flowers needed weeding and she didn't care. I talked to our daughter Heidi who was a nurse so she knew the right kind of doctor for us to go to. Heidi made an appointment with a neurologist, Dr. Armitage.

The doctor visit was horrible. I never knew Jenny didn't know her own phone number or her address. When the doctor asked Jenny these questions, Jenny said I have that in my purse. We had the same phone number for 28 years and lived in the same house for 18 years. Then the doctor asked Jenny, how many kids do you have? Jenny did not know, nor did she know their names. These were questions I never would have thought to ask.

When Jenny could not answer them, I started crying right in front of the doctor and Jenny. It was such a shock. All the little crazy things going on at home were going through my head. I just couldn't believe Jenny could not remember her own children's names. I remember getting into the car, I started crying again, and Jenny did not ask why or even seem concerned. Now the lid was off. Jenny stopped trying to hide all the little details of things she could not remember.

After testing (MRI, CAT scan, blood work, etc.) Jenny was diagnosed with having had 5 mini-strokes. Jenny and I were actually happy about the diagnosis because we both thought she would recover from the strokes. Jenny had lost her ability to write but she could still print, just not all the letters. Jenny wanted to at least print, so we practiced for a year. Night after night we would practice until we realized Jenny kept losing more letters, instead of getting better. Jenny was getting worse and she knew it. She was trying so hard and practicing so long I couldn't understand what was going on! It was really hard to watch Jenny struggling with such easy tasks. I mean Jenny was always so smart and remembered everything.

One Saturday our friends Mary Tremper and Ann Record came over to take Jenny shopping. Jenny had a great time and wanted to tell the girls thanks for taking her shopping. Jenny printed them a thank you note. I have it safely put away because it is so precious. It said "thank you for taking me shopping real fun. Jenny."

Another night we had some friends over for dinner. I had tried to make desert and it turned out terrible. I said at least I can make us coffee. Jenny jumped up and said I'll make it. I had been making the coffee for a long time so when Jenny said, I'll make it, I was very happy. Jenny walked over to the coffee maker and just looked at it. Then she walked away and into our bedroom. I made the coffee and comforted Jenny by telling her no one noticed she did not make the coffee. I don't remember for sure but I think Jenny stopped drinking coffee right after that.

In November of 2003 the doctor recommended we apply for social security benefits. They were denied. Really I couldn't blame the government for denying Jenny benefits, her systems would be so easy to fake. It was around this time that I started noticing things missing around the house. Like our phone directory, our camera, and other things like cookbooks. I know now it was the Holy Spirit that prompted me to look in the garbage for things of value, and I thank God He did.

In December we were going to Mom's house for Christmas so I decided to make some of Jenny's homemade pumpkin pie. Jenny always made hers from scratch. I had the recipe from Jenny and to my surprise they turned out good. On the way to Mom's house I had the pies on the floor between the seats of the van. All of a sudden

Jenny reached down and put her hand in a pie like you would do if you were making a hand imprint in concrete. Then she licked her finger and said "mum, mum punk." She continued licking her fingers and saying "mum."

I moved the pies and when we arrived at Mom's I carried them in and when it was time to eat dessert I showed everyone the pie and everyone still wanted a piece, so I was happy. A funny situation came up when we were ready to leave. My sister asked Mom "Where is the rest of Jenny's pumpkin pie? I didn't get any so I would like a piece to take home." Mom said it is all gone. Then my sister opened a cabinet behind Mom and pointed to half a pumpkin pie on the shelf where Mom hid it. Thank you Jesus the pies were a success!

2004

In 2004 it was back to the doctor for answers. I hoped and prayed for something simple. I did not like the first doctor so Heidi found a new doctor for Jenny. Dr. Broderick was so much more personal and caring than our first doctor. Jenny liked him also. Jenny's innocent personality came forth when she called Dr. Broderick a "hottie hottie." He just smiled at Jenny. He ordered more testing, and when he asked for a new MRI, I said I haven't paid for the last one yet. Dr. Broderick upon realizing I didn't have insurance, gave us the MRI for free. After more testing the doctors said Jenny was an Alzheimer's variant.

I didn't want Jenny to know this diagnosis because she was a nurse and would have known it was the kiss of death. This was the first time in our marriage I had to hide anything from Jenny, it was really painful. Sometimes while talking I could not look her in the eye and she said, "You're hiding something from me, aren't you?"

My workplace was in our 3700 square foot garage attached to the house. So I could walk to work and I had people working for me. I was either with them or in the house with Jenny and I never had time to be alone. If an occasion came up where I got even a couple minutes alone I would just burst into tears. I seemed to stay strong until I was alone and then I would lose it! Sometimes I cried in the shower, so Jenny would not know.

I was still trying to keep my business going and trying to keep the house but Jenny's care was demanding more and more of my time. I built furniture for the unfinished furniture stores. The orders were getting backed up and the storeowners were very sympathetic but they had customers that were not. So the business was starting to fail. I was taking care of Jenny during the day and trying to build furniture at night. It seemed everything in our lives was upside down. This worked for a while until Jenny stopped sleeping. I sold my business in June 2004 and lived off the proceeds of the sale for the next five years.

Along with this Alzheimer's diagnosis I was told to start going to the Alzheimer's association. At the Alzheimer's association we met Clarissa and Ann. I remember after meeting Jenny a couple times Clarissa was talking to a group of people and said, "When Jenny walks into the room you feel love walk into the room." I know Jenny is love, and she radiates love to me but for Clarissa to say she felt Jenny's love too was really saying a lot. Thank you God for Jenny's love, which is your love manifesting. Thank you God for Clarissa and Ann and all the hours they dedicate to helping others.

The Alzheimer's association did help especially with legal papers I would need in the future. I went to a lawyer and by the time they drew up the power of attorney, medical power of attorney papers, and a host of other legal papers I would need in the future, Jenny had changed a lot. When we first went to see the lawyer, Jenny was still trying to print her name "Jenny Johnson." But in the month or so it took for the lawyer to come up with the papers to sign, Jenny was only able to print her first name.

In June of 2004 we had Taylor with us and one night he got so frustrated because he could not clime a rope straight up. Jenny had me write Taylor a note. Jenny said. "Dear God. Thank You for making me special. Everybody has things they cannot do very well, like climbing a rope. But it is a lot easier to be mad about things you cannot do then to thank God for the things you can do. Signed JENNY." Then she added with a little work, "You can get better at writing. With a thankful heart you can be your best at everything. Signed JENNY." Thank You Jesus for letting me be with Jenny and for letting me see her sweetness!!!!

Jenny was doing some things that were really childlike and yet so cute. She would ask me if we had enough gas every time we got in the car. She would even ask about gas when I was leaving a gas station. Jenny would look down the street and say okay you can go. Then smile like I'm still helpful. Jenny would wave at billboards that had pictures of people smiling.

I said all that to show that even in the middle of this disease, which was causing so much destruction, Jenny's loving, helpful, caring and precious personality was still intact, and the sweetness of Jenny was still showing in actions and with the words she could still say.

Jenny still loved to help people. For example Jenny would walk up to someone in a store or church and say you look great, I love your hairdo. Most people would smile and say thank you for telling me. Then Jenny would look at me and say, "See I make happy." I just loved her more and more. Jenny is truly a great example of God's love!! I thanked God for these precious moments, and for allowing me to be with my Jenny.

Once Jenny developed a really ugly spot on her neck and leg. It was hard and about the size of a quarter. So I called Dr. Nash and set up an appointment. The day we went Jenny was really doing good. As we sat in that waiting room some of Jenny's old nurse friends came out to see Jenny because this was the office that Jenny worked at. Jenny did not seem to remember them but she asked me, "Is this a doctor's office?" I said yes, and Jenny replied, "Ron why are we here?" I said for you to see Dr. Nash and Jenny got this worried look on her face and said, "Oh Ron, tell me, where do I hurt?" Jenny was serious when she asked me. I could not laugh and embarrass Jenny and I could not cry and embarrass Jenny either. Dr. Nash gave Jenny a prescription and it took care of the spots.

I think Jenny's happiness comes from knowing the Father like she does. I think that is why Jenny was never materialistic. For Jenny to help others was as natural as breathing and giving everything she had was as simple as washing your hands. When the children needed anything she couldn't do, Jenny always directed them to God, like "Jesus will help you ride your bike, just ask Him." Jenny always put the needs of others first and nothing was second. I felt sometimes I was falling in love all over again and again.

I remember Jenny loved to go to JC Penney's to shop. We never bought anything but we would go looking. Night after night we went to Penney's. One spring day we were at Penney's and they had all the mannequins dressed in little shorts and some with mini-skirts. As we walked by Jenny said I want one of those, she was looking at the mini-skirt. Jenny weighed 207lbs. at that time, and a mini-skirt was not going to look good on her. She insisted so I got the biggest size on the rack and we went to the dressing room. The girl at the dressing room reluctantly let us in and I got the mini-skirt on Jenny. I turned Jenny around to look in the mirror and she looked at herself and said, "Who is that?" I thanked God big time!!!!

APRIL

In April, Jenny had her first seizure. We were sleeping and Jenny let out a scream at one o'clock in the morning. I woke up to see her body locked up and her eyes rolled back in her head. It lasted what seemed like forever and there was bloody foam coming from her mouth and I had no idea what was going on. The ambulance took her to the hospital and we stayed there for three days. She still has seizures. The medicine is helping, I guess.

I believe it was around then that our driver's licenses needed to be renewed. We could always go together because Jenny's and my birthday were around the same time. Jenny had not driven for over a year but she wanted her driver's license. She was unable to pass the eye exam.

So we made an appointment in Columbus to have them test her peripheral vision. The man tried for hours to have Jenny tell him the right answer but Jenny just didn't understand. When they ask for her driver's license Jenny just handed it to them. She even thanked them for trying so hard. When we got in the van to start home Jenny started screaming, nothing I said would comfort her. After about an hour and a half I pulled the van over again and said you have to stop screaming Jenny. I tried to hug her but she did not want me to. It was one of the worst days. To see Jenny in that pain and torment and to have no way of comforting her was horrible.

I told her it is just a piece of paper you still can drive, nothing has changed, and you can still drive. She reached in her purse and showed me her car keys and said I never had an accident I will still drive. She didn't know over a year ago I had changed her keys to some old car keys left over from cars we had sold. Her keys didn't fit our cars now but having car keys meant freedom. For months she would ask me to let her drive. So I would take her to a deserted park and let her get behind the wheel. I would put the car in drive and the car started to move ever so slowly. Jenny would get the biggest smile on her face! She was driving!!! "See, I not wreck!!!" I really, really miss those days. They were so awesome because Jenny was so happy!!

Jenny's ability to talk in complete sentences was gone. Jenny was leaving me at such an alarming pace; it was truly frightening. I remember explaining to her I needed to do the laundry because Jenny would put a whole bottle of laundry detergent in each load. Jenny looked at me and with tears in her eyes. She said, "Just one more thing." Life was slipping away with no way to stop it! Cooking and Jenny's second love, baking, were gone also.

Jenny still wanted to be helpful but it was hard to find a way to let her help. One night I decided to make homemade cookies. Jenny wanted to help so I gave her the eggs and said crack them and put them in the bowl. Jenny cracked them and put them in the sink drain then she looked at me like, I did it right didn't I? It seemed that every day I lost a little more Jenny and my heart.

Around this time Jenny quit taking showers by herself. She needed help. It was not hard to help but it was hard to watch the progression of the disease." Shortly after I started helping Jenny take a shower Jenny would forget to keep her eyes closed while I washed her face. If the soap got in her eyes, you'd better look out she would attack me. I prayed about it and God said, "Just mist her face with clean water and wipe it off." I have been doing that ever since. The cool thing is no soap has been on Jenny's face for eight years and everyone says what beautiful skin she has. Thank You Jesus!!! My Jesus tells me everything I need to know about caregiving. I love you Jesus!!!

My sister Pat would visit my mom every Wednesday and help mom with whatever she needed. So Pat suggested taking Jenny with her on Wednesdays. Jenny was very happy to go and it seemed like a great idea. Pat went out of her way to make Jenny smile and be happy! Mom enjoyed Jenny coming over because she was helping also. Then one day on the way to Mom's Jenny got mad for no reason and started acting up in the car. Pat said it was dangerous and she was right so that ended that. Jenny never seemed to miss going, it was just another thing gone.

I think it was around this time in life that Jenny started moving things around. I thought I could leave her in the house for a couple minutes by herself. This proved not to be a good idea. One day everything in the freezer was in the wash machine. Jenny would turn on all the hot water faucets in the house and let them run. Never the cold water just the hot water. Another time Jenny had turned all the burners on the stove to high and left them on. One day I forgot to put the dish-washing soap away and I came in to find Jenny with green soap running out of her mouth and down her face. I realized I could not let Jenny alone for even a minute. I was learning how to Jenny-proof the house.

At this time in my life I knew God just enough to know He could change all of this. I talked to our parish priest and he said to look on the Internet for help. That was not the answer I was looking for. I started searching for help but not on the Internet.

Paula was my best friend's sister who moved from Wheeling, West Virginia to Cincinnati years ago. We became friends with Paula and her husband Gary before this started with Jenny. Paula is on fire for God so I turned to her for help. She gave me books on healing and God's power being alive and well still today.

I didn't know it then but Paula was starting me on a journey to know and love Jesus like I never knew was possible. Paula was always quoting scripture. I did not understand the power of the spoken word then, but I have learned and now have a deeper respect for the things Paula was teaching me.

I did not realize then but everywhere I turned for help up to that point, people were helpful in legal matters and technical advice, but nowhere was hope for Jenny to recover. Paula was the first person I remember talking to that offered true help and wanted to teach me how to have a relationship with God. I was praying and so were our friends but I just wanted God to heal Jenny. I didn't realize God wanted me to know Him. My life was being turned upside down and in the middle of this I was supposed to learn more about God? Give me a break! Jenny is dying! Jesus, just heal Jenny—you're the only one who can.

Thank you Paula for helping me get past myself and on to a love relationship with Jesus. I am so blessed to know you and have your prayers over all these years.

2005

In 2005 Jenny and I went back to the doctor for more tests only to find out Jenny's diagnosis was changed to Pick's disease. Dr. Broderick was just starting to tell me Jenny's diagnosis was changed when he had a family emergency and had to go. So I went home and got out Jenny's medical books and started reading about Pick's disease. I called my sister Pat and she did a ton of research for me. Eventually Pat found a chart to show the stages of Pick's disease. My sister Pat is a nurse with a lot of degrees and when I need to know anything medical or understand doctor terms, my sister Pat is the one to call. She has spent hours on hours helping me with medical information.

The evidence showed and the doctor said Jenny had about 3 to 4 more years to live. The doctors had no way of helping Jenny; that is, no medicine to stop the progression or slow it down. I thought, "Three or four years is not enough!" I started really searching for God and His answers. Being Catholic all my life, I knew just enough about God to make me dangerous. I knew I needed help and He was the only one who could help us. So I turned away from doctors and on to God.

This proved to be the best decision I have ever made! In my search for help from God I seemed to be turning away from being Catholic and turning to other churches, mostly non-Catholic. It surprised me that the information I was getting about healing was not really taught in the Catholic Church. I was learning a new way to pray. I was actually talking to God and hearing Him.

I started doing something that Jenny really liked. It started by accident. Our bathroom was a little cold in the winter so I bought an electric heater to warm it up. One day while trying to get Jenny in the shower I dropped the bath towel on the floor. It landed right in front of the heater, so when I finished showering Jenny, I picked it up to dry Jenny with it. The warm towel felt so good to Jenny and had a calming effect. I never forgot to drop the towel in front of the heater after that. It was so nice to find something so comforting for Jenny. I now realize it was not an accident but a blessing from God

Himself. Thank you Jesus for showing me how to make Jenny comfortable in a time when things were really rough.

I was reading the Bible more and more. One day I read a scripture about how God rejoices over us with singing. It was really a tough day with Jenny because as I was reading the Bible, Jenny's bowels let loose in our kitchen. I carried Jenny into our bathroom and I cleaned Jenny up. I locked Jenny in our bedroom while I cleaned the kitchen up. Jenny was upset and was betting on the bedroom. When I opened our bedroom door I saw another mess on our carpet and wall. I immediately picked Jenny up to clean her in the bathtub again. After cleaning Jenny I carried her to the living room and went to clean our bedroom wall and carpet. While cleaning that mess I heard Jenny vomit in the living room. I again carried Jenny into our bedroom and cleaned her in our bathtub. As I was cleaning the mess, I asked God, "What song are you singing right now?!!!!" I'm glad He didn't tell then because I was in a crappy mood. (Smile—Get it? Crappy mood?)

After cleaning Jenny the third time she was tired and thank you Jesus she fell asleep on our bed. This was a thank you Jesus because it gave me time finish the clean up, and I thanked Jesus for the tools, water, soap and everything I needed to clean up the mess.

I think it was around this point that Jenny would go into our bedroom and get in my underwear drawer and put my underwear on her head and walk around. I would take it off her head and she would just get another pair. Sometimes Jenny would rip the sheets off the bed and pull them around the house (I think there was a cartoon character that did that). Jenny also seemed to have friends she talked to, or I should say babbled to, Jenny would walk up to a mirror and talk to her reflection but no one was there. This might sound strange but I miss that so much because Jenny seemed to be comforted by the person in the mirror. At this time most of her words are gone.

In December 2005, we went Christmas shopping. Jenny and I were in K-Mart when Jenny walked past a talking deer head. She started babbling back too it. It has a motion sensor to tell it when to talk, so Jenny just stood there and looked at it. It just looks at you but as soon as you move it talks again. Jenny would start to leave and it would talk. Jenny was fascinated; people in the store would look at her and Jenny did not care. I called our sons and they bought it for Jenny's Christmas present. On Christmas we hung it in the living room and it just fascinated Jenny again. A couple months later, however, I had to take it down because for some odd reason Jenny became fearful of it. I miss Jenny and long for our relationship. Today is a good day for a miracle. Thank you Jesus!

I Love You

The trials begin to pick up, but love stands strong. When we woke today, Jenny's bowels had let loose sometime in the night. I started to get her up but she was fighting me so I decided to get her some milk and give her a drink first. While in the kitchen I said out loud, "Jesus, I have not heard Jenny say I love you for a long time. Please let Jenny say I love you." I walked back into our bedroom and Jenny raised her hands up to me like she wanted a hug and said, "I love love love you!!" I got back in bed with her and into the mess of the night. I got the biggest hug ever. Thank You Jesus, I love you too!!!! I do not remember Jenny being able to say I love you after that.

2006 was the year of hospital stays. At night Jenny would just start screaming and sometimes hold her stomach. I took her to the emergency room and they would run tests, but Jenny would not sit still for x-rays. They could not get good pictures and the pain seemed to vanish so they sent us home. After five trips to the emergency room I told the doctor no more x-rays until you sedate her. The doctor got mad and said, we don't sedate until we know what is wrong. He walked out of the room mad. I knew after five tries at x-rays, the nurses could not hold Jenny still and so what is one more blurry x-ray going to do? Now I had the doctor mad and that was not good. Jenny was in pain and that was not good.

A couple minutes later, two nurses came in with a needle and a bag of medicine. I asked, "What are you doing?" and they said, "We are going to sedate Jenny." I went out of the room to find that doctor and I hugged him and thanked him and I told him, now you find out what is wrong with my Jenny. They got a clear picture and the doctor said she had kidney stones. They said she had a very large one but it was ready to drop down, so they started to hydrate Jenny for 24 hours to see if it would drop down by itself. When it didn't, they operated and got them out, but what a time. It took six times in the emergency room, three days in the hospital, and then a couple office visits before this was over.

In May of 2006 our son Jason thought I needed to have a break from watching Jenny. He knew a friend that needed some extra money and was willing to watch Jenny a couple times a week for four hours at a time. I had to take Jenny to her house because she had two small children, but I told Jenny she was going to make some money babysitting Shannon's kids. Jenny was excited to be a help to Shannon.

When I went to pick up Jenny, I would give Shannon some cash and she would hand it to Jenny and say thanks for helping me with the kids. Jenny would get the biggest smile and look at me like, "I'm still making money." I only took Jenny over there a couple times because Jenny started having problems with the kids. She was taking their toys and not sharing. When we stopped going, Jenny never asked about it. I missed Jenny when she was gone to Shannon's, and I think Jenny missed me, but it sure was cool to see her little face light up when Jenny thought she was being helpful and making money. She was receiving love by believing she was giving it.

In June of 2006, my best friend Joe Coleman and his sister Paula came to see Jenny and I. While at our house Paula volunteered to watch Jenny while Joe and I went to Sunday Mass. Upon arriving home we found Paula praying for Jenny and almost in tears. I didn't see Jenny, and asked what is going on? Paula explained to us what happened. She said as soon as I left for church, Jenny started looking for me. Then Jenny went to the closet and curled up in some blankets and hid on the floor saying, "Don't hit me mommy, please stop hitting me mommy, don't hit me mommy, it hurts mommy." Jenny stayed in the closet until she saw I was home.

I was glad church didn't last too long. I do not know much about Jenny's childhood because she wouldn't talk about all those years in foster homes. I was really glad that Paula and Joe came that weekend because we talked a lot about the Lord and our relationship with Him. After Joe and Paula left I became very sad to the point of crying. I wanted to hold Jenny but she wanted to walk. I walked along side of Jenny and realized I was sad because I wanted to have a good conversation with Jenny. I miss my Jenny.

One morning after breakfast while I was doing the dishes, Jenny came over by me. She picked up a dishtowel and started rubbing the counter top. I said thank you for helping Jenny. She got the biggest smile on her little face. I know Jenny just wants to be helpful! I want to thank you Jesus for letting me see and be with Jenny; she is such a blessing.

In July of 2006 I decided to take Jenny and our grandson Taylor to Myrtle Beach on vacation. I had been to the health stores and was trying all these health remedies. Some seemed to work and, although expensive, they were cheaper than medicine. I figured Jenny and I would be together so I thought we would be safe. Plus I thought some time away from home might pick Jenny up a little.

We had as good a time as possible. Taylor and his friend seemed to have a good time also. On the way home, we had a car accident. We were about 15 miles from Myrtle Beach when a pickup truck pulled out in front of us. We T-boned a big jacked up Chevy truck. Thank you God no one was hurt, but our truck was totaled. We rented a car to go home. We had to leave our pop up camper there because no one will rent you a car to tow a camper. This must have been really traumatic for Jenny because she went incontinent for about a month, including during the daytime.

AUGUST 2006

Jenny started a period. She had had irregular periods for a couple years, but her last period was over ten months ago and I had thought they were over. So when she had this one it surprised me. The problem was compounded because now she did not understand them. Jenny would get her hands in the blood and start screaming. I called her doctor and they said it would be four weeks before they could see her. I called on God and thank God He led me to a pharmacist who gave me Estroplus, an over-the-counter vitamin. In two weeks Jenny seemed better. Life was a real mess for those two weeks though.

In September of 2006, Jenny woke up screaming again. This time Jenny was holding her head. I took her to the emergency room. They did x-rays and released us saying there is no bleed to the brain. The doctor talked about Jenny having Alzheimer's even though I had handed him a note saying, Do not talk in front of Jenny about Pick's disease. My note called Jenny's disease Pick's disease but the doctor called it Alzheimer's. I did not want Jenny to know about Pick's or Alzheimer's. My note said, Jenny doesn't know she has it and I do not want her to know she has Pick's disease!

Although they could not explain her screaming, something changed in Jenny. I think it was the doctor talking about Alzheimer's in front of Jenny because Jenny seemed even more distant when we left the hospital. Jenny stopped sleeping, she started fighting me when I would bathe her, she started spitting out food, and would not let me clean her teeth. She asked me to kill her. She would look at me and beg me saying, "Kill me, Ron, kill me." I had all the knives and things put up but I became fearful that Jenny might do something on her own, so I stayed really close to her. She sat on the couch for hours and would not open her eyes. Jenny cried and cried for hours and days.

It was about this time when her muscles started jerking. I was begging God to heal her, to help her, to make her open her eyes, but most of all I wanted God to help me keep her alive. She went totally incontinent about now also. I was reading the Bible and listening to tapes but I felt like a little kid trying to learn to swim by being thrown out of the boat in the middle of the lake. The vitamins, the herbs and the minerals were not working anymore. Jenny was spitting out everything I tried to give her. My heart was breaking because I was out of ideas, nothing was working, and then I realized I still have God! God must be the answer!

Then I realized how much God was already helping me with caring for Jenny. For example, Jenny could not or would not spit toothpaste out of her mouth after I scrubbed her teeth. If you leave toothpaste in your mouth all night, it turns rancid and stinks. One morning I was talking to God and asking Him to tell me what to do about Jenny's breath. The rancid toothpaste smelled worse than her bowel movements. I started showering Jenny and God spoke to me saying, "Scrub her teeth now." So I scrubbed her teeth while holding her in the corner of the tub. Then God directed my hand to the showerhead. I picked it up and sprayed Jenny's mouth and she responded by spitting out the toothpaste. Praise you Father!!!!! I still scrub her teeth in the shower twice every day; that is Gods way! Thank You Jesus; I will put my trust in YOU!

For over a year Jenny would look at herself in the mirror and just talk to her image like it was her friend. It was sad but kind of cute because her friend seemed to understand Jenny's babbling. She would move her hands while looking in the mirror and so did the girl in the mirror. Than one day Jenny hated the person in the mirror. I had to cover all mirrors and eventually all windows or anything that she could see her refection in. At night I would turn flood lights on outside, so I could see inside the house without inside lights on. This way Jenny would not see her reflection in the window and attack it.

In October 2006 we went to see Dr. Hellmann. This was a doctor Jenny worked for. After hearing the symptoms he sent us to the emergency room to have Jenny tested for diverticulitis. Thank God Jenny never had that either.

After more trips to the hospital because Jenny seemed to be in some kind of pain that I could not explain. The doctors did numerous tests and could not find what was wrong. I had explained to the doctors what Jenny did and how the pain affected Jenny. Finally the pain hit Jenny while we were in the hospital and I ran down the hall and screamed for a doctor. This time the doctor actually saw Jenny in pain and said they should x-ray her to look at her gallbladder. They found a big gallstone and planned to operate the following week.

By Thursday that week Jenny was in so much pain I took her to the hospital again. Friday night they did the operation to take her gallbladder out. They explained to me after the operation that the incision was bigger than normal because the gallstone was so huge. They kept Jenny in the hospital until Sunday night. Before they released her I said, Jenny has not had a bowel movement in the four days she has been here. So they gave her a suppository and said she will start now. You can take her home.

The following Friday I went to the hospital and told them Jenny had not had a bowel movement for nine days. They x-rayed her and found her bowels were severely blocked. The nurse said the Vicodin pain medicine probably caused this. They were going to give her a suppository and send her home again. I told the nurse how Jenny had been in the hospital four days and then sent home after they gave her a suppository. I said, I don't think another suppository will help. The head nurse tried to manually unpack Jenny's bowel until Jenny started bleeding, so they stopped. Then they gave me a bottle of stuff for Jenny to drink and said this will get her going.

I took her home and gave her the stuff, which was not easy because Jenny did not like the taste of it, and she was in so much pain. On Saturday we were back at the emergency room. This time a doctor did the manual unpack job and got the blockage out. It must have really hurt because I was standing by Jenny and holding Jenny as the doctor started to unpack her. Jenny's hands grabbed on to my arms and she squeezed me so tight that her fingernails dug into my arms, to where both my arms were bleeding. When the doctor was finished, the nurses looked at each other and said, "Have you ever seen anything like that before?" They both said no. They were ready to send me home with Jenny and I asked if Jenny could stay. Thank you God for a nice doctor—he placed Jenny in a room in the hospital.

They kept Jenny in the hospital two more days. That night and most of the next day Jenny's bowel just kept going and going. The nurses and I changed Jenny's sheet at least 30 times. Finally her bowels seemed to slow down, and the nurses came in to check her blood pressure. I asked if they could stay with Jenny so I could go get a cup of coffee because I had not eaten or had any to drink in almost 36 hours. They said go get something. As I was walking down the hall I heard Jenny start screaming so I ran back to her room. Both nurses said all we did was try to change her like they had been doing all night and most of that day. Jenny calmed down the minute she saw me.

A little while later a psychologist came into the room and started asking me questions about Jenny. I asked "What is this about?" She told me that Jenny's reaction to the nurses when I was out of the room was a sign that Jenny could be being molested now, or maybe as a child. I said no one is molesting Jenny now because I'm with her 24/7, but I do not know about her childhood because Jenny never talked about her childhood.

I signed some release forms and they got Jenny's records released from the state of Ohio and the records showed she had been molested as a child two different times. Once when she was six months old and she almost bled to death and the other when she was seven years old. The records showed the man had sense died. Thank you Jesus for helping Jenny through those awful times in her life. I know you must love me Jesus because right now in my mind, I want to go dig up a gravesite and crush the bones in his coffin! I know You Love me and You are working in my heart because my heart says forgive him!! Thank you Jesus for your love and for teaching me forgiveness!!!!

November 3, 2006 we went back to the emergency room for head pain. The doctor and I talked outside the room about Jenny's condition and then we went back into the room. Jenny was in the hospital bed lying on her back. The doctor asked Jenny, does the light bother your eyes? Then he turned off the overhead light and said is that better? Jenny shook her head like yes. He turned the light back on, looked at me and said, it is a migraine headache. He wrote a prescription for migraine medicine and sent us on our way. The migraine medicine was really complicated to give Jenny so I never filled the prescription.

Jenny's violent behavior was escalating to a point that it seemed Jenny was so out of control. I tried everything I knew and nothing helped. Everyone I knew had a home remedy and I think I tried them all. I remember one night I tried taking Jenny for a ride in the van. She was going crazy so I went back home. As I tried to get Jenny out of the van, her pinky finger went up my nose and I was bleeding pretty badly. It did not bother Jenny at all. It was like my precious Jenny was hidden inside some Jenny I didn't know.

Three days later, we went to see a psychotherapist. He put Jenny on Zyprexa. The first couple days Jenny was at her worst. She was even more violent so I called the doctor and he said, keep giving her the medicine she will get better. After about a week I took her off the Zyprexa because of the escalated violent behavior. There was really no down time for Jenny. While on it that week Jenny was so hyper she could not sleep at all. Her fighting and scratching, hitting and biting were getting worse instead of better. My trust in doctors was diminishing and my trust in home remedies was gone, but my trust in God was growing.

On November 22nd, 2006, Dr. Broderick looked at some new x-rays and said there is a lot of brain shrinkage which is normal for Pick's disease. I did not ask but something about the way he said it made me think the shrinkage was worse than he expected. I guess at that time in my life I just did not want any more bad news.

November 29th, 2006, back to Dr. Helm. He said to put her back on the Zyprexa and gave her Ativan for sleep. I decided to not go back anymore.

In December 2006 I decided I needed to get out of the house for a while. Jenny was having a really good day. Christmas was coming up and I wanted to go to the grocery store. You see, our friend Mary would shop for Jenny and I for months now. Mary had 6 of her nine children still living at home. Every Wednesday night Mary would grocery shop for me, because Jenny was so unpredictable. For some reason Jenny was having a real calm day and I just wanted to go out for a while. So Jenny and I went to our local IGA store. We were doing great in the produce department. People were looking at me weird because my face was scratched up from Jenny's fighting me, but I didn't care I had the rest of me hidden with long sleeves and a hat. We were out of the house and smelling the good smells of the grocery store. Christmas stuff was out and it was so nice to see.

Then Jenny and I walked into the second aisle and out of the blue, Jenny screamed, took her hand, and ripped my face open. She was hitting me and screaming. The owners came running, asking what can we do to help. I had Jenny in a bear hug and told them I was just going to try to get her to the van. They insisted they wanted to help so I handed them my wallet and my list; they shopped for us. They were so nice; they even volunteered to shop every week. Their help took a lot of pressure off Mary but she still came every Wednesday and helped. I so enjoyed her visit, she always seemed to have helpful tips.

2007

2007 was one to the longest years yet. The violence had escalated to hitting, biting, scratching, kicking, and still screaming. Jenny could literally go 24/7. It was as if she was trying to burn herself up. Jenny got her hands in her stool and would throw it everywhere. The only dependable thing about Depends is that they will leak, although not as bad as other brands I have tried. Thank God I had laundry machines in the house. The new drugs had stopped working and life was pretty tough.

I had stripped the house of anything throwable in 2006 but now everything was stripped. The pictures on the walls, even the kitchen chairs had to be put up. I even took some doors down because Jenny would slam them and I was afraid Jenny would get her hand caught and be hurt. The coffee pot was on top the refrigerator; anything that could be picked up had to be put up high. Once or twice Jenny actually flipped the kitchen table. She is strong.

Anyone that stopped by said I looked like I was at the end of my rope. Jenny could literally go all day. I drew the line at midnight. I would put Jenny in bed and lay on top of her to hold her in bed. It was not easy to do; you see Jenny weighed 207 pounds and was a fighting machine. My ears bled, my face was scratched up, and I had bite marks on my arms. I even had infections in my mouth because while showering Jenny she would lash out at me and sometimes her fingers got into my mouth and cut the inside of my mouth.

For some reason about 4 o'clock in the morning Jenny was up and going again. 20-hour days were taking a toll on me. We were confined to the house like prisoners. I had to have Jenny's drugs delivered to the house. Mr. Berry from Berry's drugstore in New Richmond is a real pharmacist with a big heart. He hand-delivered Jenny's drugs to our house. Bill has a four-wheel drive truck and delivered them even in the snow.

Happy Easter, a couple weeks ago Jenny started crying again and Jenny kept crying and crying. It drove me nuts because I didn't know what was wrong. Jenny has not had a bowel movement for a couple days and I have had her on some new medicine for weeks. She just has little messes that are hard to clean up. I mean showering her is like putting your life in her hands, and I have to shower her every time a little comes out. I have suppositories but how do you force someone into that position who is fighting you. I really don't think Jenny is fighting me as much as she just doesn't understand I'm trying to help her. I love her, and I hope my love is enough.

I know for a fact that Jenny knows her condition. She also knows she cannot express herself. Sometimes she gets so tired and I try to comfort her by holding her, but she pushes me away. I pray and pray and pray. God knows I pray.

In June 2007 I was wrecked and felt like I needed some help. I called the Alzheimer's Association and they said to call hospice, so I did. They sounded real nice on the phone and said they would come to the house for an evaluation. It turned out they were not able to help because Jenny was still walking. While they were there, Jenny started to fall and I caught her, and she said "thank you" which is two audible words, so we didn't fit the criteria for help. It shocked me to hear her say thank you because she had not said anything I could understand for almost two years.

We applied for Social Security again and this time they ordered a physiological exam to evaluate Jenny's condition. I guess you could say Jenny passed because we were awarded benefits. Finally, we had some health insurance for Jenny.

In July of 2007 anyone that saw me would tell me to put Jenny in a home. They told me stories of how the caregiver dies before the patient. I knew there had to be help somewhere so I called the Alzheimer's Association again and this time they suggested a hospital that Jenny could go to for behavior drugs.

I called the hospital and they said we could come. They originally said it would probably be three days before they would have her medicine working. The check-in was disastrous. Jenny head-butted a male nurse and hurt him. They drugged her, and when things settled down, a nurse came in to take some history. She told me I had to leave at ten o'clock because visiting hours are over at ten. They said the drug they gave Jenny would last all night. Not so, they had to drug Jenny again in just hours because the first sedative was wearing off. At midnight they said I had to leave for the night. I told them not to try to change Jenny in the morning because Jenny had been molested in one of the foster homes she grew up in, so no one could touch her but me. They put this information in her chart.

The next morning I arrived at the hospital early, and they beeped me in right away. I ran down the hallway and saw Jenny had torn up two nurses and was ready to attack Dr. Gupta. They had tried to change her Depends and she had torn them up. When Jenny saw me, she put her hands up like, "Come get me!" Dr. Gupta pointed at me and said, "You have unlimited visiting hours." I felt sorry for the girls who got torn up but they should have read the notes from the night before. I also felt sorry for Jenny to have to go through all that. I realized how much Jenny still loved me and I thanked Jesus for her love!

The next couple hours were not too bad. We went into the eating area for lunch, and when Jenny saw some of the other patients she immediately tried to comfort them. You could see her heart go out to the patients. Jenny could not talk so she just rubbed their backs, smiled at them, and tried to comfort them. Jenny actions were saying a lot more than words could ever say! Jenny's heart of pure love and her need to help others was still intact and that was a beautiful thing to witness. I love you Jesus!

Then a nurse came over and told me there are some crazy patients here and I'd better stop Jenny because some of the patients would knock her across the room just for touching them. When I stopped Jenny; her anger came out again. I started praying to find a place where Jenny could be of help and still feel useful. It was so cool to watch her pour her heart out to help others. It was like seeing the real Jenny again, and yet so sad to have to restrain her from her first love (helping others by giving of herself.)

I think that is where the violence actually came from. I mean, Jenny had always helped everyone and whenever she saw a need, she tried to fill it. Jenny's loving, caring, and beautiful nurturing side was on display and now I had to stop her? Taking away her joy of helping others was literally tearing my heart out! I ask God to please help me find some place where Jenny could be helpful.

After two days I wanted to take Jenny out of there. She had stopped eating and was shutting herself down. I believe Jenny felt useless and if she could not help others she was just going to shut down. I told Dr. Gupta this is not what I hoped for. He talked me into staying a couple more days. After ten days they thought they had some drugs working and sent us home.

Jenny was excited to get out of that hospital and into the van. We had developed a technique to get her into the van and Jenny still remembered it. I thought Jenny would be glad to see her house again but she actually seemed disappointed and upset. I think home had become a prison for her also. After all that time in the hospital, Jenny would rest at night with the drugs but never for a whole night. During the day, the drugs did nothing.

While in the hospital my sister Pat came over to see us. She helped me pass the time away and monitored everything the doctors did which was very helpful to us. Also Mary Tremper came to visit us.

One day while Mary was there the nurse came in with a new medicine for Jenny. The nurse had it ground up and in applesauce like I would do when I was at home. Upon taking it Jenny started reacting badly and Jenny's voice changed; the nurse just stood there like, what is going on. Thank God Mary was there because she picked up the paper about the medicine and saw you could not grind it up and put in applesauce. Mary told the nurse and she immediately said get her something to drink. Jenny's voice was different for a day or so and the nurse ordered the drug in sprinkles so it could be put in applesauce. I thank God for putting it in Mary's heart to be there.

After we were home for a while I bought a cell phone. Everyone told me it was necessary for our safety. With the new drugs I decided it would be safe take to the dentist. Wrong, the visit was a disaster. Jenny was not cooperative (imagine that). I had drugs and gave her some, then waited a couple more hours, and Jenny was still not cooperative. So we just went home. So much for drugs!

After being home about half an hour I could not find my cell phone. I called it from our landline and got a recording saying out of service area. I looked for it everywhere. Even in the toilet tanks, the garbage, I mean everywhere. I did without it for a month when I finally gave up trying to find it. When I bought a new one the girl at Verizon said if you do find your old phone within 30 days bring back the new one and we will give you a full refund.

So twenty-eight days later I was sitting on the couch and complaining to God. I said, "I don't like this new $119.00 phone as much as my old $39.00 phone so God will you please show me where my old phone is?" God spoke and told me to look in the refrigerator. So I went to the refrigerator and opened the door. As I did I said, "Lord, I'm in this refrigerator every day. If it was in here I think I would have seen it." God said, "Look in the other door," so I opened the freezer door and there was my phone. I thanked God and laughed out loud. I also got my $119.00 back. THANK YOU

GOD VERY MUCH! I don't know why it took me so long to ask You.

Be In Health

As you have read the year 2007 had been one thing after another. I believe my faith in doctors was getting weaker and I found myself looking to God rather than doctors for help for us.

Paula called from England and told me about a place in Georgia called "Be In Health." She was so excited to tell me because a lot of people went there and received healing from all kinds of diseases. I checked the place out and called them. They could hear Jenny screaming in the background as I talked to them on the phone. They said I could not come because the church did not have a soundproof room to put her in.

I understood the situation at Be In Health. They have people coming from around the world and it would not be fair to them if Jenny was screaming all through the teachings.

They did tell me of a place here in Cincinnati that taught the same thing with the same results. So I called them and talked to them from out on our deck so they could not hear Jenny screaming.

A couple weeks later we went to the Cincinnati conference. On the way to the conference, Jenny ripped the air conditioning vents out of the dashboard and the radio knobs were gone. I prayed for Jenny to be calm and when we walked into the church entry area Jenny was calm, thank you Jesus. People looked at me funny because of the scars on my face but at least we were there.

We went to the registration table, and as the man handed me the forms, Jenny ripped her hand from mine and lunged across the table. She scratched his face and ripped his shirt. Everyone was screaming and running away when John Wood, one of the workers, came running towards us. I said that right. He was running *towards* us. He was screaming to the top of his lungs, "In the name of Jesus I command you demon from hell to come out of her now!"

He was the first person that didn't run away. I had never heard anyone command demons to come out. John and I talked for hours as we walked the halls of the church/school. He saw a lot. I mean as we walked Jenny bit me and hit me out of the blue. He left us for a while to talk to Mike and Bryn, the people who ran the conference.

At every church Jenny and I attended in the last two years we had been asked to leave. I knew our behavior was not conducive to a good learning environment for a church setting, so I understood.

When John didn't come back right away we started to leave. As we went out the door John came from somewhere and hollered, "Ron are you and Jenny coming back tomorrow?" Truthfully I was in shock that he wanted us back! I said, do you want us back and he said "Yes, Jenny needs to hear the word of God now more than ever." I thanked God and sung His praises all the way home. I knew God was the answer and now He found us a church. Not just a church but a special church with people that seemed to care. I mean they asked us to come back after they saw what we were like. This was a miracle for sure!

The next day the service started at 9am. I had Jenny up and showered and fed in time to be on time. We got part way there when Jenny's bowels let loose. I took her back home and showered her again. Three times we started to go and had to turn around for the same reason.

It was almost two o'clock by the time we got to the conference. As we walked in the church break area, the conference attendees were coming out of the church for a break. One lady walked up to us and said, "I'm so glad you are here." She could tell by the look on my face that either I didn't believe her or that she must not have been here the night before. She smiled and said, "I was here last night and I want you to know we are glad you are here. In fact when you did not show up by eleven o'clock, Mike and Bryn stopped the conference and we all prayed that you would come." I was totally overwhelmed by their love!

They said Jenny and I could go up on the balcony and there she could walk all she wanted, without brothering people. The problem was Jenny would not go up steps, so I had to carry her and she was not cooperative. So the trip up and down was quite a chore. They also told me to give her a lot of drugs to keep the screaming down.

As the conference continued, Jenny went walking up to a young man named John that was dressed in black leather with studs everywhere. His hair was spiked and colored purple; he looked like someone you would meet in a dark alley. Jenny would rub his face and he would just stand there like I don't know what to do. One night they sent him up on the balcony to tell me to give Jenny more drugs. She was making too much noise. I asked "John, would you get Jenny's personal bag for me?" John said, "Dude I don't do purses," so I asked him to keep an eye on Jenny while I went and got it.

In less than a minute I was back with her bag, but as I approached John I smelled something rotten. I asked John if he cut the cheese and he said, "Wasn't me, Dude." I looked at Jenny, her bowels had let loose and she had gotten her hands in it. Immediately I grabbed Jenny's hands and asked John is there a bathroom up here somewhere? He ran to find out.

When he came back he showed me where it was. By now the bowel movement was soiled through Jenny's clothes also. It took a long time in the bathroom to clean Jenny and as usual I was singing to her to try to keep her calm. When we came out of the bathroom to my surprise John was still standing there. Here is this big tough guy dressed in leather with spiked hair and he says to me, "You know Ron, my dad left when my mom got pregnant with me. Mom has worked two jobs all my life to keep us in food and clothes. Until tonight I didn't know what love was or what love looked like." I thanked him for his kind words, and prayed for him.

When the conference was over Jenny did not seem to change at all. But a couple weeks later while I was cooking breakfast on the back deck of our house, I realized I did not have my earplugs in my ears and I could not hear Jenny screaming. I walked in to a quiet house. Jenny was just walking around. As the next couple days came and went with Jenny still quiet, I was in heaven! Some screaming did come back but nothing like before, and within a couple more weeks it was gone.

After the conference I wanted to tell Mike and Bryn how much I appreciated them letting us be there. A lot of people had questions and they realized the work involved in the care of Jenny, so I wrote a thank you and an explanation of why I thought Jenny and I are so blessed. It went like this:

What are the blessings in Pick's disease?

1) The doctors have no cure.
2) There is no medicine to slow the progression.
3) There is no drug or surgery to help Jenny.
4) There is no hope from doctors.

You might ask, "Those sound like negatives, so why do I call these four negatives; blessings?" Let me explain. In Jenny's case I do not have to make decisions about surgeries, drugs, or special treatments. I believe these are blessings because God made it easy on me to seek Him first; I can have all my faith in God and I am not torn between the doctor's advice and what I hear from God. To me these are very big blessings. You see, if there were drugs or surgeries or treatments, and I turned them down to have Faith in God's treatments, I would have problems from my family and probably well-meaning Christians, telling me to take the doctor's advice. They would have been actually chipping away at my faith and causing a lot of mental anguish in me. So the blessing is God made it easy for me to choose Him first and believe Him without everyone telling me to take the doctor's advice.

Also people always made the same comment, "you need a break." I must admit at that time I probably looked like I did need a break. But in my heart I knew that every moment with Jenny was a precious moment that God was giving me. I knew every smile was a gift from God. I ask, Who would cover her up when she kicks her covers off during the night? Who would kiss her goodnight and good morning? I would miss her smile, I would miss Jenny's laughter and I would miss these blessings from my God.

I love God for all the strength He gives me and by loving God first and by having faith in God I know it is God that keeps my heart from exploding! I also know that God is still in the healing business and Jenny is healed right now. Just because I cannot see her talking in the physical and she is incontinent doesn't mean a thing. God in His word said "walk by faith not by sight" so I do!

October 2007

I remember in October of 2007 Jenny and I were walking in the living room and Jenny said, "I want home." I said, "you are home" and she got frustrated. Jenny said again, "I want home," and I said, "Jenny, we are home." Then Jenny said, "I want Jesus home go to."

I said, "You want to go to heaven and see Jesus?" and she smiled. I said, "You will but I want you here for a long time." She looked like she understood and put her head down and said ok.

This was a really big deal to me because Jenny had not really said anything much for a couple years and these words were complete thoughts.

I thought to myself Jenny is like God now. You see, God has all these mysteries. Jenny is a mystery now. I mean, Jenny can hug you and kiss you, then push you away and scream in your ear, pull your hair, scratch you, and then pull you close and hug you, all in one moment of time. I think I am not going to go crazy trying to figure this out; I'm just calling it a mystery.

Around this time I think I asked God to either make me stronger or let Jenny lose some weight. Carrying Jenny up and down steps was really hard. I don't think I'm complaining, I just needed some help from my God. God answered my prayer so quickly that anyone who saw Jenny would say, "What are you doing to make her lose so much weight so fast?" Jenny went from 207 to 110 in about six months. Her skin looked great; you know no hanging or sagging.

Mary bought new clothes for Jenny and Jenny looked great. Mary was so patient with me! I would tell her what kind of clothes I wanted for Jenny and she would get them, bring them to the house, and I would try them on Jenny. If needed, Mary would take them back and never complained.

I had some requirements for Jenny's clothes. Like no back pockets. I still to this day have no pants or shorts for Jenny with back pockets. To me women that wear pants with back pockets look like men. I am not gay so I don't want my wife looking like a man. I don't know where Mary found women's pants without back pockets but she did, and if that was not good enough she would not let me pay for them either.

I could handle 110 pounds very easily. So God not only gave me the gift of a smaller Jenny like I asked, He also made Jenny even more cute and adorable! I could not praise Him enough. I'm the most blessed man on earth. I love you Jesus!!! I really believe that if I had had to put Jenny in a home and walk down the hallway by myself, my heart would have exploded. I thank You God for making it possible for me to take care of Jenny!! I am so blessed to be this blessed by YOU!!! I want to thank you Jesus for answering Jenny's prayer, the one where she asked You to make her forever loveable to me. You have definitely made Jenny forever loveable to me!!!!! THANK YOU JESUS.

Bryn gave Jenny and I a complete set of teachings on CD and I listened to them every day. I had the workbook so I repented for every kind of sin imaginable. I spent weeks doing this, thinking I must have missed some sin because Jenny was not healed. I had Pastor Henry's book that talked about spiritual blocks to healing. I spent hours asking God to reveal the block. I knew this would work because I saw so many people healed of everything imaginable. It seemed as though I was just missing something!

In September 2007, I couldn't believe what Jenny did. I saw her pick up a picture I had left out last night and she reared back like to throw it. Then she put it down, went to the sink, and picked up a plastic lid and threw it instead. That was a conscious decision. Thank You Jesus!!!! I believe that is real improvement!!

Later I found a note dated October 26th 2007. It said, "Today I sat on the couch and listened to some romantic music." It brought back so many memories of when Jenny and I did that. Almost all the CD's we had were love songs. Sometimes after the children were in bed Jenny and I would sit and refresh our spirit listening to soft music.

Jenny was walking around like normal and seemed unconcerned and unaffected by the music, but then God gave me the neatest gift. I saw Jenny crying as she was walking. She actually let me hold her, and not just for five seconds, but for four songs. It was like going back in time and Jenny was normal again. Jenny and I were crying so hard and it was so beautiful, and then as suddenly as it came, it went and Jenny started attacking me again. I prayed, God please let Jenny out! I know she is in there, I just saw her and then she went away. Please dear God bring her out again.

OCT-DEC 2007

Jenny is fighting everything. Showers are wartime. I cannot cut Jenny's nails or her toenails. She cut my ear pretty good this morning; at least it took a while to stop bleeding. Jenny is going further and further into her own little world. She just walks around talking to someone or something I cannot see.

Sometimes Jenny walks right by me like I'm not there and other times she looks at me like I'm her long lost friend, or she attacks me. I'm just not sure. I do know I love the tender moments and wish they would last more than 4 or 5 seconds. I wish most of all we could have meaningful conversations again. I just miss my Jenny!

My sister Pat got me a book titled *Losing Lou Ann*. She thought it might help reading about someone going through the loss of a loved one. I read it and could not help thinking about all the little moments he missed by putting her in a home. It really got to me when he took Lou Ann out of the home to go to the doctor. She was so excited to leave the place that she ran down the hall without her shoes. She was answering the doctor's questions until she realized she was going back to the home. Then she got real quiet. On the way back to the home, he took her past their own house and said who lives there and she said, we do! At one point Lou Ann escaped the home and came to their real house and walked into their bedroom at midnight and went to the bathroom and then got into bed. But he took her back to the home.

Pat was right; it did me good to read his book because it allowed me to see even better the blessings from God of taking care of Jenny at our own home. THANK YOU GOD FOR THE STRENGTH AND LOVE YOU HAVE GIVEN ME! I LOVE YOU JESUS! I don't want to miss a minute. Jenny is still precious!!!

On November 2, 2007 I noticed Jenny was not snapping her fingers to the music any more. If Jenny liked the music playing she always snapped her fingers. I played some of her favorite songs but she didn't snap her fingers any more. I thought where is my Jenny?

November 11 was our 35th anniversary. I had decided not to let it go by without a party. Around the first of September I had started calling people that I thought would like to celebrate with us. I called twenty people and got eighteen answering machines and two maybes. No one called me back. In October I had called again and had no one confirmed either. So I added more people to the list and still had no confirmations. I decided to just forget it.

But a week before our anniversary, people started calling wanting to know what to bring! I started to panic because everyone was coming and I had nothing prepared. So I called Mary for help as usual. She went to the store and even bought decorations for the house, a detail I had totally over looked. Eighty some people came, the house was full of laughter again! Jenny was smiling at people and walking around. I had given her six Ativan, which is enough to make the average person ready for an operation but Jenny was still going strong.

A nurse friend of Jenny's said "Ron go talk to your friends I'll watch Jenny." I said, "You haven't been around Jenny for about two years and I don't think you realize how capable or how fast Jenny can get into things." She insisted I go and talk to my friends, plus it was really nice of her to offer. Within seconds Jenny knocked over a beautiful cake someone brought. As people tried to get control of her she had knocked over more stuff. As they were cleaning up the mess, Jenny was picking up food, taking a bite and then putting it back on the tray. Jenny was walking around and having so much fun watching people. She was just as excited to see people as I was! Plus, she is so cute.

I found in my notes about Jenny's Journey this paper I will share with you. The day after our anniversary party Jenny was crying a lot. I think she is thinking about the party and all the people that were here to see her. I haven't seen her this depressed for a long time. It must be terrible to have that much brain working and yet she cannot tell me what is going on. I guess by now you have the idea that I love my Jenny and to the best of her ability Jenny still loves me. Life will be so cool when Jenny is healed and we can communicate with each other, hold each other, and love each other.

Jenny can tell me if she is thirsty by picking something up and trying to drink it. Today she picked up an apple and beat it on the counter top until juice came out. So I peeled her an apple and sliced it and she ate it. Life for Jenny must be so frustrating and yet if someone says, "how are you?" Jenny will say "good." I love her so much and I want another 35 years minimum. The first 35 went so fast it is hard to believe.

One day, Jenny slept in and when she woke up, I was lying next to her. We were facing each other on the same pillow. Jenny raised her head up like she was going to tell me something but the words would not come out. She laid her head back down for 3 seconds and raised it up again and tried to talk again but the words would not come. She laid her head back on the pillow and started to cry. She did not get mad or angry, she just cried. I cried too because I wanted to her talk and I wanted to hear what she wanted to say. I thank you Jesus that Jenny did not get angry, and I thank You Jesus that Jenny will talk again. This was an awesome moment in our life and I thank you Jesus for it. I thank you Jesus that I don't miss these treasures and that You have seen to it that I am able to take care of your Jenny!!!!

In December I started making plans to sell the house. I knew I was going to run out of money and although I knew I had enough to stay in the house another year I also knew I needed to list the house for sale. I started giving more stuff away. At first it was kind of hard but the Lord was helping me.

I called Be In Health again and they said Jenny and I could come if I could control her. Also I had to be ready to leave if they asked me to. I put our dining room furniture up for sale because it was the only way I could figure to raise the money for the trip. One day Paula called and asked me if the dining room furniture had sold yet. I asked if she was interested and Paula said no, but you don't have to sell it to go to Be In Health. You guessed it, Paula paid for our trip down there.

The Motor Home

In January of 2008 I started talking to God about where we were to go when the house was sold. Because of the economy our house was worth a lot less than I had expected. Because we were without insurance those couple years, I had borrowed almost $80,000 against the house to pay those hospital and doctor bills. My nest egg in the house was virtually gone. So where would Jenny and I go?

I knew some friends that had a twenty year old motor home for sale. It was a one-owner and very well taken care of. They had it for sale for almost two years and knew I was interested but I couldn't come up with the money. I started praying about it every night because I didn't want to be in government housing. I don't have anything against government housing or living in government housing. I just did not want to be held down to living in anyone place. I felt like a prisoner in our house the last couple years and I did not want to live that way anymore.

I just could not figure out how to come up with the ten thousand they wanted for the motor home. One morning after feeding Jenny, I thought I heard Jesus say, "Sell your van and your pop up camper and you will have enough money to buy the motor home and a small car to pull behind it." It was a perfect idea and I thanked God for it. It was not just a way to buy a motor home but a whole new way of life and I would not have to be in government housing. Thank you God!!!!!

A couple minutes later the phone rang, my cousin Mike called and told me his son was rushed to the hospital last night and they didn't think he was going to live. So Jenny and I went over to support and pray for Jason. In the course of the day I told Mike about the motor home I was thinking of buying. He told me his brother Dick just bought a new car to tow behind his motor home and the old one was not sold yet. I called Dick and bought his old

Saturn for one thousand dollars. It was perfect. I wanted a Saturn because they do not require a tow dolly or a trailer to tow them.

I put our van and our pop-up, up for sale. The first people to see the pop-up bought it. So I paid Dick for the car and went over to pick it up. I saw the Saturn still had the tow bar connections on it. Dick said I even have an old tow bar if you want it. That saved me probably six or seven hundred dollars. I was so happy, it seemed everything was coming together fast. A couple weeks later the van sold and we made plans to get the motor home.

Before we left home I bought insurance from a company called Good Sam. The motor home broke down twice and thank God for Good Sam roadside assistance. We did manage to make it home. There our son Ronnie came over and we tuned it up, put all new hoses, belts and fluids in it. I thank God Ronnie came over to help because I realized some of the things I just could not have done myself and he is a really good mechanic. I am blessed that I have him and he had both the time and the will to help.

Jenny and I then left for Georgia. The motor home was running so well and it felt great to be in our new twenty-year-old motor home. We only went about twenty miles when the amp gage started showing a total discharge. God was looking out for us because we were right by the welcome center to Kentucky so I pulled in.

I turned off the motor and you could hear something sparking. I got out to disconnect the batteries when I saw smoke coming from under the hood. I ran back in and got Jenny out and took her to a safe place. There was a couple coming from the bathroom so I asked them to watch Jenny while I tried to put out the fire. They said I'm sorry but we are in a hurry. They left and just that quick a trucker saw the fire and asked what he could do. I said please watch Jenny, she falls down real easy. I fought the fire with fire extinguishers from truckers and the ones that were in the camper. Someone called 911 and by the time the fire trucks came, the motor compartment and all the wiring, hoses, etc. were burnt up.

In the meantime I had to get our clothes out of the camper and start washing them so we could still go to Georgia. The inside of the motor home was intact. The whole night was spent doing laundry. I made about four trips to the camper and back home trying to get stuff cleaned and I packed in the little car. As the sun came up I got Jenny up and off we went to Georgia.

Jenny didn't like being in the little car. She was becoming combative to the point of being dangerous. She hit the gear shifter and threw the car into reverse at 70 mph. She would hit me and pull on my clothes while I was driving. I was hoping for a relaxing trip. I was really new at knowing Jesus and I had been awake about 28 hours when we stopped at a rest area. Finally I just asked God how we are going to get to Georgia. I'm tired, I cannot think right, and Jenny is going crazy in the little car. Jesus spoke to me and said, put a pillow between Jenny and you.

I did and we took off again. It worked!!! Jenny could not see the radio or the gear shifter or any of the controls. She sat in her seat like, what happened I cannot get into anything. I love you Jesus!

GEORGIA

We arrived at Be In Health on Sunday around noon, registration started at 2pm so we walked the hallway for a few hours. Originally we had reserved a camping sight but when our camper caught on fire I called the church and changed our reservation to a cabin. When they witness Jenny's condition they asked me if she could go up and down steps. I told them I just carry her up and down steps, so steps are not a problem for us. The receptionist needed to check if that was okay with whomever.

This took a really long time, Jenny wanted out of the hall way and was fighting me. I was frustrated, tired, and hungry and wanted to go to our cabin and shower and rest before the Sunday night service started. Thank God in the hall way I met Jerry a man from Montana who was there to go through the conference also. He had an extremely bad back but a great personality. I thanked God Jerry was there because he made the wait more tolerable.

The conference was great. They let me hook chairs together and make a playpen for Jenny in the back of church. The teachings were almost the same as the ones in Cincinnati, but the deliverance sessions were conducted differently. We made it through the long week; it seemed that Jenny's bowels let loose every day. I was bringing three outfits for Jenny every day and doing laundry every night.

Lunchtime was a hoot. Jenny would not sit down, so I fed her on the run. After the second day everyone knew to protect themselves as she walked by or they might be wearing their drink and food. Everyone knew her name and we made a lot of new friends. I don't think anyone had seen anything like this, not even the staff. Jenny truly loved lunchtime and being around people. She learned real quick who would smile at her and who would not. It was really a nice break from our prison at home.

While at the conference they played a song by Chuck Girard tilled "I Will." I loved it so much that I went to the bookstore and bought it. Chuck sings to God about how much he loves God. The words resonated with me: "I will love you forever, I will want you forever, and I will need you forever, until the end of time." I found I had a problem singing the song to Jesus when I was alone in the camper, I found myself singing to Jenny. I tried to sing it to Jesus but every time I started singing the song Jenny would open her eyes and look at me. I loved singing it to Jenny but knew I was supposed to be signing it to God, so I put it away.

On my way to Georgia I was praying that I had missed some small detail in Cincinnati classes and that this detail would be the key to see Jenny's healing. Nothing happened. That is, Jenny didn't seem any different. I had bought some of Pastor Henry's teaching books on fear and envy and jealousy but even after studying them I could not get to the root of Jenny's illness. I figured it must be something from her childhood or something from one of her foster homes or maybe something passed down from her father who was dead (at least we think he's dead). Maybe he had been a Free Mason and had taken those terrible oaths. I spent days doing deliverance from Mason oaths just in case he was in the Masons. I was getting a little disgusted; I was starting to feel like maybe I was on the wrong trail, but I was witnessing great miracles (my friend Jerry's back got completely healed this week) and the good news was Jenny needed less behavior medicine.

THE MOTOR HOME

Upon arriving home I had to start dealing with the insurance company about the motor home fire. After a couple weeks they said it could not be fixed. They were going to total it. I was upset because I knew I could never find another one-owner 37ft motor home in that great shape. I mean in the last two years the previous owners had replaced the motor, exhaust system, the awnings, refrigerator, toilet, DC converter—they were all new. I was sitting in our living room and talking to God. I said, I thought you lead me into that camper, I mean I prayed about it for over a year. I thought I was hearing from you God when you said sell your van and pop up camper and you will have enough money to buy the motor home and the small car. Just then the coolest thing happened. I heard from Jesus again! I heard Him say, "Go over to Holman Motors and see what I can do for you."

I picked up Jenny and put her in the car, and we started for Holman Motors. As we pulled out the drive way I said out loud, "Why am I going to Holman Motors now, I mean I know they close at 7pm and it is 6:55 now." I didn't get an answer so I kept going because I wanted to be obedient to what I heard. When I arrived at Holman motors it turns out they were having a sale and were open to until eight. As I walked in, the salesman approached me and asked if he could help us. I told him I was looking for a used motor home in the 10,000-dollar price range. He kind of smiled and said, "Sir you are just in the wrong place. Holman Motors does not sell or carry anything in that price range. You need to look elsewhere." I said, "I have it on a higher authority that you have something out there on your lot for me." The salesman looked at me puzzled, paused, and said, "I don't know what that means but the used motor homes are way out that way."

I was finally able to get Jenny out to the used motor homes. A cool thing about Holman motors is they put the lowest price on the windshield and you do not try to talk them down. You just accept the price or you don't. The salesman was right—all the used motor homes were 8 to 10 times more then what I had to spend. Then I found one motor home with no price on it. I literally wedged Jenny between two motor homes so she could not fall and I ran for the office. I found the salesman and told him there was one motor home without a price on it. He said it is closing time now. I said my wife is still out there, please get your price book and get out there. I ran to check on Jenny who was still okay, and he came out in a golf cart with the book.

He then got a startled look on his face and said, "I have been here for about 10 years and never seen a motor home on this lot for this price." They wanted $11,900 for it. I said that must be the one I'm to look at. He unlocked it and I carried Jenny up in it and set her on the couch. To my amazement she fell right to sleep! I looked at everything, checked everything, and tried everything. The salesman said if you want to drive it you will have to come back tomorrow and I said I would. I asked if I should put some money down on it. He said no, this is not our normal price range and so I don't think we would have any customers looking at it.

That night I had my son Ronnie look on the Internet for used motor homes and he could not find anything close to it for the price. The next morning Jenny and I were having breakfast when the phone rang. It was the insurance man saying they have a total amount for the old camper. They are going to give you $11,815 dollars. I said that's great, when can I expect a check? He said in one week.

Jenny and I went over to test-drive the new motor home. I couldn't stop smiling as I was thanking God over and over on the way to Holman's. Then I said, Jesus you know there will be at least a 1000 dollars tax on the new one and where will I get the money for the tax?

As we drove it off the lot for our test drive, I saw a pickup truck with two people in it come on to the lot and stare at the motor home. We liked the test drive but found the alternator was not working. The mechanic said it will take a week to get the right one in, is that okay? I said our check from the insurance company would not be in for a week anyway so that is fine. Then the salesman said I think you need to put some money down because those people in that pick-up had looked at the camper last week and they want it also. I said tell them it is sold and I put some earnest money down.

A week later the check came in along with a note from our insurance company stating "if you buy another motor home with in thirty days the insurance company will pay the tax on the new one up to $11,815 so God even paid the tax! Praise God, Praise God, and Praise God!!!!!!!!!!!!!!!!! THANK YOU JESUS!!!!!!

On our maiden voyage I took our new motor home over to the welcome center in Kentucky and parked in the same place where the other one burned up. It was easy to tell I was in the exact parking place because the black burned up stuff was still on the parking lot.

I then started our generator and had lunch with Jenny in our air-conditioned motor home. Thank you Jesus!!!!!!!!!!!! I love you Jesus!!!!

I knew our new to us motor home was going to take us places we never dreamed of because God Himself got it for us. God's gift made it a lot easier to sell our own home. We listed it with a realtor and prayed for a quick sale. Our son Jason decided he wanted it and I said, take over the payments. We did refinance and I got 40,000 dollars to live on for the next three and a half years. That had to hold me over until I could start collecting Social Security. You see all the retirement money I had set aside for retirement was already used up in mostly doctor bills and living expenses already.

The morning after our test drive Jenny fell out of bed at home and thank God she was not hurt, so I decided to put the mattress on the floor. While I was taking the bed apart Jenny started playing in the toilet. I cleaned her up from the toilet mess and as I started to clean the bathroom floor, Jenny ripped the sheets off the bed. She was dragging them around when she went to the closet and hid, as if from her mom saying, "It hurts mom please stop, it hurts." I was able to comfort her and Jenny started walking around again. I guess I'm blessed not to know what went on in Jenny's childhood. I know I am blessed to know and love Jenny and to know she is so strong in her faith in God to overcome it all!! I know the only reason Jenny is so strong is she knows Jesus so intimately!!! I love you Jesus.

Dr. Broderick put Jenny on Depakote sprinkles for seizures and one of the side effects is loss of hair. Jenny's beautiful long hair was falling out and looking really thin. One night some friends, Bill and Cindy, were over for dinner and they told me to cut Jenny's hair shorter so it would look thicker. I looked at their granddaughter who had a little face like Jenny's. Her hair was cut short and it was really cute, so I asked Cindy what do you call this hairdo? They said it's called a "bob."

The next day I just happened to be talking to Ann and told her I'm thinking about getting Jenny hair cut short. I saw a hairdo called a "bob." To my surprise Ann knew exactly what I was talking about and said she thought a bob would look great on Jenny. Ann told me Andrea, their daughter, could cut Jenny's hair.

I called Andrea Record and made an appointment. The day came for the haircut but Jenny was not interested in getting her hair cut, or she just didn't know what was going on. I got her in the chair and knelt down in front of her, wrapped my arms around her and the back of the chair, to hold Jenny in. She was still moving around, shaking her head from side to side, but Andrea got her haircut really good, I mean really good! It was like a miracle.

Ann came to help, thank God, so we tried to cut Jenny's fingernails too. Jenny got wild and knocked over a finger nail polish display. Some of the polish bottles broke, and nail polish went on the floor and on some customer's shoes. It was a mess but Andrea and Ann said, don't worry about that, let's get Jenny's nails trimmed. I wanted to pay for the damages but Andrea would not let me. Andrea would not let me pay for the haircut either. Andrea is still cutting Jenny's hair and my hair, for free, to this very day.

The day after Jenny's haircut I tried to get her hair to curl under like a real bob but I could not figure out how to do it. After chasing Jenny around the house for a while because she would not sit still, I put the brush up and decided to just let her hair be straight. Later I tried again and this time Jenny was walking slower for some reason. I still could not figure how to get Jenny's hair to curl under but by accident I got it to curl outwards. I liked that look better than a bob so I just kept brushing Jenny's hair that way. When people would comment on Jenny's hair and ask what do you call her hairdo? I said, "I call it a Jenny!"

In the late fall Jenny and I went on a weekend getaway in the motor home. Jenny seemed to really like being in campgrounds. On Sunday morning I started rolling up the carpet I put down under our awning. Jenny was walking around but when she saw me rolling up the carpet she got mad. She walked on to the carpet, folded her arms and stood there like I'm not moving. God is so good to me and gives me these little confirmations that I'm doing the right thing. Thank You Jesus, I love You!

One spring day Jenny and I went out on the back deck to walk around. We had a glider on the deck and sometimes I could get Jenny to sit on it with me. Not today, Jenny just wanted to walk. I was looking at the yard that used to be so pretty but now after two years of not being able to take care of it; the yard looked a mess. I thought, Jenny is so steady today maybe I could just cut the grass in this little spot and weed her flowers. It would be cool to have that much done.

I got our lawn mower out. The gas in the lawn mower was two years old but it started on the second try. I had only cut a strip about ten feet long when I heard a noise. I looked up to see Jenny had fallen on the deck; I ran up the stairs to Jenny, Her head was bleeding but she seemed to be okay. I helped her up and into the house where I cleaned the little cut on the back of her head. I know Jenny forgave me and I forgave myself but I didn't worry about the grass any more.

The following Friday we went to R.L.I. for another conference. After each conference I saw little changes, like I was cutting back on her behavior medicine. Jenny's behavior was definitely getting better.

New Adventures

In February of 2009 the refinance was done and it was time for Jenny and I to start our new adventure in the Motor Home. We had a ten-inch snowstorm and the snow was up to the bottom of the storage boxes on the motor home. Jenny was walking around so much and yet she could fall down at any time. So I couldn't even walk out to the motor home let alone start packing it to move. We had a deadline because Jason's lease was up and he had to move or renew. At noon the day before we had to be out of the house Mary came down our driveway in her four-wheel drive truck. She asked, don't you have to leave tomorrow? I said yes and she asked "How are you going to make it out the driveway?" You see it is two tenths of a mile long; all up hill and covered in snow. I said God knows I have to leave tomorrow and He will make a way. Mary said she would ask her husband Kern if she could come over after she gets home from work and feeds the children. I said that would be great. Mary went back to work.

A little while later another friend Robin and her four children stopped by. Robin's children are home schooled and took the time that day to see if I needed help. She said I don't see any tracks in the snow to the camper so I'm assuming you haven't packed up yet. I said your right. Robin said the girls and I will watch Jenny so you can start packing. Robin and the girls stayed in with Jenny and Josh who was 14 years old and Josiah who was 4 years old came out to the camper with me.

I wanted to get the heat on in the camper first and then fresh water in the camper. Josiah was vacuuming the camper with a hand held vacuum. After I got some water in the holding tank, Josh told me the rug in side was getting wet. I had not turned the pump on yet, so the leak had to be back by the tank, which was under the bed. So Josh and I took the bed apart. We had the mattress and stuff spread out in the camper, while we were trying to find the leak.

Sara who was 13 years old came in the camper to see if we were making progress. She looked at the mess and asked (why is the bed apart)? We are looking for a leak in the water tank but so far we cannot find it. She then asked if we had prayed about it, I said actually I forgot to ask God to show me the leak. So Sara made us all hold hands and she led us in prayer, (dear Jesus uncle Ron needs his camper fixed so him and ant Jenny can leave tomorrow) just then Josiah said I see your leak, it is by that thing. I looked and he was right, the leak was by the inlet to the water pump. All I had to do was tighten it up and the leak was fixed. Thank you Jesus.

We put the bed back together and started hauling stuff into the camper. We were all in the camper when we heard a weird noise. It was coming from outside, so we all went to the window to see what the noise was. Some guy was on a quad plowing my driveway, so I went out and ask who he was. It turns out he had bought a house in the neighborhood over a year ago. He told me he had heard about Jenny's condition but never had time to come back and introduce himself to us. Anyway he had just gotten this quad with a snowplow on it and my driveway was the only one not plowed. So he figured he would plow it for me. I thanked him and he finished plowing my driveway. A little while later Robin and the children had to leave.

Mary came that night and watched Jenny while I finished packing. She had a million questions, like how are you going to shop for groceries? Who plowed the driveway? Where are you going to camp? I said Jesus knows I only have groceries for three or four days so after that He has to make a way, and my neighbor who I did not know until today plowed my driveway. Mary was really concerned about how I would get groceries while on the road because she had gotten them for me the last couple years. I assured her Jesus would provide a way for us to have groceries.

I actually had no idea where we were going until that night. A while ago I had ordered a camping directory form trailer life. I figured I needed to go to Florida or someplace warm, because Jenny needed to have a place to walk around and the camper is not big enough. When I looked at the map of Florida everything on the map was blurry to my eyes except the town called Carrabelle Beach and it was written in red. So I figured okay Lord that is where I'm going.

The following morning the sun came out and melted the rest of the snow that remained after the plowing was finished. I hooked up the little car to the motor home and we went up the driveway without spinning a wheel. I was thanking God for providing friends that helped pack the camper and plow the driveway. I thanked God for our new Journey in life.

I was actually glad to be out of our house and looking forward to whatever God had planned for us. I did not realize or think about it then but that was a miracle in itself. Jesus was transitioning Jenny and I to a whole new way of life. The miracle was how much peace I had about it. Thank you God!!!!

Jenny had been in foster homes all her life. Growing up she had lived in many homes, some for only months, that life style had formed a desire in her to lay down roots and to give her children stability. After living in two apartments we started looking for a house. We decided to buy a house with the GI bill. After closing on the loan and receiving the keys, Jenny and I went to our new house. I remember we walked through and Jenny started to cry as she said Ron tell me we never have to move again. It was at that moment I realized how important it was for Jenny to have a stable environment for her family. Later we did sell that home and I built Jenny a brand new house to live in. We stayed in the first house for 9 years and we sold it to build another new house; we were in the second one 20 years.

Now I had to sell it or lose it to the bank. I prayed and asked God please don't let Jenny be mad at me when Jenny is healed, I asked God to give Jenny understanding about how it was I lost her house and all of Jenny's little treasures. The cool thing was I just gave everything we had to friends and most said when Jenny is healed she can have her stuff back. God is so gentle on me.

We had only gone a little over one hundred miles when we hit an ice storm in Kentucky. I pulled into a rest area and started looking up campgrounds close by. I found one and we were able to make it there. The camper stayed nice and warm, our holding tank heaters worked so the holding tanks did not freeze. Thank You Jesus! The next morning I called the highway patrol and they said one lane of the highway is open. I thought, that's all I need, so off we went. When I went outside to unplug the camper I noticed our little car had more than a half inch of ice on it.

That day we only made it to Alabama because the storm had dumped a lot of ice in Tennessee also. The next day we made it to Florida and to warm weather. After setting up in the campground I got Jenny out and she started walking around like she owned the place. I decided to take her over to the Golf and see if she liked the sand. I set her on a picnic table to take her shoes off. I carried her down to the sand, but Jenny didn't like it. She could not walk in it right and that started making her mad. To calm her down I picked her up and while praising God for a safe trip danced in the sand with Jenny in my arms. I then carried her up to the picnic table to put her shoes back on.

To my surprise a couple was already having a picnic at that table where I had left Jenny's shoes. So I ask if it was all right for me to set Jenny down and get her shoes on her. They said sure and as I put Jenny's shoes on her they started asking about Jenny. They watched as I tried to answer their questions and observed how I had to be near Jenny to keep her from falling down and had to keep turning her around so I could hear them. They observed for ten minutes or so, when the lady asked (how do you shop for groceries?) I said I haven't figured that out yet. She said we live about 30 miles from here and there is a Walmart store there near our house. So if you need groceries you call me and I will watch Jenny while you shop. I said what are you doing tonight? She looked at me and said you are serious aren't you? I said yes I am. I went back to the camper and called Mary to tell her I had not been in Florida an hour and Jesus has already worked out my shopping. Then I made a list and off to Walmart we went.

Coming back from Walmart I noticed a little sign it the shape of an arrow that said Carrabelle Christian Center. I just knew Jesus wanted us to go to church there. On Sunday we went and met Pastor Don and his wife Lisa. Lisa volunteered to trim Jenny's fingernails. This was the start of a lifelong relationship. Again Thank You God for looking out for us and putting such nice, loving, and God centered Christians in our life. It was really nice to have Jenny's fingernails done. You see I had lost clear sight in my left eye about two years ago. The doctors at the V.A. wanted to do lazar surgery but I refused to let them. To do things close up like cutting Jenny's fingernails was really hard for me to do. Thank you Lisa!

We started meeting more nice people at that church, and during our second visit we met a little boy named Matt. He was ten years old and fascinated with Jenny. He started feeding her cookies as she walked around, it made him feel really big to be feeding an adult. The following Sunday Matt brought more cookies for Jenny and started feeding her, I found his mother and told her what a special boy he was. She said you only know half the story. She said Matt will come home from school and be playing with his friends, when he just runs in the house and says Momma lets pray for Jenny, I want her healed. She said some times in the middle of the night he comes into her room and wakes us up to ask us to pray together for Jenny. I went over and with tears in my eyes I hugged him!

Jenny and I started going to Matt's baseball games. The town is so small they only have one other team to play and they always lose because the other team has better hitters. Matt told me on the way to the game that someday my team will win a game I just know it. Jenny and I just walked around at the game but Matt was happy we were there. When Matt's team did anything good all the parents stood up and cheered the team on. It was fun to be part of it. After the game everyone stopped for Mexican food. I told them I love it and would come but I usually never eat Mexican food because Jenny cannot tell me if she has heart burn or any kind of reaction to the spices.

Jenny had a great time in the restaurant and ate like there was no tomorrow. She even flirted with the waiter. Every time he walked by Jenny would say whoo whoo and just smile. Then everyone laughed so she did it more. On the way back to the camper, without notice Jenny leaned forward, grabbed her stomach and screamed. I turned on the dome light and she just started smiling. It happened twice on the way back to the camper.

After I showered her and tucked her in bed she went to sleep and so did I. In the night she suddenly sat up and screamed, I turned the light on and Jenny would smile at me. Jenny did it twice. So I ask Jesus, want should I do, I mean what can a doctor do with such mixed signs. Jesus said Jenny is just mimicking the crowd at the baseball game; I thanked God and started laughing. I then went to sleep and so did my Jenny.

One morning I was just overwhelmed with the love of God for us so I got out the Chuck Girard CD and played the "I will" song. It only played a short time when Jenny looked at me and I started signing it to her. So I put it up again, I mean that song is for Jesus.

One morning after showering Jenny, we were outside under our awning and enjoying the perfect weather. I was cooking hash browns and eggs on the griddle. Jenny turned toward me with a different look on her face. I stepped toward her when she vomited; it was all over me and the griddle, table and rug. I was able to set Jenny on a lawn chair and took my shirt off, I then went in the camper to put towels over the carpet, as I did Jenny got up and started to walk away. I quickly ran after her and carried her into the camper; as I carried her to the bathroom her bowels let loose and her Depends did not even come close to holding.

I was trying to get her nightgown off when she vomited again. Now I'm standing bare footed in bowel movement and have vomit on the camper walls and all over me. I was able to keep Jenny in the shower while I grabbed another towel to wipe the mess off me so I would not get it on Jenny as I lifted her out of the shower. I also took off my shorts off for the same reason. I said a real quick prayer that no one would look in the camper as this was going on because all the shades were open. Thank God I was able to get Jenny on the couch and dressed again.

To my amazement Jenny fell right to sleep. So I started the cleanup. I praised God that we were in a campground that had full hook up and a laundry close by. Everything inside the camper cleaned really nice and we had perfect weather so all the windows were open and the smell was dissipating. I got showered, the laundry in the washer and with a hose, cleaned the outdoor rug and the outdoor furniture. It was really amazing to see how easy the cleanup was and how fast the smell left. Jenny was sleeping so I fixed a nice breakfast and had some time to relax before Jenny woke up again. Thank You Jesus for another easy clean up and for all the connivances that are at our fingertips.

We loved our time at Carrabelle Beach and loved everyone we met. There is something special about being there. Even the girls that cleaned the campground bathrooms were special. They would see me having a rough time with Jenny some mornings and the next thing I knew my laundry was folded and sitting outside my camper door. I loved being there with such nice people.

Carrabelle is a fishing village that never let big high-rise motels on their beach. It is like unspoiled, real laid back with mom and pop everything. No chain stores except Subway and an IGA store. Two gas stations and some mom and pop restaurants. The closest traffic light is 13 miles away and the only one in the county. The whole village is surrounded by national forest land on three sides and the Golf on the other side. Carrabelle Beach is truly a paradise of people that love God and share that love so freely with everyone! They are not materialistic and that makes them free to love you freely. God is truly alive and well in the hearts of the people of Carrabelle Beach! I believe God blessed Jenny and I with a very special blessing of knowing them.

One day while talking with the girls that worked in the campground office about God, I mentioned meeting a lady on the beach that had a mentally challenged child with her. Jennifer (one of the girls in the office) said (it was you, I knew it) I said what are talking about? She asks me (did you give the mentally changed girl cookies to feed the sea gals?). I said yes I did. Were you on the beach dancing with your Jenny in your arms? I said yes, Jennifer smiled and said the woman on the beach was Pastor Julie my pastor. She said during the Sunday service Pastor Julie had talked about watching a man pick his wife up and dance with her on the beach. She explained how it touched her heart.

Jennifer went on to tell me about a healing service Pastor Julie has the first Tuesday night of every month at her church. So Jenny and I went to the healing service that week. Pastor Julie is truly dedicated to her congregation and dedicated to pasturing and loving everyone that she meets. She has a huge heart for helping people and when she met Jenny; her love over flowed in the prayers she said with passion and sincerely calling on the name of Jesus to heal Jenny. Jenny and I were truly blessed to meet Pastor Julie and to be prayed for by her. Jenny and I loved being at Carrabelle Beach, but felt it was time to leave even though we had no particular place to go.

We went to Dayton, Ohio to visit with the Walk family. We camped in Kurt and Robin's driveway for almost two months. We had a lot of fun and great fellowship with them and their friends. Their children are fantastic in my estimation. They won or placed in the top 10 of the Bible bee contest for the state of Ohio. Our friendship is forever cemented together!

While at Robin and Kurt's house Jenny's condition was changing more. She actually started sitting down some. I looked at this as a blessing because it was hard to keep up with her all the time. Now Jenny loved to sit on my lap and just be held and I was loving holding her. If I left the room for a minute Jenny would start looking for me. So when I entered the room again I would say (HELLO LOW BABY) in a deep voice and immediately Jenny would smile and laugh. Others tried to mimic me but Jenny new it was not I and would not respond to them. It made me feel pretty special. Jesus loves me so much.

One night I wanted to take the Walk family out to dinner for being so kind to Jenny and I. They chose to go to the Olive Garden restaurant. The waitress came to bring the bill and ask us not to leave a tip. She said it was a privilege to serve us and to watch a true Christian family! Jenny and I were really blessed to share in the lives of such a great family.

While staying at the Walk's we met their friends the Waller family, the Wallers have twelve children and a really huge love of the Lord. He gave up his cushy job to become a farmer and be with his family. Things were really going great for them when the Lord said move your family (12 children) to Israel. They did and now have a great ministry growing grapes and telling people about God. They live their belief in God and that is what makes their testimony so powerful!

From there we went to Montana to see Jerry. You know the guy with the bad back in the hallway in Be In Health. While on the way out to Montana, Jenny's walking became more unsure. I started using a wheel chair while in stores and carrying her more then before. Jenny hated the wheelchair and she truly hated the way people looked at her while in the wheel chair. She would just hang her head and look at the floor. I tried to let her walk but she would just stand and then fall. I could not shop that way, so I had to use the chair while in stores. One thing that was really cute was when I would carry Jenny into a restaurant, people would tell me she was smiling real big. Jenny actually liked being carried so much, that sometimes she would laugh out loud. I loved the way caring Jenny made her so happy. Jesus so loves us He gives me these special moments of Jenny's laughter. I think I said this before but I'm saying it again because it is true I LOVE YOU JESUS ALL THE TIME.

I don't think I said this but while in Georgia, Jerry's back got completely healed. His health insurance had sent him to every specialist in the United States and he had many surgeries; then he was told it was oxy cottons for pain and a wheel chair. After two years of that Jerry said okay boys I did it your way, now it is time to try Gods way. He asked God to heal him and God did it completely. Thank you Father and Jesus and Holly Spirit for healing Jerry's back and letting Jenny and I witness this great miracle!!!

We never thought we could afford to go to Montana where Jerry has a ranch, but Jerry came up with a plan, he let us stay in their drive way two months free which covered the cost of the Gas out there and back. We had an awesome time. The weather was great. Dora, Jerry's wife has her own garden and is a fantastic cook. We felt like kings there. Fresh fruit and vegetables, fresh eggs, milk, and meat all prepared by Dora and Jerry. Dora made homemade ice cream, jellies, and even homemade yogurt. The coolest thing at Jerry's house was how they just gave everything away. It seemed that needy people came almost every day to get free food.

Jerry and his sons love hunting and are really great hunters. They processed all they killed and froze it to give it away all year long. Dora gave away her home made jellies and anything she canned. It seemed that Dora was cooking or canning something ten or twelve hours a day. Her kitchen was always full of good smells. Jesus really blessed us with knowing Jerry and Dora and letting us see firsthand how you can use every blessing Jesus gives you to show His love to others. I believe Jesus never let them run out of food because they never horded there food trying not to run out. Watching them work to take care of anyone that pulled in the driveway was like watching Jesus; love is the biggest and best driving force on earth!! Thank you Jesus for letting us see your love first hand!!!!

When Jenny and I left Montana we headed for Georgia and another conference. While at Jerry's we realized I had missed a lot of the teachings because I always had Jenny to take care of. I was always distracted. So I drove Jenny and I to Georgia and Jerry flew down to meet us. Jerry watched Jenny while I went to the conference uninterrupted. Jerry and I both thought there would be some breakthrough for Jenny. It didn't happen, so I continued searching, asking God to lead me to whatever it was I was missing. I mean I knew without a doubt that Jesus was still in the Healing business. There must be something I didn't know, some missing link.

Anyway I decided to stay in Georgia for thanksgiving and Christmas. I was still hoping I would find the missing link. After going to almost ten conferences I found myself-being judgmental. They teach you in the conferences not to be judgmental but I noticed when I saw someone sick or hurting I would start wondering "What sin did they commit?" What sin brought this disease? I started really questioning the teachings. I was noticing some negative thoughts in my head. I needed some time alone with God to sort this out.

Finding the Missing Link

Jenny and I are still in Georgia. Our friends Kevin and Heather gave me a DVD from Pastor Thurman. He has an amazing testimony about has Granddaughter. After watching it 10 times I told the Lord I wanted to go see Thurman. I GPS'ed his address and figured I needed $410.00 in gas money. So I ask Jesus for financial help. To days later I was in church at Be In Health when a man I didn't know came up to me and put something in my left pocket. I said what is this? He said don't ask and don't look until after service. A few minuets later another man put something in my right pocket. When I as; he said the exact same words as the first guy.

After service I carried my Jenny to our car and then checked my pockets. The left had 15 $20.00's in it and the right had 3 $ 50.00's in it for a total of $450.00. I thanked God over and over and made plans to go see Thurman.

Pastor Thurman is so personable. He prayed for my Jenny. We stayed a week and had some one on one time with him. I know we learned a lot form him and surely enjoyed being with him. My spirit told me it was tie to move on so we headed for our loving Pastor Don and Lisa in Carrabelle Beach Florida.

Carrabelle seemed different, the joyful atmosphere was missing, people were doing all the things they always did but there was a heaviness everywhere I went. Even when you did simple things like getting gas or going to the library people were looking down; they didn't look you in the eye. Everywhere you went and everyone you met was talking about the oil spill in the Gulf of Mexico. Everyone knew it was coming to Carrabelle Beach and it would destroy the fishing and the oyster beds there. Fishing and collecting oysters are the main source of income for the whole town. If the oil comes the town is destroyed. It was really sad to see the morale of the people so low.

We stayed February and March. We spent a lot of time going to the picket area across the street from the campground. There we prayed for a lot of people and met a lot of nice people traveling through. We also spent extra time with Ray and His wife Jimmy this year. They are so great to be with. We saw Matt and his parents and watched him play baseball. Our time went so fast.

The night before we left Carrabelle Beach, Jenny and I went to Pastor Julie's healing service for prayer and to give the gift of Jesus love. I had asked Ray to come and he did. While sitting in church with Ray, God gave me a vision; I said Ray, God just gave me a vision. Ray asked, "What was it?" I told him I saw everyone was standing on the beach with their left hand on the shoulder of the person next to them and there right hand in the air; as they were rebuking the oil from coming into the bay. Ray got excited immediately and said that is just what this town needs HOPE!!!!

Jenny and I left for Georgia the next morning. The campground we went to does not get cell phone service, but on Sunday morning my phone rang. It was an excited Ray on the line; he said the vision was coming true. I said "How in the world did you organize it so fast." He told me he went to Pastor Don and the two of them started brainstorming and came up with a plan. They let every pastor that would bring their congregation to the beach Sunday morning talk for a few minutes.

One pastor said they had to pray for wind from the northeast to keep the oil out of the bay. He no sooner had he said the words and the wind blew out of the northeast and people got excited knowing that their bay was going to be spared. God kept the oil out the bay and fishing and oysters are still a big business in Carrabelle. I thank God for keeping the oil out of the bay. I thank God for the faith of Ray and Pastor Don and for their vision to put together a plan so fast. I thank God for all the faith of the people in Carrabelle and the church leaders that brought their congregation on Sunday morning. God bless you all!!!!!! Enjoy your faith in God as you fish. Isn't God the greatest!!!!!!

I went to Georgia again to see if I could find the missing link. I mean I had seen so many miracles there and at the Cincinnati conferences. I still felt I was missing something. I had been through the teachings about ten times and spent countless hours doing the deliverances on Jenny and myself. I knew there was progress in Jenny; I mean she was not violent anymore and she was completely off all her behavior medicine. Yet physically Jenny was still declining. Her walking was, well it was gone and she was still having the grandma seizers. Sometimes her face muscles would like freeze. It was horrible to see. I mean I'm looking at Jenny's eyes and it is like there is this little Jenny in her head saying get me out, please Ron get me out. I stand in Faith with my Jesus that He will heal her and is getting her out. I praise Jesus that He is with Jenny and I always! I cannot be defeated!!!! I have Jesus!!!! I just know Jesus is real.

Finally one day I was up by the church and I started talking to Peggy, one of the workers at the church. As we talked Peggy asked "What is wrong?" I told her I love Jesus with all my heart and I know He is real but sometimes I feel like I'm giving up on God. I didn't want to give up on God, I mean He had done so much for us but I just could not figure out what else to do.

Peggy asked me "How is your relationship with God?" I used to think it was good but lately I'm not so sure, I mean I look for the sins in my past all the time I just keep looking for the missing sin to repent for. I pray for God to reveal to me the sin I missed, He knows I will repent. Peggy said that's your problem. You need to concentrate on your relationship with God, I look back on that day and laugh because I was looking for the missing link and when Peggy told me what it was, I was almost mad. I thought just one more thing to think about!

I really hadn't realized I lost my close relationship with God because I was spending all my time focusing on the devil. Every time I saw decline in Jenny I would spend a lot of time casting out the devil. I would war against him and check all my notes and look for sin issues I have missed repenting for.

So I was always looking and asking God to reveal the sins in our lives that may cause this disease. I would repent every day for something and forgave everyone for everything I could think of. Concentrating on the devil was pure stupidly. It was like saying I'm not going to watch television but I'm going to sit in the room with the television on and look at it; I just will not watch it. I mean God was right there with me all the time but I was so focused on the devil; I gave Jesus no time to talk to me anymore. Jesus in His word says to resist the devil and he will flee. Suddenly His word became simple; to resist the devil you focus on Jesus. It is so simple, once you realize that. I mean it is a choice; I either focus on Jesus or my circumstances. I cannot love or focus on God while casting out devils all day. I just cast out devils one time and then except on faith that they are gone. I resist the devils temptation by focusing on the love of Jesus. Like I said I Have Jesus so I cannot be defeated, all I have to do is believe in HIM!!! The lights came on in my mind.

COFFEE TIME WITH JESUS

Jenny and I went back to our camper and sat outside under our awning. I said okay God I know we had a good relationship but obviously I lost it somewhere along my way. So I ask Jesus; what does a relationship with you look like? I sat quietly and waited for an answer. Jesus answered me saying "what was it like to date Jenny?" I said Jesus you know, I could not wait to see her, to hold her hand, to spend time with her, to talk to her, I wanted to know everything about her, I wanted to provide for her and I wanted more then life itself to bring joy into her life. Then Jesus said the coolest thing. Jesus said "It's four o clock, go in and make us some coffee." I started to cry and I asked Jesus do you want to have coffee with me? Jesus said "yes we need to spend time talking together today and every day." Immediately I went into the camper, made coffee and poured us both a cup.

Now I have coffee with Jesus every day and I look so forward to it. At night I ask Jesus to wake me up early and we have our coffee time together every morning. It is the most wonderful time of the day. I believe I learned a lot at the conferences, I learned how to forgive others, I learned a lot about discerning my thoughts. Now I know that the best thing in life is having a relationship with Jesus. Jesus and I talk about everything. I was so excited to have this relationship back, I got out the Chuck Girard CD again but I still wanted to sing to Jenny instead of Jesus. I prayed that Jesus understood and I knew in my heart that He did.

Jesus started revealing to me how important this relationship with Him is. Jesus was truly setting me free of the past. Yes that is right; the truth of knowing and having relationship with Jesus is what sets you free from the past. All the years I spent searching the past looking for the sin I could not find could have been productive time telling people about the love of God. I will not waste one moment more searching my past for sin. Instead I will seek the Lord with all my heart. Ministry sets us free if we believe we repent one time and then stand in faith the rest of our life that God forgave us. If we fell we need ministry all the time we have not experienced the love of Jesus in our heart yet. Jesus said my truth sets you free. My relationship with Jesus was starting to come alive again and I was beginning to be joyful again. I could see Jenny was responding also. My love for Jesus was growing fast again!!

We left Georgia and went to Cincinnati to see our boys. After a nice visit with them we went to see Robin and Kurt and the children again. While there we heard from another friend about a preacher called Curry Blake. After listing to the teaching I started to look at the Bible a different way. I wanted more uninterrupted time with Jesus and so I went to a state park. Jesus and I were getting to really know each other and it is great to have my friend Jesus back in my life. Jesus was teaching me that I was His brother. I mean we have the same Father so I must be His brother. Our coffee time together was becoming even more awesome!

I'm going to back up for a minute so you can see where I came from. All my life I was told Jesus came to forgive our sins. I was sin conscious all my life, I mean I was told all my life I was a sinner saved by grace. I spent my time trying not to sin, I prayed not to sin. At the conferences I learned all about sin and how to repent and cast out devils and war against devils. At the conferences I became even more devil conscious. I was taught how devils have all this power and how the sins of the father can be handed down from generation to generation. It seemed so unfair to me.

I remembered going to Moeller, a Catholic all boys' high school. I remembered being taught about the sin most boys do at that age with themselves while alone was a mortal sin. You could go to hell for that. I got so upset every time it happened; I got upset even if it was six months apart. Then one day while in school our teacher, the priest ask for a show of hands (how many of you boys do it). Almost everyone raised their hand. The priest said (just as I thought 90% do it and admit it; while the other 10% lie) and everyone laughed. I thought heaven is going to be a very lonely place. No one seemed too concerned, not even the priest. If it is a mortal sin and you're going to hell for it, why are they not concerned? I think this is where I picked up a lot of confusion about sin and our relationship to God.

I remember crying out to God and saying how is this war fair? How do we learn the rules? I mean the devil has thousands of years to perfect his skills and according to their teachings he can start messing with us while we are in the womb. Almost all the teachings were from the Old Testament. For years I was almost totally sin conscious and just thought about how not to sin. I was trying to love God but it was work. I felt God was disappointed in me, because I was a sinner, so why would God want me around anyway. I found myself trying to please God, to work for God, but not really seeking God except for protection and in my case for a Healing for Jenny. I was in fear of what the devil could do and anyone I met that was not in fear must be in denial.

Then I started listing to Curry Blake's teachings about God and Jesus and he encouraged me to read my bible.. I read in my bible how Jesus defeated the devil and He gave us the same power over the devil that he had. Jesus never gave the devil attention; Jesus simply told them to GO! I probably had heard that before but it seem like the first time to me and this time I understood it.

Suddenly the Bible was a book about life and how to live a God pleasing life of power and authority over sin. I wasn't just trying not to sin I have power and authority over him. I was born again so I had Jesus living in me and I could tell the devil to go and he had to obey. This was revelation to me. In fact I didn't even have to tell the devil to go; he just went when I simply seek relationship with Jesus. The knowledge of knowing Jesus and I are brothers and Jesus lives me is what makes the devil flee. Not acknowledging the devil by screaming and spending time talking, warring and casting him out over and over. Do it one time and stand in faith it is finished!

I only had to cast the devil out one time and then accept the fact he was gone by faith. By Faith I will accept the fact the devil has to obey. Jesus did forgive me and now I can forgive myself and love myself, I am a child of God and He talks to me because I am His son and I know it. Like Jesus said all things are possible!!!! I will not waste my time trying not to sin; I simply will not sin because I will spend my time loving God with all my heart mind and soul!!!

Being in Love

When I fell in love with Jenny, I did not try to prove my love for her by spending time with her friends or trying to please her by doing things for her friends. I did not try to learn what Jenny was like by asking other people about her.

No I proved I loved Jenny by spending my time with her and making what she wanted to do a priority in my life. I went directly to Jenny to know her. I want to love God so I go directly to God to know God. If you make knowing God a priority in your life; you will know God but if you make His priorities you priorities then you are loving God and God knows you. I don't mean for an hour on Sunday, I mean 24/7. The joy and peace of mind, the comfort of knowing Him is yours, in just setting your priorities on Him. The devil will find some other person to tempt. That is right the devil will flee when you put your focus on Jesus the one who already defeated him.

You can know of God without knowing God. I mean you can quote a thousand Scriptures and go to church and sing and wave beautiful flags and still not know Jesus. Jesus said my sheep know my voice and follow me. When I was trying not to sin I knew God. I knew he loved me and sent his son to die for me. I can live next door to you for twenty years and know your name and your children's names but still not know you. But I can start to know you in one hour if I sit down and listen to you personally. What would cause you to listen to your neighbor for an hour? In the case of Jesus; you cannot be satisfied with knowing of Him! If you spend an hour listening to Him you will hear Him and before long He will be your best friend. Trust Jesus and you will hear His voice and develop a personal relationship of trust in God. Trust in God and the devil is a thing of the past.

Now all the devil could do is tempt me. The devil has some real creative ways to tempt me; but that is all he can do is tempt me. I resist the devil by focusing on Jesus all the time. Because I know Jesus loves me; any time the devil brings up the past I don't war against or do battle against the devil, I just focus on Jesus and the devil has to flee, THE WORD OF GOD SAYS SO! All I do is believe and trust!!! My relationship with God was changing; I no longer went to him with request, I went to Him to know Him and the more I got to know Jesus the more I fell in Love with Him.

In the past Jesus and I had a relationship for a while and some of the lessons I learned at the conferences were good information. But I had let the devil come between God and I. I mean I was spending so much time casting out and warring against the devil I never had time to talk to God anymore, I had all my attention focused on the devil and what he could do. I think some of my problem with my relationship with God was; I saw God as the go to God. I mean I only went or talked to God was when I needed him. (God help me) you fill in the rest. We have all prayed like that. Can you imagine having a spouse like that, or college children who only call when they need something? Yes you could love them but it would not be easy.

My God was patient and gracious enough to still hear and answer my prayers, but while listening to Curry's teachings I started learning that God wants us to be friends. Like I said God in His word said He is our Father and that makes Jesus my brother, so I'm a Son of God and a friend of God. I am not just a sinner saved by grace I am a Son of God!!!! I am not a servant; I am a Son who serves. Open your heart and let God in and be His Son!! Seek God not just the reward. The reward is automatic when seeking God first, because God is the reward!! When I dated Jenny the reward was being with Jenny. Heaven isn't the destination; knowing God is the destination and we can know God here on earth so we can have Heaven here on earth. God said so in the Our Father, (on earth as it is in heaven). Life cannot get any better than that!!!

My sins are forgiven and forgotten by God. I no longer need to spend all that time on the devil which got me nowhere. I can now spend my time on Jesus and I know Jesus does not bring up the past. Jesus said our sins are removed as far as the east is from the west and I believe Jesus! I love my coffee time with Jesus but we have communion 24/7. Jesus loves me, Jesus wants to use me and I want to be used by Jesus, I have purpose in life, I am here to spread the Good News!

So now I read the Bible and realize that Jesus not only came to forgive our sins but to empower us with real power over the devil. The devil is no longer this big guy with a head start of thousands of years to figure out how to outsmart us. Jesus showed us while He was a man how to defeat the devil. When you know for a fact that Jesus the Holy Spirit lives in you; the devil is defeated. I read how

Jesus wants us to proclaim His word boldly. The devils did not want me to know that!!!

The devil actually had me looking at my past to find more sin, and then he made me feel more unworthy of the love of Jesus. How is that loving God? How does that bring me peace and Joy of God?? I'm going to concentrate on my past so I can peel off one more layer of sin today and another tomorrow if I just concentrate on the past. How is that loving God??? I'm going to love God more by focusing on God. Think of your transformation as Saul to Paul. Paul could have spent years repenting of killing Christians and for the sins of Saul. Paul chose to repent one time and then he became a great man of God by living the rest of his life for God not crying out begging for the forgiveness and pealing off layers because he knew God had already gave him.

I could not have a relationship with Jenny if I never thought of her, if I am always looking back at my past to try to clean myself up; I would have no time to love her. Actually I would be useless to her. When Jesus ask me what was it like to date Jenny; He knew the answer; when I meet Jenny I went full steam ahead to know her. This is the same thing I need to do to know Him. The more I knew about Jenny the more I loved her and Jesus is the same way!!! Please just ask Jesus to know Him better, don't strive, and just listen for His voice!!!

Another tactic of the devil is isolation. The devil makes you shrink into yourself; he wants you to want to be alone all the time. If you have an opinion the devil will tell you to shut up; it will only make people mad and the devil says who wants to listen to you anyway. I know because I listened to the devil most of my life. I always told jokes, I made people laugh, and I talked politics, but I rarely told anyone my thoughts about Jesus. I'm not the only one; look at the world today! All you hear is politics, sports, hunting, money talk, economy, travel, and negative talk about religion. These are the safe topics. Call a Christian a hypocrite and most people will agree with you and no one will defend you.

Try to talk to someone about God and what he has done in your life and receive comments like "he went off the deep end". I heard a report that 90% of people when asked what the preacher talked about in church Sunday morning would not remember, within one hour of leaving church. I believe as soon as we leave church the devil starts talking and says lets go eat, then we have to hurry to get this done and if you want that, get another job work harder and oh yea that other thing you want is on sale, so just put it on your credit card and save some money its only on sale today. I bet we have all heard the devil and most people don't know it. I know I was caught up in material life and I did not take time to listen to God. What I thought was going to make me happy, only delivered momentary happiness!! But the Joy of knowing and loving God is joyfulness forever!!! Jesus told me to get the worldly stuff out of the way and then you will hear what I Have to SAY!!! Thank you Jesus for our relationship!!!!

Now I am taking time to listen and to read about Jesus. Jesus came to be our example of Boldness and show us how to live boldly. Jesus is my example of how to love my way to Him. Jesus loved us first; He loved us while we were still sinning. Jesus did not say to the Father (I'll go when they clean up their act) no He came to us while we were sinners. The devil is the only one that holds sin against us! No I take that back, we hold sin against our selves because of lack of knowledge. I can guarantee you that anyone that is depressed, broken hearted, or needs pills to get through the day does not know Jesus!!

Jesus came to forgive us our sins and to give us a future of hope, love and joyfulness of knowing the power and authority we have here on earth. Jesus told us to make the devil His footstool. Being depressed and broken hearted and needing pills to get through the day is saying God you are not helping me and we blame God for our problems. We ask God why did this happen? The devil is laughing himself silly. Jesus says read my Book I gave you power and authority over this so why are you asking Me to take care it. Just tell him to go!!!! He has to obey you when you ask in my Name!!! Prove to him you know Me and I will prove to you I love you!!!!

The devil wants to hold us in the sins of the past to rob us our future! When you wake up and think I cannot sin today, I will not sin today, I'm going to be good today, and you are setting yourself up for failure. Wake up in stead and say Jesus what are (we) going to do today, I have the love of Jesus in me and I'm going to give that love to everyone I meet. I cannot even think that way without getting excited and I actually live that way and it is exciting. My life is full of hope and joy knowing Jesus dwells in me and I get to give Him to everyone I meet! Life is sharing the Joy of knowing Jesus and if you're not Joyful all the time just ask God to help you die to yourself and live for Him. Joyfulness is guaranteed!!!!

I wanted to meet Curry, so Jenny and I went to Denver Colorado. Curry was starting a church there. On Sunday Jenny and I went to Curry's church. There we meet Joe Funaro the pastor of Curry's church. Joe is a tough ex-Marine that still bench presses a thousand pounds. I saw him melt like snow in the sun when he met Jenny. His big heart went out of his tough marine chest and Jenny and I have been in love with Joe and his little wife Elsa ever since. What a blessing to meet these two, on fire for the Lord and who are fearlessly doing the work of the Kingdom. Joe talks Scripture 100% of the time. Elsa is herself a great preacher and a woman of God. Joe makes himself available all the time. Just like Jesus!!!

We then went to Colorado Springs to a Curry conference on how to heal the sick, raise the dead and preach the word boldly. I had started praying for the sick to be healed already and seeing some results but I wanted to go to an actual conference. It was great and we saw a lot of miracles. We were encouraged to have a better relationship with Jesus.

Relationship with Jesus is not just a Sunday morning thing. God is for us the whole week. I was really starting to fall in love with Jesus like I fell in love with Jenny. I didn't want to miss a minute of Him, our relationship was growing fast and I loved it! I was starting to get my self-worth from God not from man or my accomplishments. Nothing but knowing God is important to me. Jesus is my brother! I'm loved by God! Life is not about me; life is about telling and showing people how God loves us. Jesus not only redeemed us and forgave us; He came to Prove He Loves Us!!! My sins are removed and I am free to be who God created me to be, a Son of God and a brother of Jesus; a co heir in the kingdom of God. Thank You Jesus!!!!! You restored all that while here on earth and by rising from the dead you proved yourself to be truth. Praise you Holy Spirit!!!! Praise You Holy Spirit and praise God You live in Me!!

I'm just starting to know God and I'm not begging God to heal Jenny anymore, because I know by faith it is done. I believe faith in

God's word makes Jenny happier too. She seems more alert and the people we meet seem to see it also. I'm starting to walk by Faith and not by sight. Wow that probably sounds contradictory, I mean I just told you how I see improvement and then say I'm walking by faith and not by sight. I mean I am now thanking and praising God for Jenny's complete healing even though I don't physically see it. Asking God for something takes no faith. You're just asking.

Faith is believing and thanking Him before you see the result of what you are believing Him for. I now believe the Holy Spirit of Jesus dwells in me. We are one! I can do anything Jesus did! Jesus himself said all things are possible to those that believe and so I believe all things are possible. I know when I pray for someone to be healed and then touch them Jesus flows through me into them and they get healed. I myself cannot heal any one, but knowing Jesus dwells in me and flows through me and believing that truth I can touch the sick and watch God heal them. Jesus and I have become one and so if I touch someone then Jesus is touching them and they receive the love of Jesus. It goes way beyond cool! It's fantastic!!!! I don't say and do these things to make myself-look good, I do them to give the love of Jesus to those in need. I know Jesus lives in me so I don't care if I look good to you or if you think I am crazy; I look good to Jesus and He loves me!!!

Thanksgiving was coming up so I called the boys and told them (if one of you will volunteer your house I will come home and fix you a big dinner.) They said we are going to Thanksgiving dinner at Heidi's house this year. You see Heidi had moved to California about four or five years ago. She is a drug rep and her husband works for Toyota so they just transferred out there. We had only seen Heidi once since they moved. I called Heidi and left her a message (I said how good it made me feel to know the children would be together for the holidays). Three days later Heidi returned my call and said you can come too if you want to. I was really excited and said we will come. After I checked the mileage and our finances I realized it would be too much money and I called Heidi back to tell her we could not come. Two days later she called me back and said she checked with the boys and they were going to split the gas money three ways, so Jenny and I went all the way to California for Thanks giving. Heidi found us a place on the beach to camp and we had a great time!!! THANK YOU JESUS!!!!!

God always takes care of us. While on our way to Heidi's house our exhaust system started leaking, the fumes were coming into the camper when we were stopped at traffic lights. I had Heidi get on the Internet to find a number for Bank's exhaust systems. I called them on Friday after Thanksgiving. They said they were having a one-day sale. This was the first sale, Banks ever had, in the history of the company. I saved over four hundred dollars. I know some people would call that luck, but I don't believe in luck just blessings from God.

The installation department at Bank's exhaust systems was so busy from the sale they could not install the system for four weeks. I told them I wanted to be in Cincinnati for Christmas and ask if they could find a place along the way. They did in Phoenix, Arizona. The guy that did the job was more than professional. He is super and so is our new exhaust system, it boosted our power and our mileage. Thank You Jesus for no more fumes in our camper.

As we were going through New Mexico I stopped at a rest area for coffee and our lunch. Jenny and I were eating when Jesus said to me "you have friends in New Mexico." I could not remember anyone from New Mexico so I picked up our address book and started looking through it. Sure enough Tom and Sue live in New Mexico now. We have been friends for thirty-eight years.

We had an excellent dinner and then went into the living room to talk. Their son Mike came over to introduce me to His wife and new son Miles. Mike is like a stand up comedian. I was laughing so hard at his stories my face started hurting.

Then his wife ask Sue for 5 extra strength Tylenol. A little alarm went off in my head. I ask are you going to take them all now. She said I have to because about 30 years ago I started with an eye problem that gives me pressure in my eyes and terrible headaches. Also now beside the headaches she was getting lumps on her head in her hair.

I ask her not to take the medicine for ten minutes. She asks why. I said I believe God is going to heal you tonight. Can I pray for you? She said yes. I did and her husband Mike started timing God. About seven or eight minutes later she sat up and asked who are you? I'm just a man who believes in God. Her eyes didn't hurt and the lumps were gone. Praise God and live in Praise. I just saw my first miracle, isn't God the best. I know there are probably people who will read this testimony and say that is impossible. All I can say is God cannot lie so why would He tell us to go heal the sick if we could not do it. You see we can become so close to God that we become one with God so He can flow through us and use us to do the work of HIS kingdom. Thank you Jesus I love you too.

Jenny and I arrived in northern Kentucky December 21st. There were about four inches of ice and six inches of snow on top the ice. It was very cold but our camper was built with all the water lines inside the camper and the heater did just fine.

We made it to our boy's house for Christmas Eve. Our rule was no presents for anyone; just have a good time. When Jenny and I arrived at Ron's house their sat a big present for me. I was a little upset because I had nothing for them. They both said dad we just had to get this for you. After dinner I opened the present and it was a loud, obnoxious, but very cool air horn for the motor home. I was excited to get it installed and my cousin Mike said I could pull the motor home into his heated garage to install the horn. Ron came and installed the air horn for me. It works great. Thank you boys!!!! I am literally having a blast with the horn.

Christmas at mom's house was great. My brother Kenny had mom's house looking festive. Christmas decorations looked so cool. Kenny did them just like dad used too. We had a nice dinner and all went well. Jenny had a good time also, she ate very well and we didn't make any messes. Thank you God for a wonderful Christmas.

WHERE IS MY COFFEE?

In 2011, we left Kentucky heading for Georgia to see friends. The church has a weeklong celebration and Kevin and Heather were coming with their son Ariel from Texas. We got stuck in traffic in southern Kentucky for hours. We finally made our way to Tennessee and stopped at a campground. While putting the leveling blocks under the rear tires I could smell gear oil. The next day I went to the office and they told me of a place not too far away that could work on a motor home rear end. I called the guy and he told me it would take a week to fix it. Parts and labor would range between $ 2500 to $ 3500 dollars and I would have to stay in a motel for the week.

I went back to the camper and started praying about it. I decided to fill the rear end with gear oil and try to make it to Georgia. Our friends were coming from Texas and we wanted to be there. We made it to the church campground and met Kevin and Heather. I was so happy to see them because they have such a depth of Godly knowledge and they can articulate their beliefs so well that I love just being around them and watching them express their love of the Father so boldly everywhere. We all wanted to go to American Pie; a pizza restaurant we all like. Derrick the owner was glad to see us and would not let us pay for our dinner. Derrick always goes out of his way to be kind to us. I knew Derrick had a motor home and so I ask him who he would recommend to work on mine. He gave me the mechanic's phone number and told me what a great guy this mechanic is.

The next day I called Kevin the mechanic. He came out and looked at the rear end, ordered the part and fixed it for under four hundred dollars. I was so happy and just kept praising the Lord to everyone I saw. We stayed for a month in Georgia because an ice storm came through and everything in town closed down.

The weather warmed and off to Amy and Brandon's house to see them and their 5 year old Josie who always gives me ten thousand hugs. They have a horse farm and free camping in there yard. It is always great to stop in and see them. I would stop in if I only got five thousand Josie hugs but don't tell Josie that. I love Amy's good cooking and just hanging out. They are so helpful and I learn a lot about forestry from Brandon. There is a peace and gentleness at their home that makes your stay there a great time. Thank you God for leading me to Brandon and Amy's house and to ten thousand Josie HUGS!!!

We then went to a state park in Florida. We stayed for a week because I just wanted to be alone with the Lord and Jenny for a while. I was thinking about going to Texas for a conference that Curry was going to do or we could go to a conference in Florida that Andrew Wommack was going to do. I had pretty much decided to go to Texas when Ray from Carrabelle Beach called. He wanted to know when we were coming to see them. I said you just made up my mind. So Jenny and I went to Carrabelle Beach.

It is always great to go back to Carrabelle and see friends. The whole church welcomed us and we are so blessed to be there. Across the street from the campground is a roadside park. I would take Jenny over there every day and look for people to pray for. One day a car pulled in and two big black men and a woman got out of the car. As Jenny and I approached them it was obvious that one man could hardly walk. So I asked him if I could pray for him. He just stared at me. Then the other man said by brother can't talk. I said that is okay I just want to pray for him. He got a big smile on his face and said go ahead and pray for my brother if you want to. So I commanded the infirmity to go and then thanked God for healing this man. Nothing you could see happened but the lady hugged me so tight and said thank you for praying for my son. Jenny and I got to pray for someone almost every day while we were there. Spreading and sharing God's love is more fun than going to Kings' Island for a whole day. I love you Jesus and thank you for this awesome Journey you have Jenny and I on.

Last year before we left Carrabelle Beach, while attending church Sunday morning Jenny and I were in the entry area of the church. They play their music real loud and I love it, but it hurts my ears. I think it is from being around wood working machinery most of my life. Anyway I don't know if it is hurting Jenny's ears so we go into the big entry area of the church.

That Sunday a young girl came back there with us. It was obvious that she was in a lot of pain. When I asked she said she fell and hurt her back like two weeks ago. So I asked if I could pray for her and for her not to take the pain medicine for at least ten minutes. She said yes and she did not take her pain medicine. This year we naturally went back to Pastor Don's church and upon seeing us the young girl came running and said my back has been fine ever since you prayed for it. I said I love my Jesus and I love seeing His work. Now that is a welcome back; I love you Jesus!!!

One day while having my coffee time with Jesus I suddenly realized Jesus was upset with me. I mean for over a year I had always poured Him a cup of coffee. Somewhere along the way I had stopped pouring Jesus an actual cup of coffee. This morning I heard Jesus say where is my coffee? So I got a cup and poured Jesus a cup of coffee. Then I felt He wanted cream and sugar. Jesus had never told me He wanted cream and sugar before, but I jumped up to get the milk and I turned and looked at the cup of coffee and in my mind I saw Jesus point a finger at the cup and sugar came out the end of His finger, then I saw Him point another finger and cream came out. I said you need a spoon and as I reached for the spoons I looked and saw his coffee was stirred. I sat down and just marveled at what just happened and Jesus said (everything is at your fingertips when you are in Me.) I saw all this in my mind, just as you would see a dream in your mind except I was totally awake! Jesus is so amazing!!!!!!!!!!!!!! So if you have coffee with Jesus, expect the unexpected and remember that everything is at your fingertips when you are in Him!

Our coffee time is so awesome and Jesus is so present that I know He is sitting right across the table from me and I can ask anything and get an answer right away. For example one morning I said (Jesus, I always describe Jenny as precious; how do you describe Jenny? And immediately I heard the words DELIGHTFULLY PRECIOUS) I started to cry because I knew Jesus feels the same way I do about my Jenny)! This is why I say Jesus just wants a personal relationship with you!

Jesus said my sheep know my voice and follow Me. How are you going to know His voice if you never listen to Him???? I know for a fact that the most awesome time in my life is the time I give to Jesus! We are on personal time and I love my personal time with Jesus so much that I am learning to have it all day long!! I think most people think of giving time to Jesus as going to church on Sunday and maybe Wednesday night. They see this as going beyond their obligation. I to love Sunday worship and fellowship but to me loving God; has become a life of freely giving always. The more of God's love you give away the more you get to see people transformed and the more you see people transformed the more you see God's awesome love working. God is blessing Jenny and I with the honor of watching Him flow through us! Thank You and we love You Jesus!!!!

Another morning I was experiencing an extreme closeness to Jesus. So I got out the Chuck Girard CD and turned on the, "I will" song. As I sung to Jesus (I will love you forever, I will want you forever, I will need you forever,) Jenny woke up and started smiling at me, I started signing to her instead of Jesus. I turned off the song and laid my head on Jenny's chest. I said I'm sorry Jesus I always try to sing this song to You but I look at Jenny and the words are the way I feel about her also! Just then with my head still on Jenny's chest I heard Jesus speak to me. He said "Ron you are not singing that song to me I am singing that song to you!" I started crying tears of joy and the joy of the Lord was in me to the max. I pray that everyone can experience that Joy and His love!! It truly is a love that surpasses all understanding!! Jesus in his word says He rejoices over us with signing and now Jesus told me what song He signs to me!!!!! YES I LOVE MY LIFE WITH JESUS!!!!!!!

I cannot imagine or even begin to understand how the creator of the universe, the creator of the world, the sun and whole human race, GOD has time to be so intimate with me! I love you Jesus seems so easy to say but has so much meaning. I dedicate my life to you Jesus, so you can have all of me. I want Jesus to have all of me!! I will live and have my being in You Lord!! Today and forever!!! YOU are the most high, the most Supreme Being and You know Jenny and my name and You call us by Name!! I believe the most important relationship you will ever have is your relationship to Jesus and the Father through Jesus. You will never have a relationship with them without listening to them, without learning what is important to them, and without a desire to hear their voice and to manifest their love on the earth. As my friend Pastor Dan put it, you are the best Jesus has here on earth and He is okay with that. Jesus is just looking for people who are submitted to Him!!!

Miracles Across America

Sometime later we went back to Georgia, to the Be In Health church. This is the church where I first heard the "I will" song. I asked the pastor to play the song during the service and then let me explain to his congregation what God revealed in this song. During the service they played the song and everybody sang along because the words were on the overhead projector. I then told the congregation what Jesus said to me about the song and Jesus said He is no respecter of persons, so I believe Jesus today, right now wants to sign this song to all of you individually.

I then ask the church to play the song again only this time please don't sing, just receive from Jesus, the perfect love of Jesus. I then walked back to my seat and held Jenny. I had my head down listening when someone tapped me on the shoulder and said Ron you need to see this. I looked around and everyone, I mean everyone, even the pastors of the church were crying. God's love is that perfect and that powerful!!!! YES JESUS I LOVE YOU AND I KNOW YOUR LOVE FOR US IS PERFECT!!!! Isn't it amazing what the perfect love of Jesus can do!!!

From Georgia we went to Ken Lake state park in Kentucky. We met our friends Robin and Kurt and the Waller's there. The Waller's have a ministry and rent the whole park for the week. There friends come from all over the U.S. to celebrate God's feast day together.

These people have a lot in common. They home school their children, most live on farms with out electric, they dress almost like the Amish and they will not touch pork. There is a peace about them that is contagious. Their children are the most respectful children I have ever met. Although the way I dress Jenny and I did not conform to their standards they made us fell very welcome.

While walking Jenny in the wheel chair every afternoon, a little girl about 3 years old would see me coming and she would walk in front of Jenny and just stair at Jenny. The fourth time she stood in front of Jenny she ask me "is it hard to dress your baby?" I really love children and I love their questions and if I had known her better I would have hugged her till the cows come home.

From Kentucky we went to a church north of Atlanta. Our friend Pastor Joe from Colorado came to preach the good news so Jenny and I went to see and hear him. Joe is on fire for the Lord and spreads the word in a powerful message, about who we are in Jesus. The more I learn about who I am in Jesus the more I can help others learn about who God created them to be. When you have that knowledge down deep in your heart the world is a safer place to be. The word of God is the love of God, you cannot separate the two and God says His perfect love cast out fear; so I fear not.

We moved on to Myrtle Beach to meet with up with our longtime friends Philip and his twin daughters Claire and Faith. We camped near the ocean and had a great time. The weather was great for beach goers. I decided to take Jenny to the pool. When I carried her into the water, she responded with a big smile. While in the water I hold Jenny's shoulders and walk backwards so her body just floats along with me. She seemed so happy and it must feel so good to finally be off her backside.

Jesus had a big gift in store for me the next day. I decided to take Jenny to the pool again, as I carried her into the water I sat her little bottom in first. As soon as Jenny felt the water on her bottom she looked at me and said FUN just as clear as you read it just now. I was so amazed that I almost dropped her. God is so amazing and God's love for us goes beyond understanding. What a gift to hear Jenny talk and the word she said was appropriate to the situation. I know I am blessed beyond any material possession and I want to thank you Jesus for bringing such Joy into my life.

We left for Cincinnati to see Ariel our granddaughter, the boys and Mom. Ronnie invited us to his house for dinner. Ronnie is an excellent cook and I never turn down any of his cooking.

While eating dinner at Ronnie's, I suddenly had to use the bathroom. I asked Jason to hold Jenny in the chair I had her tied in. Jenny was leaning forward that night so I had tied her into the chair. When I came out of the bathroom, Jason was asking Jenny "what is my name mom, who am I mom, do you know who I am mom" as I approached them Jason suddenly leaned back and said mom is crying dad. Then he looked at me and asked, why is mom crying? I said I believe mom knows who you are but she cannot get the words out. Jenny stopped crying and we finished our dinner. We all went into the living room and started talking when Jenny suddenly leaned forward and screamed to the top of her lungs! Everyone jumped and Jenny just sat back like nothing happened. The boys asked, "Why did mom scream?" I said sometimes it takes 30 to 40 minutes from the time you ask a question to the time you get a response. I believe that scream is a response to Jason's questions. I believe it is sheer frustration that Jenny cannot answer Jason, because she knows who Jason is.

A couple weeks later Jason and I were talking on the phone about the night mom cried, Jason said he now thinks maybe mom got her hand into the onions Ronnie had that night and that is what made her eyes water. He said the scream might have been a gas pain. I said Jason I know you think I'm crazy when I talk about how the devil works, but do you realize; you are letting the devil steal this precious moment away? God gave you a precious moment with your mom and you explaining it away. I'm telling you that is the work of the devil.

About a week later I was getting ready to hit the road again. I needed something from Lowe's and I wanted to take Jenny to Chipotle. Before we left to go to Lowe's, Jason called and we realized we would up that way about the same time, so I ask him to meet us at Chipotle. He said he would and as we were eating, Jenny suddenly turned her head toward Jason and started staring at him. Jason asked me, "Why is mom staring at me?" I said I think she recognizes you Jason. Then Jenny started crying again. I said Jesus just confirmed it was not onions or gas pain was it. Isn't Jesus awesome!

For some reason I wanted to go to Michigan for a while. So Jenny and I took off for Ludington, Michigan to see some friends we met there six years ago. Kim and Bryan were camped next to us and helped me through a rough time with Jenny that week, it was around the start of Jenny's violence. We have been friends ever since. So we meet in the same campground but they could only stay one night. We still had a good time and as usual it was great to see them.

I decided to just head north. Life was a little boring, I mean I had not prayed for anyone or seen any miracles for a while. I talk to Jesus every day and started asking Him what is going on? No answer. The next Saturday Jenny and I went north to a town called Charlevoix. It turns out to be a tourist town. It is beautiful, the weather was great, there are parks and a drawbridge, and a beach on Lake Michigan, and a lot of walk ways for Jenny and I to walk on. So we walked and as we did we saw the same couple three different times. I knew God wanted me to talk to them.

They didn't seem to be in a hurry and they were holding hands like young lovers. I started to talk to them about God naturally, and to my surprise they were receptive. After listening about a half hour the lady started smiling, she said my husband is a pastor of a church here in Charlevoix. They invited us to their church for Sunday worship. We continued talking and I told them about Jenny and I being full time campers. Margie said our church has a campground. Wow how cool is that. On Sunday Jenny and I went to service and met some of their congregation, including Pat, a woman who was leaving on a mission trip the coming Saturday. Neil and Margie showed us the campground. We moved up on Monday.

We were also invited to a lighthouse lunch to feed the poor. As Jenny and I walked into the lunchroom I tried to pray for a guy that had his hand bandaged and a scar on his arm. He got upset and left. I thought to myself, I have only been here one minute and I have already drove one their customers away. We were also invited to a Wednesday prayer meeting with the city officials, to pray for the city. It was really cool to see the city officials asking for the guidance of God in their decisions. On Thursday we went to the lighthouse lunch again and the same guy got up and walked out when I ask to pray for him again.

The campground was closing for the winter so Jenny and I started looking for another campground. When Pat came by and asked us to house sit her house while she was on her mission trip. Free camping and free laundry, I'm in! Pat's trip got delayed for a day so we went for a walk Saturday evening. We went to a parking lot were some kids were playing Christian music. As we sat there listing to the music I was trying to hear the words because I had not heard some of these songs before. I could not concentrate because my eyes kept drifting over to a dress shop across the street. I asked the Lord "do you want me over there? Is something going to happen that you need me over there?" No answer. Then a woman started preaching and I was trying to listen except I was still distracted by the dress shop. Finally Jesus spoke to me these words, "that is what you were 7 years ago." So I asked "7 years ago I was a dress hanging in the dress shop window?" "No! 7 years ago you were just hanging around taking up space!" I started laughing to myself and then told Pat what Jesus said to me.

The women preaching finished and the music started again. I went over to the women and told her what the Lord had said to me about the dress shop and she thought it was funny. She asked if I wanted to share that with the crowd there. When the music stopped she called me up to share. After I shared and everyone laughed, she did not ask for the microphone back so I asked the crowd if they knew Jesus was still a healer today.

I know Jesus was giving me boldness to face this crowd and so I started talking about Him. I thought I talked about five minutes but later I found out it was over thirty minutes when I ask is there anyone here that would like to be healed. One guy in the back raised his hand. I invited him up front and Jesus healed him of Turrets Syndrome, his name was David. So David and I praised God for couple minutes and then I ask if anyone else wanted to be healed of anything. To my surprise no else wanted to be healed and so I just went back to be with my Jenny.

The woman got up and started preaching but I could not hear her because I was just so overwhelmed, thinking about what Jesus had just done. Then some rough looking guy stood up in front of us and went to get some free popcorn. I watched him shuffle across the lot and my heart hurt for him. He was in such pain, he looked so hungry, my thoughts were racing and I wondered why he did not answer the call to be healed. I ask Jesus, can I pray for him? Immediately I heard the words "do unto others as you would have them do unto you." When he set down again with his popcorn I walked over and asks him, can I pray for you?

He looked at me and said FOR WHAT? To be healed of course. He said you are not from around here are you? No I'm not. If you were you would know I am not worthy of a healing. He went on to say how bad he was and how 28 years ago he got high on drugs and stepped in front of a truck trying to kill himself. He has been paralyzed on his whole left side ever since. We talked about the unconditional love and forgiveness of Jesus and he let me command his muscles to work in Jesus name. Then I kept talking to him about Jesus. He really did not seem to be listening but I kept talking when I heard in my head "make him walk." So I ask him to walk! I stood up and held out my two hands.

I was so excited to see him walk that I did not notice he used both his hands to get up. As he tried to walk he said my left leg does not hurt. The left leg started moving and he said it again (my leg does not hurt). Then he started walking around in circles in the parking lot. Some lady felt the excitement behind her and as she turned around and saw him walking she said in a loud voice "look at step and a half he is walking" everyone started looking at him and gasping at what they were seeing. I felt prompted, so I went over and ask step and a half "what is your real name?" He said Jimmy and I said I think people are going to have to call you Jimmy again. He looked at me and said "I would really like that."

Jimmy continued to walk and then ask if we could get together to talk some more tomorrow. David had come over with us and we praised God for the miracles. David wanted to talk some more also and so we all decided to meet after church in the parking lot. Jenny and I went to the camper; I was so full of joy and so excited I knew it would be a year before I could sleep. To my surprise Jenny and I did sleep really great that night.

In the morning the excitement of last night had really set into my heart, how much Jesus loves us!! Jenny and I went to church and then out to the parking lot. It was cool because David pulled up with Jimmy and we started talking. David asked me (guess what Jimmy was doing when I picked him up) so I did. David said Jimmy was stepping up on the curb and then down off the curb. So I asked Jimmy why were you doing that? Jimmy looked at me and said for twenty-eight years I could not do that.

We started talking about the unconditional love of Jesus, when Jimmy said I wish I could believe that! I was shocked when I heard him say that. I said Jimmy, Jesus healed you last night to show his love for you; Jesus took your pain and as I said that Jimmy looked at me like someone just turned on the light. He started smiling and said that's right; Jesus does love me doesn't he! Jimmy said it again, Jesus does love me! We talked for a long while and I needed to change Jenny so we went to the camper. Jimmy now has a large print Bible that he can continue in his quest to know, love and serve the Lord.

David had his own ministry. He would find hurting people and help them. He traveled to other towns and even Detroit to find these people. Most of the time he seemed to find drug addicts and help them get off drugs. He was fearless in his pursuit to help these people. He would put himself in harm's way to help others like we would cross the street. I mean he was fearless. On Tuesday night we went to a Bible study together. Jenny and I were not in the room two minutes when David said (Ron is a healer, so if anyone needs healing just let Ron pray for you) I was totally embarrassed and looked embarrassed too. Then David said don't be embarrassed Ron just pray for someone and God will prove me right. A couple people did receive healing that night, and it is so awesome to watch God work. Praise you Father and Son and Holy Spirit for another awesome night and for letting Jenny and I see the love you three have for this world. Your level of caring and Your level of love is so much more vast and more powerful than anything anyone could imagine! My heart is just singing!!!!

On Wednesday David brought another guy to our camper. He had been gut shot in a drug deal gone bad. He was dumped in a dumpster and then shot 9 times with a 9 milliliter and left for dead. He had enough life in him to dial 911 and then pass out. The police tracked the 911 signal to him and got him to a hospital. There he laid in a coma for a long time (I believe it was months) and then after a vision from Jesus and Mary he came out of the coma. The doctors were putting him back together piece by piece. It is a fantastic testimony by itself.

David brought him to the hospital that day for another leg operation. When they got to the hospital they found out the operation was to be done on 10/1/11 and this was 9/1/11 so they were a month early. They left the hospital and David brought him to our camper. After we prayed he said it did not change, the pain in his legs was still there. So we talked some more and then the Holy Spirit said tell him to walk. So I ask him to walk outside and see if the pain went away. David and I watched out the window and literally watched the miracle take place. He walked around David's car and then started running and jumping and laughing out loud and we all praised God. It is just beyond description of words to watch the Joy of the Lord!! Thank you Jesus for this awesome journey you have Jenny and I on. Jesus I know you came to show us the love of the Father and you did show us His love. Your love and the love of the Father are one and the same. It is really cool to see Your love in action and to know there really is nothing impossible for You and there is nothing impossible for us when we call on the name above all names Jesus Christ of Nazareth. My desire to know You and love You grows more every day!!!!

On the following Tuesday we went to the lighthouse lunch again. This time I did not ask Chester if I could pray for his hand. I just walked over and grabbed his hand and prayed so fast he never had time to react until I had finished praying. Then he just sat there. I went up by Margie and Neil and sat down, when Chester got up and started walking toward us. He came right up to me and said is that your camper at the end of Pearl Street? I said yes, he said I had a tree to cut down right down the street from you and if I had known that was your camper I would have stopped in to see you. I said stop in any time you want. I believe we are friends now and isn't it great to see God's love in action!!!

It was starting to get pretty cold up their so Jenny and I decided to head south. Our friend Larry called from Oklahoma, to tell us about a friend of his called Dan Mohler. Larry said we should go see Dan; he is going to be in Delphos, Ohio. I looked up the town and we were close, so we went. The first night I heard Dan preach I was overcome, the gospel is the same no matter who preaches it, I mean Jesus is the same today and forever, right! But some people have a way to make it come alive and deposit it right in to your heart.

Jesus said to write His words on the tablet of your heart, and He uses Dan to make you want more of the word in your heart more then any one I have ever met. I have heard it said (it is not what you say but how you say it)! I believe I am more empowered by God since I heard Dan then I ever was. If you want a sample go to (www.neckministry.org) I guarantee you will find a whole new meaning to the word LOVE and in that meaning you will find a whole new You! I guarantee you will love the new you!!!!

Your relationship to Jesus and what Jesus did on the cross is going to become so real that living will take on a new meaning. Dan's love of the Lord is so real and when you get it, your love of the Lord will be so real that as Dan puts it (you never back slide; you front slide right in to the arms of Jesus every day). The presents of the Lord will be alive in you and overflow in to everyone one you meet the rest of your life. People will want what you have, your Joy of knowing Jesus will over flow on to them and you don't have to say a word, just start living it.

If you want proof read the testimony of Todd White or listen to it on the web site. Be encouraged not discouraged. Please check it out for yourself.

One day Curtis called and said come meet us in Tennessee. So Jenny and I headed to meet them. On our way to Tennessee we were heading south on I 65, the expressway is one that creates a thump thump in the camper for hours. Jenny was in the passenger seat and very alert. The thump thump was kind of bothering me but not her Thank You Jesus. As we were driving, a lady in a car that was passing us got my attention and as she pointed to the bottom of the camper. I took the next exit and upon coming to a stop turned around to go out of the camper when I saw the problem. A water line had broken and water had flooded the floor of the camper. I said a prayer for the Lord to show me the leak and make it somewhere I could get to it without taking a lot apart. The first place I looked was under the sink and there was the broken water line just hanging there.

I got my map out and saw there was a campground about ten miles from me. I called and ask by chance do you carry water line parts and he said no but the next exit you come to has a Menards store right at the top of the exit. So we headed there. The parking lot was sloped so I was able to let the water still drain out the side of the camper while I went into the store. Jenny had fallen asleep so I decided to run in myself. On the way into the store I was talking to Jesus and ask that this not be a wild goose chase. Please let me find the part, I knew from my plumbing years that this was no ordinary part. I went to the plumbing department and just put my hand into one of the many bins of fittings and like Jesus lead me to the right part instantly. I looked at the fitting in my hand, almost in unbelief and then looked in the bin and this one was the only one there.

I could hardly believe what happened when a sales person ask is there anything I can help you with. I said do you carry nipple extractors and he took me to where they were. Back when I was in plumbing they only sold them in sets of four for about $80.00, but here they sold them separately and the one I needed was ten dollars. I went to the camper and fixed the leak. Then to the campground and ask if there laundry was open all night and it was, Thank You Jesus. I hooked up the water to our camper and turned it on and there was no leaks, Thank You God. Jenny was soiled so I put towels on the floor to soak up the water while I waited for our water heater to heat our water to shower Jenny. I went to the laundry and to my surprise the dryers only cost fifty cents. I have been full time camping for two and a half years and have never seen dryers for under a dollar. Thank You Jesus.

I had electric heaters blowing on the floor along with a fan to dry the remaining water in the rugs. I showered Jenny and we ate our dinner. We were so blessed the weather was warm and we could have the windows open to help with the dry out. After I got Jenny in bed I started thanking Jesus for all the details He took care of for the easy fix. I mean the whole day was one miracle after another. As I was thanking Him I suddenly ask what caused the leak anyway. Jesus said when you were on the highway and the camper was going thump thump the water line was bouncing until it broke. Jesus said you need to strap it up so it cannot bounce and break again. So I strapped the water line and I spent the rest of my awake hours that night Thanking Jesus for being my very best friend! Jesus is my best friend and I LOVE having Him with me every step of the way!!

The next day I went to the campground office to see if there was an extra charge for using the electric heaters. There was and the lady thanked me for being so honest. We then went to Tennessee to meet up with Curtis and some of the other families from family week. It was so awesome to see everyone again. It is so awesome to see real families love each other and brothers and sisters love each other. When I say I am in heaven, while I am with them, it is true. There is no materialism, no disrespect, and no lack of love for each other that I witness in other campgrounds. There is contentment in their life that translates into unconditional giving of themselves. I have been blessed to be part of their celebration and blessed to share it with you.

My camper was parked where I could see them but I was not able to get a site right next to them. One morning a new camper pulled in alongside me, and because I do not dress like them, that is I still wear my shorts and tee shirt, people automatically assumed I am not part of their group. So this man said to me "did you notice them people up there?" I said yes and it just happened that Curtis Tucker's little girls were doing dishes by the water faucet and as they did the dishes they were singing. People would stop and listen to their voices, they are truly a glimpse of the sound of heaven. I relive their beautiful voices in my heart a lot. The man then said those people come here every year and we come to just be near them. There is something special about the way they live. He said even their children are special. I said I noticed it also and I think it comes from their love of God and His love of them.

One day after a Bible study at the park shelter, they started playing music and the women and girls went in the grass and formed a circle to sing and dance to the Lord. The playground was not far away and other kids were playing when they saw these women and children dancing. Later a lady who had her grandchildren at the playground said to me "my grandchildren ask me who are they dancing for? The boys are not even watching them." The grandma told them I think they are dancing for Jesus.

She said their comment was very convicting to her. Suddenly she started thinking about how suggestively her grandchildren dress and dance. I don't know if that day changed their life but I hope it did. I pray for them to come to know the savior of the world and that His message does not limit us; it sets us free! Jesus I love you with all my heart and I love to see you moving in the hearts of others. The freedom and joyful life we have in You sure beats all the material in the world! The sad thing is the devil has us all looking for material things to make us happy when the only real Joy in life is having a relationship with you Jesus. Jesus please let Jenny and I be a good example of your love everyday of our lives. I live to manifest You in all I say and do!!!!

From there we went up to see our sons in Cincinnati. It was a quick visit and then off to Wheeling W.V. to see my best friend Joe Coleman and his lovely wife Renee. What a joy it was to spend time with them and free camping in there drive way was pretty cool too. We went to Joe's fresh fish store for lunch every day, his fish sandwich is rated the best by Gourmet magazine. I know Jenny and I love it. If that is not good enough Renee is a great cook also and their tender loving way of taking care of Jenny and I will be etched in our memory forever. Jenny and I are so blessed to spend time with them. Joe and I met in the navy 41 years ago, when Joe and Renee married 40 years ago, Joe asked me to be his best man. Than a year later when Jenny and I married I ask Joe to be my best man and so I guess that makes us the best men. I know it makes us best friends!

We went to North Carolina to see Curry Blake. His message was great also and real similar to Dan's. I like hearing who I am in Jesus Christ from both of their perspectives. They light my fire to read and study the Bible so I can stay uplifted, and convey that uplifting to everyone Jenny and I meet. At this stage of life I am learning who God sees me to be. I want to have the mind of Jesus and the eyes of Jesus and although I read the Bible and Jesus talks to me, it is still very important for me to be around like-minded people.

I have this awesome time with Jesus every morning and then commune with Jesus all day but it is so nice to have fellowship with like-minded people also. It seems the best place for me to find like-minded people, are these conferences. At this one I met John and his wife Penny and Maylin and her husband. We have stayed in touch ever since. They are very uplifting to talk to and are on fire for the Lord. So any time I am in their area my spirit lefts and my heart jumps for Joy knowing we are going to spend time together and talking about my favorite subject: Jesus.

You see traveling like we do Jenny and I run into so many people that are completely materialistic and do not want a relationship with God at all. It seems they are almost afraid that a relationship with God will put demands on their time. They are searching for happiness and looking for something material to fulfill them, it is really a shame and if they go to church on Sunday morning or not is okay with them. I'm sorry if that sounds judgmental; I don't want to sound that way, it is just an observation. I want all my conversation to be about the life of Jesus and what He has finished on the cross. I do not want to talk about material things. So when Jesus puts me in touch with people like Maylin and her husband and John and Penny I get excited when they call because I hear what God is doing in their life and it is truly uplifting.

I thank God my Father and Jesus my brother for this awesome journey and for the awesome people he puts in our life.

From there we went to Ashville. The campground we stayed at was almost empty. It was high on a hill and had a pretty view. We saw the Billy Graham chapel and museum. It was really cool to contrast it with the Loretta Lynn museum we saw earlier this year. While camping near her museum we meet some people that had free tickets to Loretta's museum and they shared them with us.

The whole museum was about her dresses, her gold albums, her cars, her busses and her friends. The Billy Graham museum was free to everyone and all about God and what He has done. In his museum there was a picture of an old man that asked Billy to come to a tent revival with him. Billy was 16 years old and said I have better things to do. The man than enticed Billy by telling him the revival is about an hour's drive and I don't like to drive at night, so if you go with me, I will let you drive. Billy drove the man and that night gave his heart to the Lord and the rest is history. We never know what one simple act of kindness will turn into. I liken the old man that didn't want to drive at night to the mustard seed of faith the Jesus talks about. When a seed the size of a mustard seed is sown in faith and with the love of God then look out because it can turn you into a lifelong love of Jesus and powerful man of God!!

While in Ashville I started suffering from withdrawal. That is I had not prayed for any one in a long time. So I talked to the Lord and asked Him to find someone for me to pray for. I usually find people in the campground laundry but like I said there was no one else in the campground. So I programmed my GPS for a Walmart and Jenny and I went.

It was almost Christmas and the Walmart was extremely crowded. I felt like we were in the way just being there. So I picked up a couple things we needed and went to the check out. The lines were long and everyone was just standing there but there was still no one in obvious need of prayer. When I finally got up to the checkout girl I suddenly felt heaviness about her. So I asked her, are you excited about Christmas? She said I'm excited for it to be over. So I asked, are they working you to many hours, and she replied I wish it was that simple. I ask, "What is the problem?" and she asked, "Do you really want to know?" I said "Yes I do." She looked me right in the eyes and said yesterday is the first anniversary of my son being murdered. I ask what happened to him. She said

Last year he was at a Christmas party and it was nice out, so everyone was outside in the yard of the apartment complex. When he heard a man screaming and hitting his wife. So he went to them and bear hugged this man from the back. Her son was really big and strong so the man could not get loose. He told the man I will let you go when you calm down and stop hitting your wife. The man did calm down, so her son let him go and her son went back to the party.

Two hours later the man came out of his apartment and approached her son with a big smile on his face. Everyone including her son thought he came to thank him for helping him cool off. When the man got right up to her son he pulled out a knife and stabbed him right in the heart. Witness said her son fell straight to the ground dead.

I ask her if I could pray for her and she said yes. I think I shocked her though when I reached across the conveyer belt and put my hand on her shoulder. With tears in my eyes I ask God to repair her broken heart. Then I said it is not just broken Lord, it is shattered and I thank You Lord for repairing it! Then I said I want to ask you Lord for one more thing for this dear lady, I want you to make this Christmas the best Christmas ever for her. She opened her eyes and said that is impossible. I said nothing is impossible for my Jesus. She said that is impossible. Just then God gave me a little vision; so I said I just saw you sitting in an easy chair with your feet up, I described the room and the wallpaper it was Christmas night and you had a smile on your face and you said I don't believe this, but this is the best Christmas I have ever had. She looked at me surprised and said I have a chair like that and you described my living room, I smiled at her and said I know; and you are going to have the best Christmas ever. Just then I heard the lady behind us crying. Jenny and I walked out of Walmart with so much joy in our hearts that it is totally unexplainable. I love my Jesus and I love to watch Him transform people. I am so blessed to have Jesus for my best friend! I hope and pray you do too!!!!

From Ashville we started heading for Cincinnati to see our sons and mom for her Christmas. We stayed at East Fork Lake campground, they have 340 camp sites and only hand full of full hook up sights and we were blessed to get one. Actually I think most nights we were the only ones there except a homeless man we met that was living in his car. I felt so sorry for Jeff; especially the day he had his little girl with him. I invited them into the camper and we talked for a while, he told me the park rangers were going to make him move on. He had a job doing the dishes at a restaurant but it was not enough money to pay for an apartment. I did what I could and we exchanged phone numbers and although I called I never got a call back.

The Joy of the Lord

Around January 1st 2012 we started heading south, when the phone rang, it was our friends Joe and Erin, from Nicholasville, Kentucky. They wanted us to stop by and camp in their driveway. I said "no" because there were some tree branches that would need to be trimmed and I would need 30 amp electric. To my surprise Joe had already handled those problems. I thought to myself, this is a serious invite. Jenny and I went and what a time we had.

Joe and Erin were so accommodating and so attentive to our special needs. We were welcomed by their friends and families and overwhelmed by the love of them all. It was as though we were special in some way. They did everything humanly possible to make us feel at home and we did feel at home. The coolest thing about being there was everyone they knew prayed for Jenny and I. The love and prayers and the fellowship seemed endless. We had Bible studies and prayer time every day that was so awesome. Our days were filled talking about Jesus and His love for us all.

They have two children a six year old, Zechariah and a three-year-old Regan. After Jenny and I were there about a week I started calling Regan, Reggie. One night this little three year old stood in front of me with her hands on her hips and said Uncle Ron my name is REGAN! Not Reggie. I said okay Reggie I will try to remember that. She gave me a look that would melt the hardest of hearts and said you already forgot!

One day Zechariah and I went to the hardware store together. Zechariah noticed one shoe of the man waiting on us was built up about six inches. He asks the man if he could pray for him. The man said I guess so. Zechariah held the man's hand and my hand so the three of us formed a little circle. Zechariah closed his eyes and said "devil! we don't like you so in the name of Jesus you have to go! Then he opened his eyes and asks the man what is your name? The man said Bob. So Zechariah said Jesus in your name I command

Bob's leg to grow out right now." Nothing seemed to happen so we got what we needed and went home.

That night Erin had some church business to do so we ordered pizza. When the doorbell rang Zechariah ran and opened the door but instead of getting the pizza he asked the man if he needed prayer for anything? The man was kind of shocked, he thought for a second and said the roads are rough sometimes my pizza's get messed up in the car and then people don't want to pay for them. Immediately Zechariah took the man's hand and prayed for smooth roads and that everyone would pay for their pizza and give the man big tips. The man smiled real big and said I like the way you pray. I thought how cool it was that Zechariah prayed for this guy even though he had no obvious need for prayer.

The next morning during my coffee time with Jesus I asked the Lord about Bob's foot. I said "you know Jesus when Zechariah prayed for Bob yesterday; his prayers were so innocent and heart felt and full of compassion, that I was praying for Zechariah to see Bob's foot grow out. I thought how seeing it would grow Zechariah's faith." Jesus said did you notice it did not deter Zechariah's faith? I thought for a moment and realized, you are right Jesus the first person he saw after that he prayed for (the pizza man). Just then pastor Joe our friend form Denver Colorado called and after I told him about Zechariah he said Jesus just spoke to me and said tell Ron all your prayers are that innocent to me! I love you Jesus and I love you more every day!!!

Jenny and I stayed at Joe and Erin's house the whole month of January. We had such a nice time. It seemed we were always praying for someone or being prayed for every day. Joe's friend and partner in business Budd came by almost every day and is an awesome guy that has visions. He is very encouraging to be around also. One day we all went to pray for a friend of mine named Larry.

It was about a two-hour drive each way and so we had time to interact with the kids and pray more on their level. All though I can play and rough house with kids all day, I personally have a hard time trying to explain or teach them the Bible. Budd, Joe and Erin were like experts conveying the gospel message and it was awesome to hear the questions Zechariah had. It was another wonderful day in the life of Jenny and I. I cannot wait until Jenny is talking to me about all these great times. I Praise God for His love for us and for the Hope we have in Jesus and to see the healing manifest in Jenny!!! I really miss her even while I am holding her in my arms!

Erin is such a great cook; we never had the same meal twice in thirty days. We even made Jenny's homemade bread, it turned out great and everyone that came by to visit, left with their belly full and happy. It was really cool to see people react to Jenny's homemade bread the same way they used to when Jenny made it. Jenny always made six loaves at a time so there was plenty to give away! Even the smell of the bread baking was bringing me back home to Jenny's kitchen.

Thank you Joe and Erin for such a blessed time at your house. Thank You God for making the bread taste so good and for letting me see the smile on everyone's face as they ate Jenny's bread. I really believe that Jenny enjoyed the smell of fresh baked bread and eating her bread again. I love You Jesus and I Praise you for the tender loving care You give us every day! I praise you for Joe and Erin's friend ship and their prayers.

Around the first of February we decided to move on. It was really lonely in the camper the first night but I knew somehow it was the right thing to do. I think it was a little depressing not having all the excitement of the kids and friends just stopping by and to think of eating my cooking again. Somehow it seemed that Jenny was a little depressed. So I put on some Christian music and in no time we were laughing and I was talking again. Jesus knows just what we need, for His word says the Joy of the Lord is our strength. So Jesus brought Joy into the camper. I love having Jesus as my best friend and brother.

As we headed south we stopped in a campground where you can wash your camper and ours needed to be washed. That afternoon I noticed I needed new front tires. Turns out there was a tire place like 2 miles from the campground that could put tires on for me. They said it would take five days to get them in. That night I received a phone call from Joel Sweeney; he was heading to a Dan Mohler conference in northern Alabama. Joel asked, "Where are you?" I said northern Alabama! Isn't it cool we were only 68 miles from the conference? If Joel had not called me I would have missed it! Thank you Jesus for putting that call in Joel's mind so we could go to the conference.

So Jenny and I drove the camper to a campground even closer to the conference. While at the conference a cold front came through and the water lines in the campground froze. I checked like three sites and all including mine were frozen. I went in the motor home and prayed for water to work long enough for me to fill the holding tank in my camper. To my surprise the water that was frozen solid ten minutes earlier was working like summer time, and all the other faucets were still frozen solid. What a gracious God we serve. My Jesus knows our needs and fills them every day and every second!!! Jenny and I went to the conference knowing I could still shower her that night! Peace of mind is truly a gift from God and I love how God shows us every day He is in our life.

After the conference was over we went to the other campground and they put our new tires on the next day and we were on our way again.

We were heading south so we stopped at Josie's house. I guess technically it is Amy and Brandon's house but I'm not sure they know it. I love stopping there for a visit. They have a big kitchen, were Jenny and I can sit and talk but still be out of the way while Amy cooks a great meal. Josie is a lot of fun and has such cute expressions. One day I was in the camper hanging up some clothes and she said Uncle Ron that is the smallest closet I ever did see. She loves to color and one day while sitting at our kitchen table she made a black mark on my table. I had already told her these markers are not washable ones like your mom has so be careful. When Josie accidentally made a mark on my table she suddenly got this feared look on her face. Jesus prompted me so I just said to her, every time I see that mark on my table it will remind of all the fun I have with you Josie. Her little face went from worried to happy and relieved in a second. Thank you Jesus for showing me how to let your piece flow to others. I love you Jesus and I love that You care so much for us that you gave me the words to calm Josie. I love You Jesus!

From there we went to Georgia to see friends at Be in Health church. We were only there one day when Megan form Canada called. Turns out she was in Georgia also. It was so great to see her and catch up on what was going on in her life. Seeing Megan again was such a treat. She is like a walking talking Bible. I can say to Megan where in the Bible does it say this and she says it is in Mathew and also in John and it is in the book of Acts. The real treat in knowing Megan is her love of God and her love of mankind and how that translates into an unselfish giving heart that brings out the best in others. Some people use their knowledge to puff themselves up. You know like "look at me I'm so smart" not so with Megan. Her heart is to help people on their journey to find the truth in God's word! I will say Megan does it really well. I love her relationship with Jesus and how it manifests out of her heart. Her love of Jesus is an awesome love to witness!

The first Sunday we were in Georgia we were invited to a Bible study, I never turn down an invitation like that. While there I ask everyone if they could tell me something God had done for them this week. No one shared; in fact I think the question caught them off guard. Any way I started sharing and after a little while some woman interrupted me to ask if I would pray for her. I said sure, what would you like me to pray for?

She had a whole list of things but then said I don't want you to pray for any of that. I said what then? She said I want your countenance and I want your Joy. I ask her to stand up and as she took my hands she started smiling and her friend said you are smiling!! I said I don't think I need to pray Jesus has already lifted your Spirit. She started laughing and every one joined her laughter and the Joy of the Lord filled the room. It is always awesome to share in the Joy of the Lord.

I learned about Cindy, a girl that was literally living in a bubble. So Jenny and I went to see her. We talked with Cindy for hours and her circumstance were about as inhuman as it can get. Her standard of living is a prison of fear. I never witnessed fear like she has before. I mean she is literally in a prison! She has fear of absolutely everything, even of contaminates in the air she is breathing. She lives in a little aluminum shed with nothing. Someone has to bring her special food. She has to go in some kind of special bag. I could go on but it is a prison. I had not witnessed anything like it.

The second day there I was able to get Jenny out of the car to let Cindy meet her. Immediately upon Cindy seeing Jenny her true heart for helping others came to life in her. It was a big miracle right before my eyes. Cindy had a thousand questions and in them completely forgot about her own problems. I believe I saw the real Cindy that day and I told her if there was some way for me to hug you without contaminating your space I would.

Megan and I spent countless hours over there and just could not break through the fear that controls Cindy. It is so sad to see what the spirit of fear can do if you come into agreement with it. I believe the spirit of fear manifest as other sins to disguise itself. Like self-pity or a spirit of confusion. It was the so sad to see her in such bondage.

While in Georgia I received a push from Jesus to start writing down some of the things God has been giving us. So I wrote the story of when a guy in a campground talked to me about guns. Then Jesus prompted me to write the abortion story, and the one He titled "don't pray the problem" and so many more. My computer was fixed and so I wrote. I made copies and just hand them out, it is so cool to see people read them and receive help from them. My friends Will and Joel have encouraged me to put the stories in a book, I have and Jesus titled the book the Joy of the Lord. It is free call 513 377 1727

Early one morning about 3am Jesus gave me some insight to Jenny's healing. I was so excited and could not write fast enough so I kept asking the Lord to slow down. Right as I got finished I saw two women walking by my camper, it was about 8am, we had shared our faith in Jesus before so I thought I have to run out there and tell them what the Lord shared about Jenny's healing. I jumped out of my seat and went to the door of the camper when all of a sudden the joy left like someone flipped a switch. I stood there dumfounded with my hand on the doorknob and said "What happened, Jesus?" Jesus said "look down." I did and realized I only had my underwear on. I thanked the Lord for stopping me and started praising Him for these awesome revelations about Jenny's healing. Jesus is the greatest and He is my Brother!!!

I know I am the most blessed man on this earth. I believe Jesus has given me such Joy in taking care of Jenny. I know that I love every moment with her. It is even hard to stop holding her long enough to write this book. I spend a lot of time right here in the camper just holding her. These are precious moments and I do not want them to end. Some times when Jenny tries to smile at me her face mussels just jump around but I know in my heart that she is trying to smile so I thank her and tell her how much I love her and I thank my Jesus for giving me this wonderful time with Jenny. Jesus is my best friend for sure!!!!

Jesus in His word said the power of life and death is in the tongue. Every miracle Jesus did He spoke into existence. So I speak life into Jenny and the mind of Jesus and the eyes of Jesus and the heart of Jesus! I speak love of Jesus and His wisdom, the understanding and the knowledge of Jesus Christ my brother to be in Jenny. I speak for Jenny to awake and rise up to be who God created her to be. I speak love and then thank God he hears my prayers and honors my prayers. I love my Jesus and I know he loves us beyond all our comprehension.

My imagination goes crazy trying to figure how the creator of the universe can talk to me any time I ask Him to. Jenny and I are so blessed to know our past is just that, the past! But my future is walking in righteousness' and in the glory of the Lord Jesus Christ by the Holy Spirit who dwells in us, I know there is nothing impossible for me!

JENNY'S CONDITION

I guess I should give you an update on Jenny's condition. It is really hard to do because it is like admitting failure in the word of Jesus. It is like saying or giving power to what the devil can do over my prayers. I do not understand it at all but I want you to know I will not come off my Faith that Jenny is healed and I will never doubt the love of my Jesus has for us. I will tell you her condition right now. Telling you this does not change the fact that Jenny is totally healed, all it does is describe to you what is going on physically.

It has been over three years since Jenny has walked. A little over a year ago Jenny's bowels stopped working so I have to manually unpack her, in a way this is a blessing too because I have not cleaned a bowel movement off the floor for a long time. There are some occasions when she does have a movement on her own and some of those have actually been on the toilet. Praise my Jesus!!!

I have to give her small bites of food and watch her drinking because she sometimes chokes. Sometimes I have to use a mixer to get Jenny's food smooth enough for her to eat. It has to be the consistency of yogurt. Jenny can make decisions about food. She will take a small bite and then if she likes it she will open her mouth for more or spit it out if she doesn't like it. Those are decisions Jenny can make. I believe they prove beyond any doubt there is still a lot going on in her brain.

Some times when Jenny is eating she actually falls asleep while I'm feeding her. I wake her up and she starts chewing her food again and eating more. She is so cute to watch and if she smiles it makes my week! Thank you Jesus for every smile from Jenny, I know it is a gift from YOU!!!! Thank You Jesus for Jenny being able to still swallow! Thank You Jesus that Jenny doesn't choke. I love you Jesus!!!!!

Jenny can still make her face try to smile and she can open her eyes by herself. I believe Jenny is trying to talk and sometimes she gets out a word at an appropriate time. Jenny still loves it when I carry her. Sometimes I think she gets excited when I put her in the car almost like she knows we are going somewhere. These are awesome displays of the love of God for us! I praise My Father and Jesus for these displays and I really believe being part of Jenny's life even at this stage is an awesome blessing! Thank you Jesus for these gifts that bring such Joy I cannot describe how my heart sings for Joy every time You bless me with another day of Your love and Jenny!!!

Some times when I put the straw in her mouth she will blow into the straw instead of sucking, thank You Jesus for cups with lids. Jenny usually gets it right the second time. Jenny is down to 94pounds and holding. Her body sometimes stiffens out and it is hard to sit her up to eat. So I pray and Jesus always helps me out there also. Every day I mist her face with water to clean it because she doesn't know to shut her eyes and so soap is out of the question for the last 9 years. Everyone that sees her says her skin is so beautiful and it is. The cool thing is when I wipe her face with the softest towel I can find Jenny coos like a baby. I visualize Jesus wiping her face and saying it is perfect and it is!!!

For some reason for about a year now Jenny keeps her hands closed. I can open them and get all her fingers straight except her baby finger on her left hand. Jenny keeps her arms folded like an X over her chest all day and night. It makes dressing her a little awkward but I don't mind. Jesus shows me how to dress her also! I can still straighten her arms while she sleeps but as soon as I let go they cross again.

Jenny's legs cross also. When she first started crossing her legs I thought it was cute. She looks sophisticated. Now they are crossed all the time, even while sleeping. I put a pillow between her legs at night to keep her from getting bed sores. Having Jenny's legs crossed has become a problem. Have you ever tried to get Depends or clothes on someone with their legs crossed? In the shower it is a problem also. I thank God we live in a camper because the tub is so small, it actually helps me to keep Jenny standing up during her shower. Jenny's muscles start jumping around when she is standing, so I ask God to give her the strength to get a shower and He does. Thank You Jesus for giving Jenny strength to be showered. I love when Jenny is clean and praise Jesus for the water to clean Jenny and for her strength!

One of the best times of the day for me is when I have Jenny showered and dressed for bed. I pick her up in my arms and lay her in bed. She opens her eyes and looks at me with such trust and love that it takes me back to when Heidi was two years old and I would tuck her in bed and Heidi would look up at me the same way Jenny does. Jenny's eyes are so pretty and pure that I know I am looking at the majesty of my Jesus! The work of Jesus is perfect!! The love of Jesus is perfect and I love Jesus partly because He trusts me to take care of one of his most perfect, delightfully precious children. Jesus himself said Jenny is delightfully precious and so I know that is the best way for me to describe Jenny.

I love to get up in the morning and have coffee with Jesus and I cannot wait to have coffee with Jesus and Jenny. I know without a doubt it will happen. I also know there are some people reading this right now and saying "don't get your hopes to high Ron, you will be disappointed." Those are words of the devil because the Bible says to live by faith and not sight. You see I told you how Jenny is doing and what she looks like and the circumstances are probably robbing you of your faith in God. When Lazarus was dead for three days, his loved ones had no faith in Jesus to do anything. Jesus called Lazarus from the tomb and out he came. I don't go by circumstances, I go by FAITH and not my faith but rather faith in the name of Jesus, the name which makes every nee bowel down!!

I bet most people read these last 8 or 9 paragraphs and say Jenny is dying; but Jesus said nothing is impossible for Jesus and I believe and trust and have all my hope in Jesus! So my hopes are heavenly high in the most high Jesus and my Father God. When you know Jesus, your hopes should be heavenly High and there is no such thing as to high. My hopes are Jesus high.

When I pray I always say Father God. I was listening to a CD the other day and found out what the words Father God stands for. Father means to come forth from and God means source of life. So saying Father God means to come forth from the source of life! All good things come from God and now I know I am calling on the source of life when I pray. I mean you might as well go to the source! I love you Father God and thank you for being my source of life!

The world says "what you don't know won't hurt you" but God's word says "my people die for lack of knowledge." Again I go by the Bible and ask for knowledge and wisdom every day, because I know what I don't know is killing me. I love my Jesus and love the love He shows us every day. If you just look and listen, you will see it too! I don't care what the signs look like; I believe Jesus and his word that says by his stripes we were healed. Done deal!!! I love you Jesus!!!!

Thank You Jesus for coming and writing the Bible for us, I really do not understand what people without faith do when a doctor says there is no hope. Do they just give up? I thank You Jesus for Hope in you! Thank you Jesus for Faith in you! I know the physical signs I see in Jenny point to death, look like death, and would make you believe that death is very close! I think I know what people are thinking when they see her.

The signs of death on Jenny are so strong that even pastors of some churches don't offer to pray for Jenny. Most people look at her like she would be better with Jesus than here like this. I see their faith go right out the door when they see Jenny, and I think back when I was the same way. I think back when I prayed for a guy named Bob who had cancer. I went out of town for a couple weeks and when I came back the changes were so horrendous, Bob looked like death and when I saw him my faith went out the door. I left and Jesus said get back there and apologize to Bob. I did and Bob lived almost two more weeks.

I am extremely blessed to know Jesus loves us and that His love wins every time! I believe that, more then I believe the sun will come up tomorrow morning. It is the love and compassion of Jesus that makes me get up every morning. I think I have given you a good idea of where Jenny's condition is. All I'm going to say is Jenny is HEALED! I praise you Jesus and love you Jesus!!!!

I told you a while back that Jesus described Jenny as delightfully precious and I think that is the very best way to describe Jenny. I pray for everyone to know and love and have a relationship with Jesus that is so intimate, when people see you they see the Jesus in you!!! I really believe that is why Jesus came, to model a life for us and for us to model our life like His! Jesus came to restore our relationship to Him, He restored to us the relationship man had before Adam ate the fruit of the tree of good and evil. I personally want intimacy with Jesus and for my life to be His love on display every day. I believe a life like that is more praise then going to church and singing praise songs.

MORE JOY

While still in Georgia, one day while doing laundry at the campground I met a young couple (Tyler and Alyssa) with two little children. It was pretty obvious they were not happy. I asked them to bring the kids and come up to my camper so I could look after Jenny and we could still talk. The morning turned into afternoon and then evening. It was really a productive day. They asked, "How long are you going to be here?" I was going to leave the next day but decided to stay an extra week. We continued to talk about my favorite subject, God, and we seemed to make some real progress. I told them about my favorite teacher Dan Mohler. I found out he was going to be in Lakeland Florida. They decided to head down there after they drooped the children off at grandmas.

Jenny and I went to Land Between the Lakes in Kentucky. Tommy Waller and family were gathering for another family week. We had so much fun there last year and could not wait to see everyone again. Kevin, Heather and Ariel were coming from Texas. Curtis, Maggie Lou and family were coming from Florida. There were probably 75 or more families coming so I won't mention all their names but Jenny and I were really excited to get there and spend time with all of them.

Jenny and I arrived and the campground was busing with excitement. It is the only place in the world that I know of where everyone shares their love of the Lord and Jesus is alive and well to such a degree that even the children are examples of the love of Jesus. Yes the children are examples of the love of Jesus! It truly is a welcome break from the worldliness of the world.

For example I remember not too long ago, I saw t-shirts and bumper stickers that said "Let me tell you about my grandchildren". Now I see bumper stickers and tee shirts that say "I love my dog." It is like the world is searching for something to love that does not talk back, is easy to control, gives you some degree of protection and gives you unconditional love. I see people in such need of love and I guess they have been so hurt they shut themselves down to human love and then channel their love into something like a dog. I see people trying to buy love in food or entertainment and material things. They are so lost! My heart goes out to them because most of them have probably been hurt by Christian's also. I do not believe they understand the Bible or the message of truth that sets us free. So they search for something or anything that brings them happiness.

The most upsetting aspect of the Christian walk today is the message in most churches is "clean up your act, repent and maybe God will accept you." That is totally backwards! The Bible says "it is the goodness of God that leads a man to repentance," change comes from knowing who God is and we Christians are to be Christ Like.

God called the apostles and some came right off the boat they were working on. They did not repent first, no they saw the goodness of Jesus and wanted to change form their sinful life. As they walked with, lived with, saw, ate and tasted the righteousness of Jesus and they wanted what Jesus had for them. They saw truth manifest right before their eyes. They longed in their own heart to be good as Jesus is good and out of their heart came repentance, I believe when God calls us we will repent and ask to be made clean for it is in the Bible that Jesus never sinned. Can you imagine being around someone that never sinned? I know just being around someone that loves Jesus and is living for Him convicts me.

I love Jesus and I love His example of life. I know in my heart that it is possible to live that way because Jesus called me! That may sound arrogant to some, I am not saying I am sinless, I am saying I seek God with all my heart and want to live before Him all the days of my life. Jesus said I give you the desires of your heart for it was I that gave you those desires. The desires of my heart are to live pure, Holy and in righteousness before my Jesus. Righteousness is impossible to obtain on our own but with Jesus all things are possible! I love your truth Jesus!!! I love you called me!!!! I will follow You all the days I live.

I think the people at family week are so in love with God and that is what makes them so special. When you know Jesus, you literally want more of Him. To the average Christian a vacation is a week at Myrtle Beach and eating in restaurants laying in the sun and doing what you want to do. To these families a vacation is getting to know who God is, its spending time listening to uplifting teachings and singing to God with words of praise. They look for ways to help others and to share with each other and celebrate the good news of the gospel.

I think it is cool that even though I don't understand their dietary laws and their customs for the way they dress, I can still love them with all my heart and be loved by them with all their heart. I don't go there looking for love, I go there to give the love of Jesus to everyone I meet and if someone gives love back then great but if they don't, I still give the unconditional love of God.

I have the up most respect for the way they raise their children and see the fruits of it in how their children respect marriage, family, motherhood, their parents and how these children respect God. I love to watch them dance for God in reverence and respect for who God is. I think it is so cool to see people that are learning to read Greek and Hebrew so they can read a non-translated Bible. Try to find that on Wall Street. I think it is so cool to see people that will scrimp and save money to go to Israel, just to have their feet on the land that God said was just for His people. I guess what I am trying to say is our life here on earth is short, like a vapor of time, I'm so glad God is transforming Jenny and I from materialistic to eternality. To do that God has lead us to people that are not materialistic. It is a true vacation for Jenny and I to be here!

I don't understand everything about the people of family week and they probably don't understand me either and the way I dress but they still love me with all their hearts because that is what Jesus did and He is our example of how to live. I want to talk about their dress code for a minute. The way these men, women and children dress is so conservative and modest that you don't see them as an object of desire but I see them as pure love, a people set apart, in the world but not of the world, I see them as Christ like in action and word. They have innocents about them and a childlike faith that is so refreshing to be around!

I wish they had a hand out to give people that would explain the way they dress from a biblical standpoint and why it is so important. I know from talking to materialistic people almost every day in different campgrounds that the people of family week are truly some of the most Joyful people I meet and to look at their belongings you want to know how they can be so joyful. I tell people it is not what you have in life; it is who you live for in life that determines your JOYFULNESS!!!!

On The Road

As we headed south we stopped to spend the night in northern Alabama and the campground host took us to a site. As I got out of the motor home I said praise God this site is almost level. The host heard me and asked if I was a praying man and I said yes. He then asks if I would say a prayer for his father who was in a hospital. His 84-year-old father fell and his daughter could not stop his hand from bleeding. The ambulance took him to the hospital and there they found his spleen had ruptured. When the doctors went in him to fix the spleen they saw he was full of cancer and during the operation he had a stroke that paralyzed him on his left side. I told the host I not only would pray for his dad but I would like to visit him also.

He ask me, aren't you on your way somewhere? I said yes but I always leave extra time to do the Lord's work. The next day we went to the hospital to pray for him. I told him I prayed on the way to the hospital and had asked Jesus what Jesus wanted to say to Earl? Jesus told me He just wants you to know He loves you very much. Earl started crying really hard. I don't think his children and grandchildren had ever seen him cry like that but when the love of Jesus comes on you it does not matter who is in the room. I know he was at peace with the news from Jesus!

After Alabama, Jenny and I started for Lakeland Florida to meet up with Tyler. After Tyler took his wife and children to Ohio he started for Florida also. Jenny and I stopped in a campground in northern Florida for the night. We had stopped here about a year ago and I had prayed for the owner, who had cancer. I pulled up to the office and there he stood on the porch. He took a double take at my camper, I got out of the camper and when he saw me he got this huge smile and hugged me tight and said it is gone! I said praise God. I was so happy for him and my heart was so joyful that God healed him. Praise you Jesus, Holy Spirit and My Father for all you do!!!! Jesus You are so good to Jenny and I!!!!!

The next day we stopped at a campground where they were going to do some work on the camper jacks. At check in the girl there got excited when I told her my name was Ron Johnson, she said my boyfriend is Ron Johnson. I felt lead to give her the prayer that Jenny said for years titled FOR A HAPPY MARRIED LIFE. To my surprise the next day everyone in the office including the owner's wife had copies and loved the prayer. There was a joy in the office that was not there the day before. It is so awesome to watch God transform people and to see how simple it is. Life really is about doing for others and the more you do the more you want to do because Joy is contagious, outrageous, and more fulfilling than any amount of happiness. Jenny and I are so blessed to be with you Jesus and to know you Jesus and most of all to know you dwell in us Jesus!!!!! I love you Jesus!!!

Finally we were in Lakeland, Florida. We went to the conference for two days when Tyler said he was thinking about calling his parents. I said is that a big decision and he said it has been years since I called them. I said wow I didn't know that. I asked, "Where do they live?" He said in Haines Florida, about 30 miles from here. He did call and his mom came that night to the conference. She looked so happy to see Tyler and after the conference came over to meet us. She had a lot of questions about us and Jesus put her mind at ease. She explained to us that her husband had to work late and would be there the next day. Tyler was so happy and excited to know he was going to see his dad, two brothers and sister tomorrow.

The conference was great and Tyler got up in front of everyone and gave a testimony. His parents invited Jenny and I to dinner on Sunday and Tyler spent the night with his parents. Tyler's grandpa called everyone and relatives from Tennessee came for a reunion with Tyler. At the party I told everyone how much I love to watch God work and how awesome it is to witness the hand of God at work. I said I never know what God is going to do with us but if you let Him use you; you will never be disappointed at the majesty of God!!!! An awesome moment came when Tyler's dad gave me a hug and said thank you for bring my son home. I said Jesus brought your son home; I was just the deliveryman. His dad smiled because he works for UPS. I thank you Jesus for loving us so much to let us be part of their family reunion.

Jenny and I decided to head to Cedar Key Florida to visit friends there. The camper seemed empty without Tyler, who decided to stay in Florida to go to school. Our generator was acting up so we went to a place to have it worked on. It worked fine while there. So we moved on. We left Cedar key and headed for Carrabelle Beach. I could not wait to see everyone there. It was a little disappointing to find out the campground we like had raised their rates so we only stayed a week. We still saw our friends and they were so glad to see us also. It was a very short visit but so worthwhile. I am going to budget my money better and stay longer next year for sure.

We went to Destin, Florida. After talking to the campground manager for a couple minutes I realized we were on the same page with the Lord and we spent a lot of time in the office just talking about Jesus. It was great! Our generator acted up again so we had a guy come to our camper and work on it. He found the problem and fixed it. About two weeks later our DC converter went out and we had a new one installed. It seemed we were paying a lot of repair bills all of a sudden.

Now that I look back on it I think how I did not worry, I just charged them. New front tires $975.00, generator repair $642.00 DC converter $433.00 and car repair $615.00. I did not pray about where the money would come from, I just knew the Lord new my need. One day a friend called from Washington State and said the Lord put it on his heart and his wife's heart to bless Jenny and me. So they did with a check for 3000.00 dollars. I thanked them and thought how cool that is. I never told them or anyone else about our need. I never went to the Lord with a need. I never know what God is going to do in our life but I know it will be cool!!!! Praise you Father and Brother Jesus!!!

We then went to a campground in southern Alabama. Our stay was free for going through a sales pitch. It was a nice campground but I really do not want to own anything. I do not want to be tied to anything. This campground had a nice outdoor pool so Jenny and I went swimming. I was amazed with the number of people that smoke and how you just could not get away from the smell. So the next day I decided to take Jenny to the beach. The beach parking lot was really crowed so I walked across the boardwalk and down to the beach. I never saw anything like this; there was music and men in bikini's everywhere. Turns out it was some kind of gay day. So I left and as I pulled away Jesus spoke to me; He said these men and boys need to hear my word also. He said they need to hear the truth, and know that they are forgiven. Everyone knows I have forgiven the drunks and prostitutes, but gay men don't think I can forgive them. That is a lie straight from the devil and as long as they believe it, they are lost but not forgotten!

A very good friend Todd White once said "If you can show me one person that Jesus did not die for, than I will pass that one up." I pray that whatever role I might have in helping these lost souls, that Jesus makes it very fruitful and gives them a complete heart of Jesus. They cannot turn away from this life style except they receive Jesus and His forgiveness. I know Jesus loves every one of us and gave His life to set us all free. I love You Jesus and it is very obvious you love us all!!!! I thank You for Your compassion and love!!! I pray for all the men in this bondage to be set free by coming to know Jesus because Jesus is calling you!

We then went back to Cincinnati. We were only there a couple days when Kurt Walk ask us to come to Dayton Ohio to talk with a men's group at his church. I was surprised and very excited to talk to these men. I was honored that Kurt thought this much of Jenny and I. We had such a great time and met a lot of very nice people. I think one man's comment stuck with me because it came right out of his heart. After meeting Jenny and I for the first time, Jeff told Kurt (that man drips Jesus everywhere he goes). I am so blessed that Kurt shared that with us and that Jeff's comment came right from his heart. It tells me a lot about Jeff's heart for Jesus! You know where the love of God flows; sin and unforgiveness GOES!!!! When the love of God grows; everyone KNOWS!!!!

One day after shopping for groceries while I was pushing Jenny to the car with cart in tow, for some reason I looked back at the front of the store. I saw a young man leaning against the front of the building. So I pushed Jenny into a safe place and ran over to see if the man needed help. I ask him and he started babbling. I thought oh Lord now what do I do? Just then a younger girl and her grandma approached us and said what are you doing?? I said it looked like he may need help, grandma said he doesn't need help he is with us!!! I said would you mind if I pray for him? Grandma melted on the spot. She said you want to pray for him? She said go ahead.

So I started to command his infirmity to leave when he started to do sign langue. So I asked the grandma, "What did he say?" She said, "He wants to know who you are." I said I am a fellow Christian who believes in Jesus and Jesus just wants to lavish his love all over you right now. Just then a big SUV pulled up and they started to get in so I thought I guess I'm done.

I walked over to where Jenny was and untied her so I could pick her up and put her in the car. I felt someone behind me and when I looked it was the young man's mom, the driver of the SUV. She said you don't know what you just did with tears in her eyes. I said your right I don't know what I did but I think I know Jesus just did. She said we were just in that store and someone got mad at my son because he could not get out of their way fast enough. Then we come out her and you pray for him. I said I don't think Jesus wanted you to go home with that hurt in your heart. She looked relieved and said well I won't and gave me a big hug and I thanked God and praised God as I watched them drive away. I love it when God uses Jenny and I to share his love. I praised God again that night for taking that woman's pain away. I love you Jesus!

Jenny and I were in Cincinnati to do some maintenance on the motor home. We naturally called John Glass who is a great friend of ours. One Sunday during breakfast with John, he mentioned going to the VA for a meeting of Vietnam vets that are still suffering from posttraumatic stress syndrome. So I ask if I could go? John called me Monday and had permission for me come to the meeting. The topic that day was helplessness, fear and anger. I listened and as each man had a turn to talk. When everyone talked the sociologist ask me if I wanted to speak. I asked her if we are allowed to talk about God in these meetings. She said yes, so I said then I have a lot to say, I started to talk when some guy across the table broke in with a story and another guy started to add to his story and the meeting was over.

In my coffee time with Jesus that week Jesus gave me some information for the Vets. So I typed it up and made copies to give to the men. At the next meeting the first guy to talk pointed his finger at me and said what you said last week really helped me. He went on to say, how he woke up at 3am this morning after having a vivid dream about Vietnam, he said he was wet with sweat and walked on to his porch and as he shook his hand at the sky asked God (how long do I have to put up with this Vietnam crap.) Jesus reminded him to forgive them. He started a long list of people he forgave and then exhausted went back into the house and slept better than he had in 40 years. Jesus said my truth will set you free and I believe that man found the truth of what forgiveness could do. I was so happy for him! I was able to give the men the message form Jesus and was told that would be my last meeting I could attend, because I do not have PTSS.

The next week Jesus gave me more for the Vets and I contacted the sociologist by phone and she let me come to one more meeting. I went and had the new message from Jesus all typed up. I was able to include Jesus and His information in their therapy section. Jesus is awesome and I believe the info will help these Vets. I bless them with freedom from the war memories and the night tear's and with knowing who they are in God. Jesus loves them for what they tried to do over there! I just hope they figure that out someday!

The second day at the campground I was putting something in my car when a guy passed by on a lawn mower. He suddenly did a turn around and came right up to me to talk. He said hi Ron and how is Jenny doing? I knew he knew us but I could not figure out who he was. Then he started smiling and said I'm Jeff the homeless guy you met at East Fork Lake last Christmas. It was so cool to see him again. I said you were bald when I meet you and now you have all this pretty red hair. He said I just shaved my hair because I couldn't afford a hair cut. I told him I called and he said someone stole his phone, while he was sleeping in his car one night. So he lost all his contact numbers. He was excited to see us and wanted to help any way he could so he gave me free firewood that whole week. I was just so glad to hear how good he was doing. He has a house he is fixing up, so he has a place to live and I sure was happy about that. Thank you God for letting me see him again. It was a blessing to see his big smile.

We also went to some spirit filled Bible studies at my cousin Pat and Margie's house. It is always nice to see them and the great meals Margie cooks are also a delight to our taste buds. My cousin Mike and his wife Christy usually come and they add a lot to the study. I love being with them and being challenged by their strong beliefs. I know God honors those that diligently seek Him and we all find ourselves stretched by the end of the night. I look forward to coming to Cincinnati to see our sons, mom and family but there is always something special about going to the Bible study at Pat's house. I know God is blessing you and your loved ones and it is awesome to see all four of you when we come into Cincinnati. The time we spend together has truly been a blessing to Jenny and me.

Jenny and I were going to leave the next day and as we sat together I gave Jenny her nighttime snack and told her (tomorrow we are leaving to go to another campground and I pray Jesus has us do some great miracles there.) Then I realized what I said and started laughing to myself and thought wow my life has changed.

Jenny and I were off to Tennessee to visit with some of the families we met at family week. Jenny and I love being part of their celebration and to hear their teachings. After being with them a couple days a couple came to our camper one night and ask (how do you stay so joyful all the time?) They needed to know the truth that sets you free. They too had been through deliverance ministries and were not free. Jesus in his word said my truth sets you free and it is the goodness of God that leads a man to repentance, not deliverance ministries. I said you do not need more deliverance you need more truth.

You know Jesus did not come just to be the perfect sacrifice for sin. Jesus came to restore our relationship with Him. Jesus told Adam; if you eat of the tree of good and evil you will surely die but Adam did not die. So what died? His relationship with Jesus died. All through the Old Testament Jesus only spoke through prophets. Now thanks to Jesus coming we can talk to God 24/7 and hear from God 24/7 so to me the main reason Jesus came was to show us the love of the Father by restoring our relationship to HIM!

In my opinion, it would be hard to talk to someone 24/7 if you did not love Him. If you don't know God and that He loves you how could you talk to Him 24/7? You can quote the scriptures, go to church and sing His praise and even try to keep all his laws but if you do all these things without love, you will not please God. His word says so! To know God you must talk to Him and have relationship with Him. Jesus said knowledge puffs up (just knowing scriptures but not living them) but Love edifies. So start talking to Jesus and watch your life change. I know you will fall in love because Jesus is so loveable!!

So the answer to the question "how do I stay so Joyful?" I simply have communion with my Father and Jesus and the Holy Spirit 24/7. My relationship with them, keeps me close to them and I hear from them all the time. They are my best friends and I am my Fathers son; they love me and I know it! I love them and they know it! So the world can sometimes be, well not so great but that doesn't change my relationship to my family. The love of my Father God and my brother Jesus and the love of the Holy Spirit is really all you need to be joyful, if you have relationship with them 24/7!!!! Jesus explained to me the difference between joyful and happiness in a teaching called MAD! It is in the Joy of the Lord book. 513 377 1727

I will tell you this; joyfulness is really the opposite of happiness. How can that be? Happiness comes from things going right for us. Happiness is momentary, it is something we make plans for and usually someone has to do something right for us. Like getting your haircut just right or the order at Mc Donald's just right. Happiness is always about yourself and what someone is doing for you. Most people think they can make themselves happy by doing something for yourself everyday like going to Kings Island. That is why I say it is momentary. It only last until something goes wrong, say you have a great time at King's Island and as you go to leave your car won't start and you call a repair truck and he says it will be a couple hours. Are you still happy?

I say joyfulness is the opposite of happiness because it comes from you doing something for others. Joy is truly knowing who you are in Jesus. You're a son or daughter of God, who were made to love and serve others. Joy is having relationship with God. Joy is knowing you are on eternity time and so you never get in to big a hurry to help others. Like visiting the sick or helping someone broke down on the highway. Joy comes from not thinking about yourself and putting the needs of others first.

If that doesn't turn you on it is because you do not know Jesus on a personal level. Doing for others is Joy if you are doing it to show people the love of Jesus and to spread the good news of Jesus. We have probably all known people who help others to make them self's look good or to get something in return. They will burn out and there will not be joy in it, because their motive is still self-gratification. If you help others to lift yourself up, you will be disappointed the first time someone you help doesn't lift you up. Let that happen a few times and burn out occurs.

If you lift someone up to share the love of God because you know God loves you and that person rejects you, it doesn't hurt you, in fact you will pray for them and ask God to help them. You see you have yourself worth already because you know God loves you and you are made in the image and likeness of God! God is love!!! So be the love of God to everyone you meet and no one can take that away. There is no burn out because God's love is everlasting!! Joyfulness can be for long periods of time because God's love is the everlasting love of joy in your heart. In a way it is kind of cool because there are people everywhere that need help so you never run out of sources of Joy. Give someone you meet the gift of God's love today!!! Check out the teaching about "MAD" it is only 13 pages long.

We left there to go back to Lexington, Kentucky to see Dan Mohler. We had an awesome time and met some really nice people again. There was a couple from Iran that heard Dan's message and started studying the word of God and now believe in the Love of Jesus and through the Internet have converted their parents also. The Love of Jesus is so cool and He is changing hearts one at a time. Isn't that cool!

While at the conference an elderly man came back and ask to pray for Jenny. As he prayed I offered to let him hold Jenny's hand. So he held her hand and continued praying, he was so gentle as he held her hand and rubbed her fingers. I felt prompted so I ask; how long has your wife been dead and he looked up at me with very sad eyes and said ten years. He continued to pray and hold Jenny's hand as I turned away to cry. I thanked God for letting me see this man's pure heart and for giving him the strength to continue loving You! He is such a fine example of your love! I believe he poured the love of Jesus all over Jenny. I know every second with Jenny is a blessing form my Savior and Lord Jesus Christ! I really mean it when I say I am the most blessed man I know! I love you Jesus and praise you for letting me know You Jesus!!!

I met a lady in a campground the other day. She told me about all her medical problems and there were a lot of them. Her husband is on disability and so is she. She said she would be in a wheel chair soon and she wanted her husband to put her in a home when that happens. Then she started crying as she told me about her dog. He has cancer again. She told me he almost died two years ago but the cancer treatment worked and the dog lived. Now the cancer came back, he is 9 years old and weights 170 lbs. She knows he is going to die soon. She was crying because she ask the Lord to please give her two more years with her dog, but I don't think the dog is going to live two more years she said.

I tried to tell her that her life, her love, and her reason for being has to be in God and not how long her dog lives. She was setting herself up for disappointment. It almost seems that people want disappointment in their life because they can get sympathy and they thrive on it. When she told me of all her problems she never mentioned asking God for help. The doctor told her she would be in a wheel chair soon and so she was making plans for that day. People just accept what the doctor says. They like their disability and are satisfied with complaining. When I ask if I could pray for her she walked away. I did give her some tracts but she said she wouldn't have time to read them. I said please take them because some day you might want to read them.

That night I was listening to a Dan Mohler CD when I heard Jesus say take this CD to that lady now. So I walked towards her camper to give her the CD when I saw her two daughters and her daughter's husband sitting by the fire. I ask them is your mom and dad in the trailer. They said they have gone home for the night. I told them I wanted to give her the CD to listen to and they said we will listen to it. The youngest girl asks if I wrote those papers called coffee time. I said yes and she got excited and said I read them and liked them. I said how cool is that? Her husband pulled his car up and put the CD in his player. I went back to my camper to take care of Jenny.

After I showered Jenny I heard it raining and noticed that the three of them where in his car listening to the CD. I just got Jenny in bed when I heard a knock on my door. It was the young girl bringing back the CD. I told her they could have it and we sat and talked for an hour or two. The next day I gave them another CD. This girl was like a sponge soaking up the word of God. I loved talking to her but I was leaving today because someone had reserved my site.

Before I left I decided to say goodbye to the people across from me. They had not really talked to me the couple days they were their but I loved the attention they gave their children and wanted to compliment them. I did compliment them and he apologized to me for not talking to us. He said I am a minister of a church in Bracken County and I have just done a tent revival so I needed some time alone with my wife and children. I said wow; see those two girls and her husband are from Bracken County and are looking for a church. I told him about them and he said he would ask them to his church. Thank You Jesus for putting them together and for letting me be some part of spreading your word. I love You Jesus your awesome!!!

A lot of people I meet say there spouse would put them in a home and just go on with their life. I want to tell you some things they would of missed. I get to see every smile of Jenny's; I get to hear every laugh. I have someone to hold, someone to love as Jesus loves. I have the honor of cleaning Jenny and being with her!! One night I fed Jenny spaghetti and did not wipe her face for the whole meal, I should have taken pictures of Jenny, she looked so cute. I get to change her, bathe her, carry her, scrub her teeth, wipe her face, in other words I get to bring peace and happiness in to her life. When you love someone, it brings great Joy into your life when you can make them smile and Jesus shows me things that Jenny loves!

Jenny can still make decisions. I know that blows the minds of people when I tell them Jenny makes decisions! I tell them if you put some food to Jenny's mouth and it does not smell, Jenny will take the tinniest little bit and then after tasting it will open her mouth for more or spit out the sample. Those are undeniable decisions! No one can tell me different! Jenny is healed by Faith in the name above all names Jesus!!!! In the name of Jesus all things are possible!!! Yes even healing Jenny!!!!

One day about a year ago when we were in Walmart, Jenny's body started stiffing out and shaking. It is usually a sign of a seizure coming on. People were staring, so I looked for an empty aisle and pushed Jenny there. I untied her and picked her up, I then set her on my lap and continued singing to her about how much God loves us. I started speaking life into her when a Walmart person approached me asking if I wanted her to call 911. I said no. I have Jesus and Jesus will make her right again. She said, I am worried for her, are you sure you don't want me to call 911? I said I am sure I have Jesus and He is all I need. I said Jenny will be just fine and we will finish our shopping, you will see. In about ten minutes we were shopping again. Thank you Jesus, Jenny's body was back to normal.

The Spider Bite

Believing in Jesus is not just for Jenny. I believe in Jesus for everything! Almost two years ago I was bit by a brown recluse spider, on the right side of my bottom. The bite area kept getting bigger; I had to wear Jenny's Depends for months to suck up the drainage. The wound was so big I think I could put half a tennis ball in it. My leg swelled so big I could not wear my shoes tied.

One day a lady saw me walking Jenny in the wheel chair and noticed my leg; she ask what had happened and I told her. She then ask if I had gone to the doctor for my leg. I said yes right away. She wanted to know what the doctor said so I told her that the doctor said his son took care of it. She looked at me weird, like, his son took care of it? So I explained: the Doctor's Son took care of this two thousand years ago. She said, you need to see a real doctor. I said I did. She insisted I needed to be on antibiotics. I told her I take pills every day and she asked what kind of pills. I said the Gospel. (I got that from Pastor Henry) She said you're impossible and walked away, then turned and said I'm going to be here for two more weeks are you? I said yes and she said I want to see if you're still alive in two weeks.

Jesus did keep me alive for those two weeks and more. The bite eventually did heal but I was still having sores all over my body. The poison attacked my joints. It made them hard to move and picking up Jenny became a real job. We went to mom's house for Christmas that year and I didn't want my siblings to know about the bite. It was painful to sit, stand, or move so I prayed that the Lord would do something that day. Jesus worked it all out for me. Jenny was in a chair next to my mom who was holding her hand almost all day. It was so cute to see. I was sitting on a hard footstool leaning back to be near Jenny. It was perfect because if I sat on a cushioned chair the cushion would naturally push on the right side of my bottom and cause pain.

Every time I felt I needed to change my Depends I took Jenny to the bathroom to act like she needed to be changed. I had Jenny's personal bag with me and my gauze pads in the bottom of it so no one noticed. It was cold out so I had long pants and long sleeve shirt on, so no one could see the sores. It actually turned in to an enjoyable Christmas for me. Thank You Jesus and Father and Holy Spirit for caring so much that you worked out every detail of the day.

After about a year of this I did go to the VA. I was just tired of the pain and the mess of it all. It was all over my hands, so people didn't want me to touch them and I was tired of everyone looking at me and saying your crazy man. People said "Why do you think God put doctors here on earth." So I caved, the doctor put me on antibiotic for 30 days. Everything cleared up but a week later it was back and a lot worse. I mean the sores were coming everywhere, some of them got so big and so ugly. I forgave myself and repented for not trusting God. God did show me He could still flow through me even with my hands a mess.

I remember when I went to Michigan and this stuff was all over my hands. I wanted to pray for people but if I tried to touch them they backed away. One day a little girl came running through our camp site while I was trying to cut Jenny's hair. She was screaming for her mother as I stepped out in front of her and asks what was wrong? She showed me her swelled up hand and said a bee stung me and it really hurts. I reached out to take her hand so I could pray for her and she saw my hands and pulled away. I said that is okay, I don't need to touch you, I command that pain and swelling to go in the name of Jesus. Just then her mother came out of the camper next to ours and the little girl ran to her mom. Still crying she told her mom a bee stung her and showed her mom her hand. Her mom looked and said it looks fine honey, the girl looked at her hand amazed and then looked over at me with this bewildered look on her face. I just smiled and she told her mom what happened. I truly love watching Jesus work.

I know Jesus is growing me up in faith. Yes I caved one time, but I realized I took my eyes off my Jesus and started looking at the problem. I will keep my eyes focused on my Jesus and not the problem. I believe I am blessed in this because the healing came from God and not the VA doctor. It just makes it easier for me to trust God. I love you Jesus for picking me up when I fall and I love you Jesus for being there when I call!!

I have taken pictures of the sours and my hands but not my bottom. I can show you these pictures if you have the stomach for looking at them.

About a half year latter I was at Pat and Margie's house and three or four of the sores on my knee were leaking to the point I used so many paper towels they put a garbage can right next to me. Mike and Christy were there also and Christy looked up brown recluse spider bites on the internet and found the things I had on my legs were called brown recluse eruptions. According to the internet brown recluse spider plants eggs in you when he bites you and these eggs can get into your blood and travel through your body and then erupt where ever. The pictures on the internet looked just like what I had.

After a while I started taking pictures of them so I could show people what God delivered me of, because I just stood on faith that the word of God is true and no matter what the circumstances look like I was not going back to a human doctor. I am sorry I let people talk me into going to a human doctor. I think if that is where your faith is then go to a doctor and live to fight another day. I have nothing against doctors or going to one because Jesus might want to flow through a doctor to heal you. So go to the doctor if you need to but put your faith and your trust in God. My faith is in God and I just caved for a month. The eruptions lasted for years but now I can say that God did take care of it all.

Thank you Jesus for your fine healing in my body. I love the fact that I don't have to sit in a waiting room and read stupid magazines to see you. I love your office hours also and the fact your line is never busy. It is cool that I don't have to navigate a maze every time I call you. I just love your bedside manners. I just love You and I'm glad I get the family rate. Oh yea I don't need an appointment, I'm actually with You all the time because You dwell in me and your love for me is oh so cool! You see why I say I am so blessed!!! Everyone needs a doctor like mine and they can have Jesus also if they just believe. I know Jesus came to forgive us our sins and I thank Him for forgiving me. Just try talking to Him and start believing what you read in the Bible.

My friend Kevin from Texas once said if people would just spend the same amount of time getting to know the Lord as they do going to doctors, their whole life would change, not just their health. If you have a doctor appointment at 11:00 PM, you leave at 10:30 to get there on time and say you get home at 12:00, counting the travel time you were gone an hour and a half. Let's say the next day you devote that same amount of time, an hour and a half to talking to God and reading the word of God. I know your health issue and your life will take a turn for the better!!!!

People ask me "do you pray about where you are going or how do you know where to go" I tell them I never pray about where I'm going and I never put out a fleece. You see it takes no faith to put out a fleece or to ask God, where I should go. Jesus said to walk by Faith not by sight (fleece). I know Jesus said without faith it is impossible to please Him. I know people that get so many details in their head, trying to figure out whether or not to do something. I just know Jesus told us to go preach the gospel to all nations, so I do. I can be going down the expressway and say "Jesus I'm tired please find us a campground," I can even get specific and ask for one with black top roads or a swimming pool the next exit says campground, so I go there and someone gets healed of cancer. It's a pretty cool way to travel. Thank you Jesus! I love to travel with Jesus! Jesus is my pilot, my GPS, and my everything!! TRUST JESUS!!!!

I know that when we die we go before Jesus for judgment. Since Jesus said he forgives our sins and they are removed as far as the east is from the west. So what are we judged on? I believe we are judged on our, BELIEVE!!!! Did you believe? You see if you believe in Jesus; you will Love Jesus and you will not sin because you know it will grieve Jesus!

You will keep all his commandments because when you love Jesus you want to make Him joyful. Don't read the Bible to see if it is true! Measure everything else in the world to see if it measures to the truth in the Bible. For example the Bible says God created this world! I believe the Bible so I don't spend time trying to figure out if evolution is true, because I know it is not. Jesus said to walk by Faith and I do! I know the Bible is true! I know that Jesus came to show us the Love of the Father, and He did! So I walk by FAITH, LOVE AND TRUTH!!!! The stakes are for eternity and where you spend it. I believe it all comes down to one word. BELIEVE or one question DO I BELIEVE GOD OR NOT????

For me and my house I Believe and thank God for things I would never even thought about before. Like I thank God for Jenny's smile, for her eyes that open, for her breathing, for her swallowing, for showing me how to scrub Jenny's teeth, for Jenny being able to suck through a straw, to chew her food most of the time, to not chock, to sit up most of the time, to sleep, to not have seizures, I thank God for her fingers that I can still open her hands to trim her nails, I thank God for showing me how to unpack her bowels, for clean water to shower Jenny in, for her strong teeth, for stopping the screaming, for Jenny not needing medicine, for her alertness, I could go on but I think you get the picture. God has shown me that these are truly gifts from Him!! God has showed me monetary gifts are momentary and really not worthy much. The gift of life and what you do with it is what I believe we will be judged on. Life is priceless, but without love it is worthless and without Jesus life is meaningless!!!! I love my brother Jesus and my Father God and I love the Holy Spirit dwelling in Jenny and I!!!!

Caring For My Baby

Jenny is amazing to me. Why? You might ask. In a word: Jesus. Yes, Jesus.

You see, while talking to Jenny's doctor this past summer, he said Jenny would not be here if not for the good care I am giving her. I know for a fact no one can add one moment to Jenny's life except God and I know Dr. Broderick was really saying I'm doing a great job. I love and respect Dr. Broderick. Jenny and I are privileged to know him. I think Dr. Broderick knows, and I realize, that helping Jenny live or keeping Jenny alive is beyond anything humanly possible.

Dr. Broderick still sees Jenny once a year and prescribes her seizure medicine. I am so blessed that Jenny is only on one prescription and does not need or take any other medicine of any kind. I think Dr. Broderick realizes Jenny's life is in the hands of God. I know for sure I do! I give praise to you, Jesus, for Jenny's life! Jenny could not even smile if not for Jesus. I believe every breath we have is a gift from God. I believe Jenny is amazing because I believe even in this state she hears and is responding to the love of Jesus. I pray for more Jenny time!!!! I thank you Jesus for even more Jenny time!! I hear people say every day is a gift from God and I give praise to my Father God whom is the giver of life, through Jesus my Brother.

In a way I feel sorry for doctors. They are limited to the knowledge they have about their specialty unless they have faith and trust in God for if they had their faith in God they too could move mountains. I know my faith and trust are in God. Like I said I respect doctors and I know they do great things for people every day. I'm actually happy they have no medicine for Pick's disease. I don't think my faith in God would not be where it is today if the doctors had a cure.

I thank you Jesus for the desire to know you and seek you with all my heart. I thank You Jesus for the cure of Pick's disease coming directly from you in the form of a healing! I thank you Jesus that I do not have why questions, you know like why is this happening, why is Jenny continually getting worse, etc. Instead I have hope in a miraculous healing, I have hope in the giver of life, and I know there is no such thing as death. So I know Jenny is going to live forever and she is healed right now! In fact I hear her stirring right now, thank You Jesus for life and for stirring awake my Jenny!

I believe Jenny and I are blessed to have this relationship with God. Anyone that has a relationship with God is truly blessed. I know as I grow up in my relationship with God and the more I study His life, the more freedom I see in Jenny's and my life. I believe most people think freedom is being able to do what you want to do. You know the world calls it (the pursuit of happiness). I've lived in campgrounds now almost four years. I see people trying to find happiness in traveling. Some are trying to escape their own children. Notice I said trying to find happiness. Traveling is just traveling. Seeing new and great places can bring happiness but like going to Kings Island it is momentary. I know the only way to true happiness is not seeking things that bring happiness but to seek God and He brings Joyfulness. I believe joyfulness is the opposite of happiness. Happiness comes from doing things for yourself and having others do things for you. Where Joyfulness comes from doing things for others. For example;

Jenny and I were camping next to a young couple. They had four children and seemed very happy. One night they knocked on our door and ask to come in. I said sure come on in and I ask what would you like to talk about. They looked a little surprised and then asked, how do you stay so happy? She said I see you taking care of you wife and she can do nothing for herself. You have literally put your life on hold to take care of her and you do it with such love. I simply told them I have Jesus in my life. My relationship with Jesus is my source of Joy! No one can take the Joy of knowing Jesus away.

They started telling me about their own childhoods. They both had a terrible past and truly terrible things had happened to them. I listened for about half an hour and ask if it made them happy to talk about their past. They both said not really. I ask who benefits form you talking about your past. They looked at me like you don't care do you? I said really I don't care about your past but I do care about your future. I said I like knowing your past history because it tells me you two are overcomers. Jesus loves when we overcome our past and Jesus loves when we fall in love with Him despite our past!

They went on to tell me how they have a lot of anger, which comes out at the worst times. Now they see some anger in their children and it is very disturbing to them. They talked about the curses being handed down from generation to generation. I interrupted them to ask, "Do you believe curses are handed down from generation to generation and if so are you powerless to stop it?" If you are powerless to stop it then I guess the anger goes on and on. They looked at each other and then ask how do you stop it then?

I asked why Jesus came. To forgive us our sins they said. Yes and does He do that? Yes Jesus forgives and removes them as far as the east is from the west. If you really believe that Jesus forgives and removes are sins as far as the east is from the west why do you think they are still handed down from generation to generation? When you repent for a sin issue in your life, the sin is forgiven. Some people think the sin is forgiven but not forgotten. To them it can be handed down from generation to generation. Jesus said forgive them Father, they know not what they do. In your case you need to forgive your parents for they knew not what they were doing. Jesus came to be our example of how to live and how to forgive. I mean Jesus said Father forgive them when they were pounding the nails in his hands! So do you think you should forgive your parents for your terrible past?

Jesus showed us the importance of being born again. When we are born again we have a new blood line. That is we voluntarily switch bloodlines and have a new Father. Original sin is removed along with the curses of our earthly parents. So we are no longer tied to the past we are free to be who God created us to be!

I ask earlier who benefits form you dwelling on your past. They said I guess the devil. So whom do you want to please the devil or God? If you dwell on the past, it pleases the devil because you look at all the hurt and pain in your life over and over again, until the hurt seems too monumental to forgive! Jesus said what we fix our eye on we will become. Thinking about the past hurts you and benefits the devil, it pleases the devil, it makes it harder and harder to forgive and takes away your relationship with Jesus because you will eventually listen to the devil in all situations. I have heard of classes called anger management classes. They are straight from the devil. There is no such thing as anger management. The devil has our government teaching anger management. Jesus says to put off the sins of this world!!! Jesus tells us how to do it!

If you make a continuous effort to shut down the past memories of hurt and anger you can defeat the devil. If you forgive them for they know not what they do, you can be set free to think and dwell on the Jesus in you and the future you have with Him dwelling in you is more joy than we can comprehend! The truth of the word of Jesus sets us free from sin, death and anger. That is more Joyfulness than a perfect day at Kings Island could ever be. Praise God! Forgiveness is freedom and freedom is simply dwelling on the one who wants to dwell in you. JESUS!!!!!

If Jesus came right in this camper right now and sat down in front of you, could you think about your past or would you suddenly be in the joy of His presence? I guarantee you, you could not think about the past, or have anger or unforgiveness. You would be in such awe that all you could think about would be Him sitting there in front of you. Jesus is in front of you! Try to have anger with Jesus in front of you, looking at you, talking to you and wanting to spend time with you! Jesus said draw nigh to me and I will draw nigh to you. So ask Jesus to show you how to draw nigh to Him and He will be sitting in front of you and you can live in his presents every moment of your life. That is Joy to the MAX!!! That is freedom to the max. That is no more anger ever and that is no more past, it is future that is bright to the max!!! Jesus is the light of the world, and so are you when you are aware of the Jesus living in YOU!!!!

The devil came up with this thing called anger management, if you're trying to manage anger you are listening to the wrong kingdom and you will never overcome the anger problem. Anger management is like trying to drive across a river with no bridge. You will sink and be in bed with anger that will choke you and snuff out your love of life. Stop anger in its tracks once and forever! Get born again, walk in the newness of your new blood line and talk to your new and real Father God. Come in to the truth that sets you free that is the relationship you can have with Jesus and your Father.

Drive on the bridge of Hope and Live before God and I can tell you for a fact anger and the past will flee faster than a high speed bullet. Don't get in bed with anger, don't manage anger, just recognize it for what it is and kick it out by asking Jesus in to your life now, today. That is freedom the Bible talks about.

Talking about the past again and again will only reinforce the past. It keeps it up front in your mind and makes it hard to move on. So right now repeat after me. Jesus I am sorry about living in the past and letting the past rob me of my future. I today declare I will live for you and you alone. We have four wonderful children, your gifts to us and you must have known we can learn to seek you above all else and in that seeking you will be our peace and Joy that you have for us. We declare today Father that you are our Father and that makes us sons and daughters of the most high. We declare that we will live with you setting right in front of us because you dwell in us. Thank You Jesus, I love you too!!!

Jesus came to show us the Love of the Father and we will study Your word to learn how to live in that love and be that love to everyone on the earth. Jesus Thank You for your sacrifice that forever restored our relationship to you. We will take advantage of our relationship with You and live to talk to you and be with you living within us. Oh Father what better gift could you have given us then to be able to talk to you personally!!! You wanting a relationship with me is Peace and Joy and LOVE!!!! I truly need nothing else!!!

Sometimes people ask me, "How do you do this? How do you take care of Jenny 24/7? You never get time to do anything you want to do." I tell them I am the most blessed man on earth to have Jenny with me. I talked about living like Jesus was right in front of you all your life. Well Jenny is with me all my life. When I get upset about something I look over at Jenny and realize she is not upset. If I start to worry and then I see Jenny and she is not worried. Jenny takes no account of wrongs. Jenny doesn't even have to repent because she cannot sin. Jenny never brings up the past! I am blessed to live with someone that is so God like in so many ways, why would I need a break.

On the contrary I want more of Jenny in my life. Seriously Jenny is a good influence on my life even in the situation we are in. I love my Jesus for the love He shows us every day and every minute. I thank you Jesus for setting such an example for us to follow. We all need truth and you are the truth that sets us free. Thank You for our freedom!!! Thank you Jesus for protection but most of all for your truth that sets us free from disease, sickness, and gives us health, joy and your perfect love!!!

November 11, 2012 is our 40th anniversary and I am so full of joy. I really cannot tell if Jenny is excited but she is very alert and I praise my loving Father for our 40th together. After church this morning, I sat with Jenny on my lap and just held her. I talk a lot about not dwelling on the past, but today I did let my mind drift back on past anniversaries, although they were happy memories and full of joy, there was sadness also. Our children are all grown and doing their own thing. I started thinking about all the good anniversaries and eating in the dining room on Jenny's china. Our children always got excited when we ate in the dining room. Our anniversaries were always happy and thinking about them I could almost smell Jenny's cooking. I am so blessed to have such great memories of our anniversaries.

As I sat there with Jenny on my lap I started to get sad and I was looking at Jenny's little face as she was sleeping on my shoulder and I was wishing she would just wake up totally normal. The sadness started turning into regret and then some guilt came on me thinking maybe somehow I caused this. You know maybe there was some way I could have headed off the Pick's disease before it got this bad. Then all of a sudden I heard someone say to me, who is this guy you are listening to? Right away my countenance picked up and I knew I was letting myself go down the wrong path. Thank You Jesus and Father God for sending me a message through your Holy Spirit who dwells in me to get on with the day and not dwell on the past.

It was amazing to me how quickly the devil was turning the great memories of our anniversaries into sadness and then regret. We have been so blessed, I mean it, we are big time blessed! I love you Jesus and my heart and mind and my soul belong to you and You alone!!!!

The weather was unusually warm and Jenny woke up so I walked Jenny in the wheel chair. The campground was almost empty but Jenny and I enjoyed our walk even though we didn't talk to anyone. When we got back to our camper I decided to make Jenny's chocolate chip cookies. They taste great and I know they are oh so good for us! I love the smell of fresh cookies cooking in the oven and I think Jenny liked the smell also. I love my Jenny and I am so thankful to Jesus for giving me these very special times with His delightfully precious Jenny! You know this was the best anniversary ever!!!! Thank You Jesus for loving us so much!!

On the 18th we went to the church, where the 20 children invited us to. Oh I'm sorry I just jumped out in front of myself. Last weekend we met a group of 20 young teenagers from a church in Louisville. They were like sponges soaking up the word of Jesus. So I gave them all some tracks to read and they invited Jenny and I to their church. It was fun to see them again but they were in their own environment and so busy. They did talk to us but only briefly.

On Monday, Jenny and I went to Louisville to have more books printed. On the way I ask Jesus if I should only have five printed because I knew I was running really close on my monthly budget. I got to Office Max and when the clerk ask me how many books do you want, ten came out of my mouth and so I just figured Jesus new something I didn't know.

Upon arriving home to our camper, a pickup truck pulled up. It was a lady we met at the church nearby (Family Christian Center). When she met us a week ago she realized Jenny was in depends and she explained how her work (a home for mentally challenged children and young adults) was accumulating extra Depends. We literally stocked our camper in every place possible with pampers and bed pads. It was so nice of her to think of us and have the right size for Jenny. I mean I was over whelmed and just could not thank her enough.

Later Jenny and I went to pick up some groceries. At the checkout I looked at the bill surprised by the small amount. Then I realized I did not have pampers in the cart and that just saved me 24 dollars. Thank you Amy and Jesus for your thoughtfulness!!!! I look around the camper and see all these pampers and I feel soooo pampered. Jesus always comes through and He always does it by flowing through someone willing to be His representative here on earth. Thank you Amy and Thank You Jesus for taking care of my delightful precious Jenny! Thank you Amy for pampering us!

On Wednesday night Jenny and I went to church at the Family Christian Center. Pastor Pat has a great message and we have met a lot of very nice people there. He ended his message with announcements and asks his congregation if he missed anything. His wife said yes and then announced she knew of someone in the church who had a special need and ask the congregation to bless this family in their congregation. She didn't want to mention their name for fear they might be embarrassed. So they just placed a bucket at the exit.

A couple started talking to us as everyone else was leaving. They kept us occupied until almost everyone had left. Then a guy walked up and handed me a wade of cash and said the collection was for you and Jenny. They had no way of knowing our needs because I never expressed them but again Jesus put it in their hearts to give us a finical blessing. I usually do not talk about financial blessings because the blessings from God are always above them but there are some times when a bundle of cash is also needed and thanks to the special people of Pat's congregation Jenny and I are blessed again. I say again because the biggest blessing was being there with them. Thank you again Jesus!!!!

I could not believe what was happening in my heart. I mean Jesus had put love in the hearts of so many to bless us. I Thank You Jesus for your desire to bless Jenny and I! I Love You Jesus for letting us witness Your love flowing through so many others. I have been taught buy Jesus; how Jesus wants us to be Jesus on the earth; how Jesus wants us to love as Jesus loved on the earth.

I never quite understood why it was so important for Jesus to have us manifest Jesus. I mean Jesus did a great job of manifesting the Father's love! We can read about the love of Jesus in the Bible, the ultimate love story. Now I am just starting to realize why Jesus wants us to manifest Him. The best way for Jesus to create a desire for people to want to know Him is to let people see Him in them. It is awesome; we can manifest Jesus by simple acts of kindness and in doing so we can give people a desire to know why we were kind.

I know some churches love to count the number of people that recite the sinner's prayer and get saved. They usually say "if you died to night where would spend eternity?" Then people recite the prayer and the church counts them as saved. That approach falls short because their desire for Jesus came out of fear of going to hell! To me that is so short of the love of Jesus and they really have nothing to run on. I heard another preacher say "but what if they live tonight how did reciting the sinner's prayer help change their everyday life?" I think when someone can witness the love of Jesus in you they will want what you have. They will have a desire to know Jesus and in that desire Jesus will fill them with truth and love that is the truth and love they see in you! Jesus said it is the love of Jesus that will lead men to repentance. Give the love of Jesus by being the love of Jesus and Jesus will bring the increase.

I think I know now why manifesting the love of the Father is so important. I think when we manifest Jesus we get excited in our hearts and become very joyful in our hearts. This is the transforming of our minds Jesus talk about in His word. I guess Jesus gets so joyful in his heart to see his loved ones giving out of unconditional love; and watching joyfulness over flowing and spilling out of everyone in his church. I thank you Jesus for your love and for giving your life so willingly!! Jesus you are the best example of love this world has ever seen! I also thank you for your word, and the knowledge this world will be saved one heart at a time.

One heart at a time! Like a farmer plants seeds one seed at a time. I know tech knowledge has increased and so is the farmers speed at planting seed has increased but tech knowledge has also boosted our ability to plant seeds in the hearts of so many hearts at a time. A farmer plants a row at a time and a row becomes a field and a field becomes an acre and the acres become a farm. Just as the farmer can feed thousands with his seeds planted in the ground, and he will never see all the people that benefit from his work, he knows in his heart the work is needed and necessary to sustain life. So too our seeds are planted to nourish the hearts of many and all though we usually never see the result of our labors; we can walk by faith knowing our labors are touching the hearts of many. Then every once in a while we will be given a powerful glance at the love of God flowing through others and how that love is the manifestation of our hearts for God's likeness. So never get discouraged, go plant some seeds of love and even if the people don't accept them right away, rest in your belief that like the seed the farmer planted in the ground, will have a miracle of life in it and God will bring the increase.

I want to talk about me for a couple minutes. When I was only 5 or 6 years old I already loved little ones. Every year my Grandma had a party. We always called them Grandma's party. You would call them family reunions. Every year Grandma had a picture of her family taken. I was always in the front row sitting on the grass holding a baby in my lap. I was just fascinated with babies even at that early age. I loved the way they would look you in the eye and if you talked to them they would try to talk back. They watched your lips and your expressions to see if they made you happy. They would smile at you and coo at you and give you such joy. I truly love babies even when others made fun of me for holding and talking to babies, when I could have been playing games with children my own age.

I told you all that to say this. Right now Jenny is like the babies I have loved all my life. I sit on the couch and hold her in my lap like a baby and she looks right in my eyes and then studies my face expressions like the babies did. I talk to her and see her mouth try to move and I tell her she can talk to me. She tries so hard to talk and her little face makes expressions that blow my mind. I tell her I understand and smile at her, Jenny responds to love just like the babies did all my life. I tell people how God out does Himself every day. I tell them how I never knew of the joy He could bring in to our life every day and I don't understand life, but I know I have the most blessed life of anyone I know!! THANK YOU JESUS for these truly special times with my loving little wife Jenny!!!

Thank you God for letting me hold Jenny in my arms and for letting me know when I am holding her, you are holding us, so we know you are present with us! As I write this I feel so inadequate to express the love of you Jesus but I know you understand because you told us your love would surpass all our understanding and IT DOES!!

In Love with Jesus

Last night I received a phone call Joel. We talked for over an hour and most of the conversation was Joel telling me what a great guy I am. After we hung up I thought that is the third phone call this week where people told me I'm a good guy. Each phone call was a little different but pretty much the same. I ask God what is going on? Why do people all of a sudden think they need to tell me these things? I love you Father God and I think you are up to something. I guess I'll just wait and see. I thanked everyone for the kind words they spoke about me. I also praised my Father and brother Jesus because without them I really am so helpless to take care of my delightfully precious Jenny. What a gift she is and what a joy it is to have her here with me. Thank you Jesus for your words of encouragement!!! I love you too!!!

This morning as I was feeding Jenny, I was thanking God for Jenny being with me. I was praising Him for Jenny being able to swallow. I can tell Jenny's swallowing has become a big decision, it is not automatic like for most people. Smiling is the same way. Jenny has to work and think about getting her muscles in her face to smile. It seems that everything Jenny does is a conscious decision. I believe her life proves the love God has for her and His love is giving her the will power to still fight and because of the love from Jesus Jenny will not give up. She just needs massive amounts of love every day, and I know God and I are up for that. Thank you Jesus for your love every day!!!

Being in love with Jesus and knowing He loves us is so wonderful. Even being in this love relationship with Jesus, I see more negative things going on in Jenny's health then positive. It is very hard to witness; I mean I have the word of God that says He will heal all. I see the love of God every day, so I don't go by what I see negatively, I go by Faith that God has turned this around and the three of us will have coffee together real soon.

1st Timothy 1:5 says the goal of our instruction is love from a pure heart and a good conscience and a sincere faith. I know Jesus showed everyone what love is and what a pure heart looks like, a good conscience, and a sincere faith looks like while here on earth. He is our example so I will seek Him for a pure heart of love and a good conscience and I will seek Him for a sincere faith that God has given me a desire for!!! I know Jenny already has hers and what an example she is! Again thank you Jesus for healing Jenny and thank you for your love and concern for our well-being. I love you Jesus!!!!

Last night I was holding Jenny on my lap and I started singing to her, about (you know who) my Father God. In my mind I saw a huge church; I'm using the word church because I have no other way to describe it. I guess I could call it a gathering place. I mean millions of spirits where there, the church was brilliant like nothing I have ever seen before, everyone was singing, here comes the bride, I have never heard music so beautiful before. There were no seats in this church, and no walls but I knew it was a holy place and everyone was just everywhere. The music was loud but soft somehow and very comforting, I did not see people playing music but I could hear it so clearly.

The song went like this (here comes the bride, here comes the bride and then someone else sung over their singing somehow and his voice sung; now all step aside as others continued singing here comes the bride) and then as everyone parted, like to form an aisle, I saw Father God walking down the aisle holding Jenny, not holding her hand like we do here on earth but holding her somehow like in His arms as you would hold a baby. Jenny looked so radiant!!! She was smiling with her little crooked tooth showing; as Father God presented her sinless and spotless and worthy to be the bride of His son Jesus. Believe me Joy is not a feeling in heaven it is a way of life!!! Peace is not achieved like here on earth, it is knowing you made it and you are in the presence of God himself!!!

Jesus said in his word that we are to be the bride of Jesus Christ and I know Jesus let me have this vision to give me the peace of Jesus Christ. I don't know when or how all that will work out but I know Jenny is the bride of Jesus and I get to witness the marriage!!! I will see Jesus with Jenny and as I am writing this I am hearing Jesus say "you ask Me if you will know Jenny in heaven or at least know that she is there." My Jesus answers all questions and this time the answer is in a spectacular vision with beauty that is out of this world and singing that is so clear and so beautiful, my heart wants us to be their right now!!!

Something about that vision really stands out in my mind. Jenny's smile is the prettiest smile I have ever seen. She has a crooked tooth and although she never complained about it she did ask one time to have it fixed. One of the health insurance companies we had years ago had a dental plain included in it. Jenny asked if she could get her tooth fixed. I said if it is important to you go ahead, but I like your teeth just the way they are. I told Jenny I thought her crooked tooth gave her smile personality and complemented her very special face. I love her dimple on the left side of her face and the crooked tooth on the right side. Jenny has green eyes and that made her eyes special to me. I remember taking Jenny to a beauty parlor for a haircut one time and the beautician ask to pluck Jenny's eyebrows? I said positively NO. I like Jenny's face just the way God made it! I love Jenny and I love her looks also. I love God for making Jenny so cute. Jenny's eyebrows are just beautiful the way God made them. I know Jesus calls Jenny delightfully precious but He made her so cute; so beautifully cute. Thank You Jesus for making Jenny delightfully beautiful to me also and thank You for all these blessings!!!

Isn't it amazing that in the vision I could not tell it was Jenny coming down the aisle with Father God until I saw her smile? The other thing I liked about her smile was, Jenny was the only one with that smile. Jesus made Jenny so special to me! Jenny never asked about having her tooth fixed again. Thank You Jesus!

When I told some people about this vision their comment was; Jesus is preparing you for when Jenny goes to be with the Lord. I could see how they could think that. I asked Jesus if He was preparing me to be comforted here on earth without Jenny. I believe Jesus was just answering my question about will I know Jenny made it and will I see her there. Jesus saw my concern and loves me so much He decided to quite my heart by giving me a beautiful vision of heaven and Jenny being very Joyful there. In a way he let me know that he likes Jenny's crooked tooth and her delightfully precious special smile. I love You Jesus and I thank You for Your very special way of loving us!!! You know Jesus you are delightfully precious to Jenny and I !!!!!!

Before I had that little vision of heaven I had been asking Jesus if I would know Jenny in heaven? It seemed important to me, I cannot figure out how you could love someone so much and then get to heaven and not want to be married their also. I know the Bible stories that talk about heaven and the word heaven is mentioned 583 times and in 551 verses in the Bible, and of those 256 times and 238 verses are in the New Testament. So I guess it is important to God for us to know we have a place to go. The very first scripture verse mentions heaven.

Gen 1:1 In the beginning God created the heaven and the earth.

Jesus created it and I want to go. Thank You God for that special vision and for telling us about the reward of going to heaven, to be with You and our loved ones!!!

In a conversation with a friend I met the through Joel; Christopher explained to me how knowing God is not enough. He said everyone knows the president of the United States. You could study the president and read every book he has ever written, you could get to know him so well, you could know what he had for breakfast every day. If you had all this knowledge and then you went to the white house and ask to see the president, all that knowledge, all the studying, and all the research you did would still not get you in to see the president. The only way to be invited in is for the president to know you. Christopher said I believe God is the same way. He said you can study God and research God and have great knowledge of God; you can quote Bible scriptures all day and still not have a relationship with God.

I thought to myself, God is not limited in knowledge like the president and God knows us all, I mean God created us all, so wouldn't God let us in? The answer is the same, you could know everything about the president or God but if you have no relationship, all that knowledge is useless!!! Kind of like knowing someone who can quote the Bible, verse for verse but he never lives in the Joy of knowing Jesus wants a heart to heart, loving relationship with him. He has missed the real reason Jesus came!!!

I decided to ask God. How do we become more intimate with you Jesus? I already have a good relationship with you but just like my relationship with Jenny grew over the years I want to continue to grow a more personal intimate, lasting, loving relationship with You

Jesus. Jesus answered with a question. How could it be that someone could be a neighbor of yours and after twenty years of living next door to you, one day the police pull up and arrest him for being a serial killer? You are totally surprised because you never had the slightest idea your neighbor was a serial killer. Jesus said your problem is, you never really talked to your neighbor and more importantly you never listened to him either. Jesus said you never made knowing him your priority and you never sought a relationship with him! Jesus said you were content to know he did not bother you and you did not bother him. You only gained enough knowledge to be comfortable. He said you were comfortable just knowing his name and most of all you were comfortable thinking you were safe having him for a neighbor, so you did not need any more knowledge of him except to be comfortable having him next door.

I have found in my travels that comfort brings complacency, you see I love to talk about God to everyone I meet and I do talk about God to everyone, but when I have been around someone long enough I get comfortable knowing they have a relationship with Jesus and then we start talking about other things because we become comfortable around each other.

I thought to myself, Jesus you are so right! Most people have been taught the only reason Jesus came was to die for our sins; we pray a little prayer and we are saved. They never seek a heart to heart relationship with Him. This would be like me marrying someone because I like the way she makes pancakes. She may think this is easy, all I have to do is make him pancakes every day and he will take care of me. You may have loved her pancakes for a while but after a few months of pancakes you might want something different. If your relationship with God is based on something so superficial, like what Has God promised you, the first time you do not get what you think he has promised, you will think why is this happening or worse you may ask, why did you let that happen God?

Your relationship probably will not last. You will probably backslide or get divorced because your relationship was based on the superficial knowledge, of thinking I'll pray this little prayer and God is now my provider. You never grew your relationship to know Him better! You never ask God what do you want me to do today! Love is a two way street. Love is responding to the needs of your loved one every day. Don't just tell God you love Him, be His love to all you met today and every day and you will prove you Love Jesus.

The first step to a good relationship is listening! The second is responding to what you heard. I mean we want Jesus to listen to us and to respond to us, don't we? Jesus is listening and responding all the time. We need to do the same! When you hear His voice and respond you are doing the will of the Father and doing the will of the Father will bring Joy to you that can and will flow through you to others. It really is a Joy that surpasses our understanding because you and Jesus are building a relationship that will last forever.

If you listen to your bride and you respond to her, you will have a great relationship and if you live to learn more about her every day your love and understanding will grow every day!!! Jesus is the Bride, start each day by asking Him; Jesus what are we going to do today!!! Then go about your day and watch God put a circumstance in your path to share the love of Jesus to someone. It never fails and it is Joy beyond your understanding!! Never just tell someone about God, give them the love of God!!! Be willing to be the representative of God's love and watch God's love change hearts one at a time. Jesus said my burden is light and my yoke is easy and as you know He is sooooo right! Go give someone the love of Jesus to day. Please don't try to give someone the love of Jesus to feel loved by God that is backwards, give them the love of Jesus because you know you are loved by Jesus! When you know and are rooted in the love of Jesus, loving others will be easy

Heroes

We moved to Lebanon, Ohio to be closer to Mom and our boys for the season. Jesus had me finish the teaching on Hero's and I had copies made so I could start handing them out. On Thursday while passing through Red Lion, Ohio we stopped for a haircut at a barber shop I saw there. I could tell Steve the barber had a big heart the moment I walked in, because he wanted to make sure Jenny was comfortable while he cut my hair. As we talked about God another guy came and we soon had a three-way conversation going. After finishing my hair cut I went out to the car to get them both a copy of "Coffee Time." I handed them both a copy of coffee time when another guy came in. We continued talking about God when the third fellow said "I used to do nice Christian things for people but they never 'thank you' so I stopped doing them".

I just stood there thinking; Lord how do I respond to that? Just then Jesus whispered in my ear, give him the teaching on heroes, so I looked at him and said I have something you might like to read. Then I went to the car again and got a copy for him. As I reentered the barbershop the three of them were laughing, the man getting his hair cut had started reading Coffee Time and had gotten to the part where Jenny flipped me the bird. He said your little wife must have been a real flip. I told them she was. I handed the teaching on heroes to the sarcastic man and shortly after that Jenny and I left.

On the following Monday I was talking to Steve the barber from Red Lion barber shop on the phone, he was excited to tell me what happened after I left Thursday. The barbershop is on a busy street with a traffic light in front of it. Steve said the three of them were still talking about Coffee time with Jesus, when they heard a woman screaming for help. They ran outside and saw a county bus had stopped at the red light and the woman driver was outside the bus trying to hold the door shut as a man inside the bus was trying to kick the door open. The bus was a special bus for the mentally challenged and this man had broken out of his restraints and started attacking the driver. The three men from the barbershop manned the doors of the bus, while someone called 911.

The sarcastic man from the barbershop jumped in the bus with the wild man and talked the wild man into trading the ballpoint pen the wild man was attacking him with, for a roll of tape. In moments he had the man settled down and when the police came they secured him in his seat and all was well again. The three men went into the barbershop and Steve told the sarcastic man, I could not have done what you did, getting into that bus with the wild man. Steve said that was really heroic! The man looked at Steve and started laughing and then said you know the man with his wife that was here a little while ago gave me a paper to read. Steve said yes what was it? The paper is titled HEROES. All three men had a good laugh and said what a day this has been.

A couple days' later Jenny and I went to see Mom. We had a nice visit. Mom is now off some of her medicine and she is so much more alert than in past visits. It was really good to see her and I gave her a new copy of Jenny's book. This one has about 30 more pages then the first one I gave her.

This Christmas season was different from last year. Last year it seemed Jenny and I had someone to visit every night. This year we spent a lot of time in the camper but it turned out really cool because Joel had time to come over and we meet some of his friends that came over with their three children. Also one night we were invited to Will Riddle's house where we met three young men that were from Russia. Jenny and I had a great time there and the whole night went so fast. Everyone there was on fire for the Lord and their fire made my fire even hotter. It was a special time to say the least. I love you Jesus for putting friends in our life that build our relationship with You.

On another night we went to Mary and Kerns house for a great dinner. We also had great conversation. Their son Sam read the Heroes paper and said he liked the part about Mc Donald's. Their daughter Libby read it and said she liked it also. I was glad Mary and Kern and children had time to visit with us because I love spending time with them.

LUNCH WITH BOB

Around the 12th we received a phone call from Bob, a friend who said he had about a two hour window of time and if we could make it to Bob Evans he would buy us lunch. Jenny and I made it there and met our friend. Before we ordered our food, Bob told me how his wife asked him a question before she left for work that morning. She wanted to know if she were to get sick like Jenny; could he take care of her like Ron takes care of Jenny? All during our meal Bob was analyzing himself and had decided he could take care of his wife like I do except he could not carry her around the way I carry Jenny. Bob said he would have to use the wheel chair more than I do, but other than that he was quite sure he could take care of his wife if she became sick like Jenny.

We were almost finished eating when Jenny's bowels let loose. I told Bob I was going to take Jenny to the restroom to clean her up. We were so blessed to have the restroom empty and none of the mess got on the floor as I carried Jenny into the restroom. It was quite a mess. The Depends did not hold and the mess went down her legs and into her socks. The toilet did not have a toilet tank; it just had the chrome pipe and flush valve. That makes it very hard to keep Jenny from falling while I am trying to clean her. I used a lot of wipes and managed to do a good job. I got a clean outfit on Jenny and as I picked her up her bowel let loose again. I really felt bad for Jenny, I mean we share all our meals and my bowels were just fine. I'm not sure what I gave her to have her bowels like mud. The good news is she didn't seem to be in any pain.

I started to clean Jenny up again. The partitions in public restrooms are about a foot off the floor. When a man came in to use the urinal I heard him say "Whew!" as the smell was horrible and you could see the dirty pampers and wipes lying on the floor. I did not open the door of the stall but I ask him if he could find Bob out in the restaurant. I described Bob to him and the man found Bob. Bob came in and could see the mess under the partition. He asked me what I needed. I told him I had another clean outfit for Jenny in the back seat of our car and needed him to get it for us. He went and got the clean clothes and handed them over the partition to me.

I got Jenny dressed and out to the car. After I buckled her in the seat I then ran back in to Bob Evans to clean the restroom and put the messy Depends and wipes in the garbage can. When I finished in there I gathered up Jenny's soiled clothes and headed out to say good bye to Bob, who was waiting by Jenny. Bob had kind of a sick look on his face and said Ron, I don't think I could do this. I told Bob all things are possible in Jesus Christ who strengths us. He hugged me and said I think you are pretty special Ron. I thanked Bob for lunch and he handed me a Christmas card with some cash in it. I thanked him and he left.

I went back in to the restaurant to ask the manager to have someone change the bag in the garbage can or the stink will continue on. A young man went in to change the bag; I went right in the restroom after him to ask him if he wanted me to change it. It is a little messy I said. He told me he would do it and added thanks for cleaning the mess up so good. He then asked me what happened to your wife. I gave him the short version because I really needed to get Jenny home to shower her and do the laundry. It was nice of that young man to ask about my Jenny. Thank you Jesus for putting such nice people in our path everywhere we go!!

Time With Jenny

I know we went to see mom again around the 16 of December and had another nice visit. Mom is so much more alert than last year and that makes my Christmas great already and just seeing her be her old self again is such a blessing. We were there a couple hours when mom leaned over and whispered something to my brother Kenny. Kenny told me mom said I'm tired when are they leaving? I just loved seeing mom drinking her coffee and seeing her walk to the bathroom, it was a special visit for Jenny and I; but the night was over and off we went. Thank You Jesus for a wonderful visit with mom!!! Jenny and I had sat on moms couch that whole time and I was amazed how well Jenny seemed to be listening.

The weather has been really cold for the last couple days, so Jenny and I have had a lot of time in the camper. Jenny really doesn't seem to be concerned about not going anywhere so I have pretty much just been holding her and loving on Jenny all day long. Even when I go do the laundry Jenny seems to understand. I think she is doing really well. Praise my Jesus and praise you some more.

On the 19th of December we received a call from Marilyn my sister, she told me mom had taken a turn for the worse and I needed to come over to see her. We did go and what a difference a couple days make. Hospice was there and just making mom comfortable, it was really hard to see mom like that but what a blessing for us to already be in Cincinnati and close by. All her children were there except Elaine who lives in California.

We went back to see mom the next day. The nurses said she was now totally unresponsive. I leaned over her bed and said Jenny and I came to see you Mom, the nurses were right, mom had no response at all. So I leaned over her bed again and said Mom it is Ronnie the one that shook your China closet when I was bad. Mom started to laugh, the nurses sprang to their feet to see her response and mom just got a big smile on her face. God blessed me with that smile and I will hold onto that smile the rest of my life. Thank you Jesus for being so thoughtful as to give me what turned out to be mom's last smile!

On Friday the 21st of December mom passed on to spend eternity with Jesus and Father God. I believe Jesus sent her a special invitation to spend Christmas with Him and His Father and mom said I'll be there and she was. I'm so happy for her and I know her work her on earth was complete; so her death was the right timing of my Jesus and what a comfort to know mom is up there with Jesus. I know most of the time we humans think of death from the perspective of our loss. If you look at death from the perspective of life in heaven with Jesus it gives a whole new outlook on death and death can be celebrated for what is (a reward form God for a job well done.) Just thinking about Mom being in heaven is such a great joy for me! Thank You Jesus.

A couple weeks ago we were invited to have dinner and spend the evening with Doug and Ann, on December 22nd. Our dinner was great and as the night unfolded Doug asked if I had a sport jacket to wear to mom's funeral. Doug gave me a really nice jacket and a dress shirt. It looked brand new and fit perfect. It was really nice of Doug and Ann to invite us over for dinner and we had a great time enjoying their company. Now I knew I could go to mom's funeral and look great for her, because Doug's sport coat did fit and looked great. What a nice thing for Doug and Ann to do and what a great time Jenny and I had visiting them. I am over whelmed at the timing of my Jesus. He planned this dinner with Doug and Ann a couple weeks ago. Then God put it in the hearts of Doug and Ann to give me dress clothes for Mom's funeral. I would never spend the money to buy dress clothes for one event and yet God cared enough to give them to me. Jesus you are the best!!!

On Friday the 28th of December mom's body was laid at the Gate of Heaven cemetery next to Dad's grave site. The reality of it has not really set in but I know they are with my Jesus and my Father God so I have a great Joy in my heart knowing they are loved and spending eternity in heaven. Now mom and dad are in the peace and joy the Lord talked about all the time! Thank you Jesus.

During the week between Mom's death and her Funeral Jesus gave me a teaching on inheritances. It was 12 pages long and I hoped to read it at mom's Mass. I thought it was very important but I did not get the opportunity to read it. I did get to hand it out to some of the people there. Jesus said Inheritance should not be material junk; inheritance should be passing on the knowledge of knowing God and passing that knowledge to your children. Anything other than His knowledge to pass on is junk that actually might take you further from God instead of growing you closer to Him.

I know some people would disagree and call the junk "keep sakes" but what are the keep sakes keeping and what are they making you dwell on. If not God then I don't need it. For example if you think you own something and that something would be hard to give up, you don't own it, it owns you. To me keep sakes are like that. You try to hold on to them and in reality they are holding on to you. Let go of the junk and live to love and be the love of Jesus in the world! Now that is true freedom and you can hand that down to everyone and you do not need lawyers or wills!

I am free to be who God wants me to be and I do not need junk to tie me down. I told my brothers and sisters to do what they want with mom and dads "keep sakes". I love my brothers and sisters and respect their desire for those things but I am just interested in doing the work of the kingdom of God. Having the love of Jesus in my heart and knowing He loves me is the greatest keepsake in the world and the only one that will see us through life's hardships!!!

When I think about heaven I know the coolest part will be being with Father God and Jesus!!! I think just seeing them and knowing you made it will be joy beyond anything we can imagine here on earth. I believe in heaven we will have enough. Enough of what you might ask? Enough of everything. You see here on earth we consume so much of our time trying to have enough. Like money or food or whatever you think you might need.

I know Jesus told us not to worry, but people do. Jesus tells to take no thought for tomorrow, but people do. Actually we worry so much about tomorrow we lose our Joy for today. Then tomorrow comes and we start worrying about the next tomorrow. I believe we can be in heaven right now if we stop worrying. Jenny and I just trust God to provide and He does! Tomorrow is not promised to anyone and the things we worry about today are projected on to tomorrow. It is a useless cycle. Life is simple TRUST GOD and rest in His love and forget trying to hold on to Physical Keep Sakes! I know for a fact that mom loved me so what else do I need from her.

I wrote a story called your Inheritance and it is in the Joy of the Lord book if you would like I will send you one free.

Your Inheritance

The day after Mom's death while having coffee time with Jesus, He started talking about comfort zones. How stepping out of a comfort zone will make you grow in the Lord. Leaving a comfort zone is like stepping in to the unknown. Like the first day of school for a child, he is leaving the comfort of home and going into the unknown. This transition will be a lot easier for him if his mom removes the fear by guiding him and assuring him it will be okay. After a short amount of time his fear leaves and he is comfortable there also. The reward for facing the fear is new knowledge and a bigger world.

For mom her comfort zone was her family and her familiar surroundings. Fear will hold you in a comfort zone until someone helps you remove the fear. It is like crossing a bridge, only we never know how long the bridge is or what awaits us on the other side. I believe Jesus sent a comforter for mom and took her to the final reward, of being with Jesus and Father God and a new world without fear.

I believe life is about preparing and helping others prepare for meeting our creator. On Friday December 21st, 2012 at 9:30 pm mom crossed her last bridge. I thank Jesus for allowing mom to be in her comfort zone right up to her entrance into her eternal life. Mom was truly blessed to have almost all her loved ones alongside her. I believe mom had the peace of mind, knowing her loved ones were at peace with her going to be with Jesus. When we cross the bridge in faith Jesus brings us to a new level of comfort. Jesus through His example is preparing us for the big bridges in life and Jesus comforts us with His love. Thank You Jesus for loving Mom and for being her loving guide in this transition. I like to think of mom's passing this way, Jesus just gave mom an invitation to spend Christmas in heaven with Him and all His loved ones and mom said yes!

The life of Jesus is our example of how to live and how to love. Jesus uses the Bible as a tool to teach us and we have a free will to decide if we want to follow Jesus on the narrow path or walk the path of destruction while thinking it is our own path. Either way we all get to cross the bridge and stand before Jesus for judgment. If we prepare for our judgment the judgment seat will be sweet and we will be in the loving arms of Jesus.

I know mom has crossed the bridge and is in heaven with Jesus. Today I pray for everyone here to be on the narrow path that Jesus talks about and for all of us to see the narrow gate and that it is open wide for us. I know Friday night my mom stood before Jesus and was judged. I believe her judgment was sweet and she is in the loving arms of Jesus and the Father! Actually I kind of envy her when I think of the Joy in her spirit! Mom is finally able to be with Jesus and Father God. Jesus said in Mathew;

> Mat 7:13-14 Because narrow *is* the gate and difficult *is* the way which leads to life, and there are few who find it. "Beware of false prophets, who come to you in sheep's clothing, but inwardly they are ravenous wolves.

So we see by God's word that straight is the gate and narrow is the way that leads unto life and only a few will find it. I believe mom and dad walked the narrow path and went through that gate. How do you find the narrow path? Simply put; you have childlike faith in God. I believe mom had that childlike faith. I believe mom never gave up on God. Even when her prayers were not answered as fast as she would have liked; mom stood steadfast in her believe that Jesus would answer them.

In other words we choose the path. The wide path is full of earthly goods and some happiness. Contrast that with the narrow path, little earthly goods, but full of Joyfulness. In my quite time with Jesus, He explained to me the difference between happiness and Joyfulness. Jesus said happiness is the devils counterfeit of Joyfulness. Jesus showed me happiness is living for yourself, and Joyfulness is denying yourself and living for others.

Happiness comes by someone doing something for you, it is momentary, it can come and go in seconds; we actually make plans to be happy. We can plane to go to Kings Island and on that day have perfect weather, no long lines, great food, and when we go to our car to leave, if the car doesn't start we lose all our happiness in one second.

Contrast the happiness of living for yourself with the joy of living for others. Joyfulness is you doing something for others; it is forever and stays with you even in your times of need. Choosing to help others is choosing the narrow path and in doing so receiving the Joyfulness that will surpass our understanding. It is bring heaven to earth as Jesus spoke about in the prayer we call the "Our Father".

Jesus commanded us to die to self. I know mom died to herself all her life. Mom would give of her time to anyone that ask!

Luke 9:23 And he said to them all, If any man will come after me, let him deny himself, and take up his cross daily, and follow me.

I know there is a spiritual war going on for your spirit 24/7. The only way to win this war is to recognize you are in it. Yes,

First you must recognize that our battle is in the spirit world and our battle is for our eternal life and this spiritual battle will determine where you will spend eternality.

Eph 6:12 For we wrestle not against flesh and blood, but against principalities, against powers, against the rulers of the darkness of this world, against spiritual wickedness in high places.

For we wrestle not against flesh and blood. Flesh is material that can and will rote away. Blood is trying to pass on these material things on to loved ones. I believe material treasures are the curses of modern day. I have seen people work so hard to have something to hand their children when they die. People write wills so the children will not fight over their inheritance. I believe this is the (worrying about tomorrow) the Bible talks about not doing. I met a couple that thought they simplified life by only having one child, only to see her go into drugs and an alternative life style. Then the parents had no one to leave their junk to.

My parents left us children an inheritance of material things. I believe there motive was pure and they just saw these things as keepsakes. I can tell you this; Jesus gave me the best inheritance anyone can ask for. The day before mom died when Jenny and I went to see her. As I entered her bedroom the hospice nurse said your mom has not recognized anyone today. I thought to myself, mom doesn't have her hearing aid in and she doesn't have her glasses on, so maybe she cannot hear us or see us and it may be hard for mom to talk.

I leaned over her bed and said it is Jenny and Ron here to see you mom. There was no response, just then I looked at mom and leaned over her again and said I'm Ronnie the one that shuck your china closet and mom smiled and tried to laugh. The nurses came to their feet as they were really surprised by mom's reaction. I know the next day I called to see how mom was doing and my sister Pat answered the phone. She said I heard you got mom smiling yesterday. I didn't realize it then, but I think it might have been her last smile. Thank you Jesus for the best inheritance anyone could ask for!!

I am so blessed to find the truth. Jesus said our fight is against principalities, against powers, against the rulers of the darkness of this world, against spiritual wickedness in high places. Principalities are devils, rulers of darkness are devils, and spiritual wickedness is listening to devils and doing what they say. Today we could say our fight is against the principality of business, notice the word sin in the middle of bu-**sin**-ess. Our fight is always against time and against the sucking power of material. Material things do suck the life right out of you. We work hard to get them, to keep them nice, to preserve them, to keep them clean and we worry about who gets our junk when we leave this world. Sounds like false idols to me. As I walk closer to the Lord I realize anything that takes my mind off Jesus can be a false idol.

Look how hard we will work to have something nice. Look how many hours and days; we will give up with our loved ones to supply them with the right clothes and material things. While we are out working so hard for our children, the "Rulers of darkness" that is the evil spirits come in to steel our loved ones. When these evil spirits still our loved ones, we do not understand, I mean we worked so hard for our children. If we give them the chance to defend themselves, they will say all we wanted was for you to spend time with us dad. I know now I would have loved more than any material thing on earth to have more time with mom and dad. I kept thinking tomorrow or next week I'll have time and that tomorrow and next week never came. New cars, second home, season pass to see the bangles, all fall short of just having time to be with and talk to my mom and dad. Most people know you can talk to God anytime, so they put off talking to God also. I have learned that intimacy with Jesus brings more Joy then anything material could ever bring. I used to like movies but now to watch a two hour movie is wasting 120 minutes I could be spending with my best friend Jesus!

So how did mom and dad overcome all the material things of the world? They found the truth of Gods word.

Joh 8:32 And you shall know the truth, and the truth shall make you free.

The truth is we should have our hearts seeking God. We should be telling our children to seek God and His joyfulness, by putting the needs of God first in life. (Denying self) The inheritance we can pass on to our children is the truth of God's word. We can do this without involving lawyers, wills and government regulations. We are free from all that. The inheritance should be such, that no one can still, kill and destroy it. The real inheritance to pass on to our children is a relationship to Jesus that sets us free of the world and all it has to offer.

The inheritance we should pass along is the truth of knowing Jesus loves us and we are the sons and daughters of Father God. The Freedom and truth Jesus is talking about is knowing material things no longer hold us in bondage, it is knowing we will never die! Our spirit is alive in us now and forever. While here on earth we can choose to follow Jesus and walk in the love of Jesus and have Heaven as a reward, that is true freedom. Or we can live in bondage to material junk, we can choose to love the world, love material things and have hell as a reward! When I say bondage I'm talking about worry, worrying about money, bills, estates, who gets what, if your worrying about anything, that thing owns you, you don't own it.

You can choose to hug a tree, work until you cannot work anymore, save for a rainy day, work to pay life insurance, leave enough junk for your children to fight over! Supply them with all the material things you can and pray the fight for your junk doesn't start before you die, because it can.

Instead recognize your true treasure is intimacy with Jesus and you share Jesus with your children and neighbors! Approach them with a pure heart, instill in them your love of God and your freedom from sin! Instill in them the love and trust of the one who said (I will never leave you or forsake you). Knowing Jesus said in Hebrews 13:5 "I will never leave you or forsake you," is freedom from the bondage of fear and the fear of losing your junk.

Spend time with your treasures, talk to Jesus and your children, your neighbors and your loved ones and instill in them the love of Jesus. It might seem awkward at first but be truthful, tell them and show them how important they are to you. Read about the life of Jesus and share his love. Share the life of Jesus, be the life of Jesus and love like Jesus loved unconditionally. That is true freedom and when you get to the end of your life you will not need a will or layers because the inheritance you give your children is already in their heart.

I know for sure eternity is a long time. We can give so much of our life to acquiring earthly material, to being successful, to learning how to play the game here on earth and to acquiring college degrees, and in doing so forget to prepare for life eternal, we will impress everyone here with our knowledge and our junk, except the one who really cares, JESUS, and our loved ones. Remember happiness is the counterfeit of JOY. If what you are seeking only brings momentary happiness, it is not JOY. Bring Glory to God by choosing Him over the junk of the world is freedom and joyfulness. Choose God not junk! Why would I want to watch a movie or work for more junk when I could spend time talking to my best friend Jesus and my loved ones?

I know my mom and dad are in heaven and that brings me great Joy. I know I am having the time of my life right now every day because I don't look to my circumstances to bring me happiness I look to the true love of God and in doing so I know the joyfulness and freedom of a life without junk can bring. I know for a fact that God loves me. I am in true freedom from the world because I am secure in the love of Jesus. I do not need any material things and my life is full of Joy because material things no longer hold me bondage. I don't wake up worrying about payments, insurance, bills, degrees or wanting of anything. I wake up and ask God, "What are we going to do today?" My life is surrendered to God and I know God will do great things through me today. Jesus is the truth that sets us free form the bondage of material JUNK.

Life is simple, it is childlike faith. Seek God with all your heart and you will find the love of your life waiting and wanting to spend time with you! Just talk to Jesus like He is your best friend, because He is!!!! Jesus told me the way to have a great relationship is to listen, that's right just listen. Jesus said

> Joh 10:27-28 My sheep hear my voice, and I know them, and they follow me: And I give unto them eternal life; and they shall never perish, neither shall any man pluck them out of my hand.

Yes read and study the life of Jesus but most of all seek that personal relationship. Jesus said my sheep know my voice. How will you know His voice if we are to busy to listen? How will we follow Him if we don't know Him? Jesus said seek and you will find! When you do, Jesus promises us eternal life!!

> Mat 7:7 Ask, and it shall be given you; seek, and ye shall find; knock, and it shall be opened unto you:

Ask God for relationship and it shall be given to you. Seek the truth of God's word and you will find, knock on the narrow gate and Jesus will open it unto you.

My brothers and sisters and all our loved ones here today, I ask for you all too just seek a relationship with Jesus. In doing so you will have joy in your life, peace that surpasses all understanding in your heart, the cleansing of forgiveness which is freedom for everyone you know, and freedom form yourself. Knowing Jesus loves you will make you free from yourself. No one can hurt you when you live for others, because what they do or don't do; what they say or don't say is not going to make or break your day because the truth is YOU KNOW Jesus loves you. Knowing Jesus loves you is the truth that sets you free! People cannot hurt me because I don't live for their approval; I already have the love of Jesus in my heart. I live to love others as Jesus loves them. I would like nothing more than to see all my loved ones know the truth that sets us free! I love Jesus but more important than that I know Jesus loves me!!! I AM FREE!!!!

Jesus wants intimacy with you. Your relationship with him can grow to where you can ask Him anything and receive an answer. For example; one morning while having coffee with Jesus I ask (Jesus I always describe Jenny as precious, how do you describe her? Immediately I heard the words delightfully precious.) I rejoice knowing my best friend and brother Jesus calls my wife "delightfully precious". You too can have this intimacy with God, in fact the real reason God sent His son was to restore the intimacy with us. Forgiving sin was a small part of why Jesus came.

Notice in John 10:27 it also says "and I know them"

Jesus loves me and I know it! Jenny and I will see Jesus and Father God and mom and dad someday. Your relationship with God is not just you knowing God, but rather you knowing that God knows you.

You could know everything there is to know about president Obama; you could study his life; you could know what he had for breakfast today, and if you went to see him at the white house they would not let you in to see him. All that knowledge would not gain you entrance to even visit him. But if president Obama knows you; you will get right in and he will be excited to see you. It is not enough for you to know of God, you must have intimacy with Him and to do that you must know His voice and he has to hear your voice, so the two of you can become one.

Jesus rejoices over us with singing. Yes Jesus sings over us like a mother holding a little one in her arms, or when parents rejoice seeing their children make good decisions.

> Zep 3:17 The LORD thy God in the midst of thee is mighty; he will save, he will rejoice over thee with joy; he will rest in his love, he will joy over thee with singing.

Jesus will even reveal the song he sings over you if you ask and listen for his voice.

Life eternal is not having a passport to heaven; it is having a relationship with Jesus and Father God and the Holy Spirit NOW! Here on earth! Jesus didn't just come to forgive us our sins. I am not just a sinner saved by grace; I am a son of God, I can talk to my Father through Jesus 24/7 and I do. The Joy of the Lord is ours just for seeking a relationship with the one who has already laid down His life for us! Please don't read His word to see if it is true in your life, Read His word believing it is true in your life, and it will become true in your life. The best things in life are free because Jesus paid the price for me!

Please spend time with your best friend, seek Him with your whole heart, mind and soul. Teach your children to do the same and you will never worry about death, in fact you will rejoice in it. Your inheritance is in your heart!

Mom and Dad are in heaven! THANK YOU JESUS!!!!!

Mom and Dad are in the comfort of Jesus!!!! I know they know what it is to be free! I know Jesus is love and God the Father is love and the Holy Spirit is love, I know the comfort of Jenny's love (unconditional love) is the most in creditable love we can experience her on earth. I believe Jesus when he said you can accomplish in creditable things on earth but if they were done without love, you have not accomplished anything. When Jesus was talking about the commandments; Jesus said the greatest of these is love. Life is simple, read the life of Jesus and live as Jesus lived, He is our example! I have never read in the Bible where Jesus said the words I love you, but I know He does by what He did. Love is not saying I Love you, love is being love every day in every way! Love is being Jesus!!!!

Mat 5:43-48 "You have heard that it was said, 'You shall love your neighbor[a] and hate your enemy.' But I say to you, love your enemies, bless those who curse you, do good to those who hate you, and pray for those who spitefully use you and persecute you, that you may be sons of your Father in heaven; for He makes His sun rise on the evil and on the good, and sends rain on the just and on the unjust. For if you love those who love you, what reward have you? Do not even the tax collectors do the same? And if you greet your brethren only, what do you do more *than others?* Do not even the tax collectors do so? Therefore you shall be perfect, just as your Father in heaven is perfect. Yes we can be perfect for Jesus said so. Just be the love of God here on earth and God will make you perfect in His love!

Jenny and Jesus and I love you all forever!!

Freedom from Fear

We left Cincinnati for Carrolton, Ky. We went to the Family Christian Center for church service and were able to give the pastor's wife a copy of Jenny's Wheel Chair. The people are so loving towards us and you can see the love of Jesus in their eyes as you talk with them. Kim met with us again and restocked us with pampers. I have packed every nook and cranny of the motor home with pampers and pads. I feel so honored and blessed. Truly Jenny and I are so blessed to have this supply of pampers. Thank you Jesus for putting your love in the hearts of the people of the Family Christian Center and for their heart for Jesus! It is truly amazing to see your love flowing and to let us be part of your world Jesus.

My Jenny is doing pretty well. She has been sitting up and not stiffing out as bad as before. Her eyes are open a lot more and I believe she is responding better. Her swallowing is better also. Things can change from day to day. Like yesterday Jenny didn't eat hardly at all. Today though she will probably eat better again. If I go by my circumstances I would be on a roller coaster ride every day of my life for I don't know how many years. I just stay steadfast in the love God has for Jenny and I and I do not in any way lean on my own understanding.

If we could understand everything we would not need God, faith, or hope! If you do not believe me just look at the really smart people who think there is no God. They have no faith, hope and don't believe in God! They believe in their own understanding, which makes them their own God. Hitler was really smart and thought he was God. He thought he could create a perfect race by killing all the people that did not believe the way he did. His life didn't turn out too good. I guess you could say leaning on his own understanding did not work out to good for him. I hope he was smart enough to ask for forgiveness before he died.

I want to thank you Jesus for letting me see your love in the world. I want to thank you Jesus for the blessings of Love Faith, Hope, Trust and wisdom! The wisdom to know I do not need to know or understand everything. Thank you for the wisdom to know your word is sufficient, Your love is more than enough, and you give us hope beyond our reasoning. Jesus you are my hope and faith, trust and love and because of You I do not need human understanding. I have Faith, Hope and Trust in You Jesus and I understand that is all I need!

Yes Jenny's condition changes every day. We have some pretty good days and some rough days. There are some days where I just sit and hold Jenny on my lap. If I let my circumstances determine my mood I would probably cry most of the time. If I did not have Jesus and His word written on the tablet of my heart; I truly would cry in hopelessness every day. I still cry some days but not for Jenny's condition, I cry for people that do not know Jesus or they only know Him and see Him as a bus ticket to heaven. They see Jesus as their liberator, the one that will rapture them out of here. I know where they get that message and I cry some times because they have not experienced the love of Jesus and the hope of Jesus and the trust of Jesus. When Jesus is reduced to a bus ticket to heaven and all you think about is being good enough to get on the bus then you have totally missed the reason Jesus came. Getting out of this world is not the goal!!!! The goal is to transform the world one person at a time like Jesus did! Jesus is our example and we should emulate Him and His work in every way and in every day!!!

For a preacher to teach you to only think of Jesus, as a bus ticket to heaven and limiting faith in Jesus to you having a better day, is truly the biggest tragedy anyone could put on their congregation. I believe that is why I can carry Jenny into so many churches and no one not even the preacher offers to pray for her. All there hope is in going to heaven not bringing heaven to earth like Jesus did.

The last two Sundays, Jenny and I have been in different churches and both Sundays the preacher has started his service by announcing that half the congregation was out sick. Both of them prayed but neither of them actually commanded the devil to take his hands off their congregation. The devil knows the power we have with faith in the name of Jesus but he has somehow gotten us to just pray for a better day and monetary blessings. That sounds like life is all about me and me having a better day and more money and security in my job. I wonder if Jesus ever worried about having a better job. I remember reading about Jesus feeding about 5000 people with two fish and five loafs of bread. Jesus simply took what he had and blessed it and thanked His Father for it and it was enough for all. Jesus did not worry because he knew he was loved and therefore he knew his Father would provide everything. Sounds like my burden is light and my yoke is easy to me!!! I give you thanks Jesus.

What happened to denying self; you know pick up your cross and follow me!! Jesus is more than our provider, protector, and creator, Jesus is our source of Joy. Jesus said "The Joy of the Lord is our strength. There is no strength in sadness, in fact sadness brings depression and depression makes you want to sleep all the time. We can call it depression, or whatever the doctor calls it but it really is just unbelief. If we just believe in Jesus and His word there would be no such thing as depression.

I see people upset about Obama care. I think to myself, "What do you need it for anyway?" If you have Jesus in your heart and not just on your lips the world is at your fingertips. I believe that is why I see so many people unhappy; without the love of Jesus, without His hope and without His Trust. I have no idea what motivates them to get up in the morning. I know spending time with Jesus is and will be my motive forever. I live to be the love of Jesus on the earth. I pray to be Jesus on the earth. Yes Jesus what are we going to do today????

January 10th, 2013

I was holding Jenny on my lap and kissing her when she actually botched her lips up for more kisses. It was incredible to say the least! I haven't seen Jenny respond like that in over ten years. What a blessing form God! It was so amazing to see her little lips botch up for more kisses. I'm in heaven right here in the camper. Jesus said bring heaven to earth and I experience heaven every day except today it was so real to see heaven in Jenny's little face. Nothing monetary could ever even come close to the Joy of watching Jesus flow through Jenny. I probably give Jenny one thousand kisses a day, but today I received two back and they were right from Jenny's heart. I praise you Jesus for this wonderful time with You and Your daughter Jenny.

January 14th we decided to head to Florida and to warmer temperatures. Jenny and I went to Destin, on the way our brakes on the motor home started locking up really bad. I ask the Lord to send someone really honest and knowledgeable to repair the brakes. Jesus answered my prayer with Bruce's repair service and now the brakes work perfect. Thank you Jesus!!! Thank you Bruce for a great job and a job well done. You know Jesus is so amazing to me! Thinking about the brakes on the camper. They start locking up on the way to Destin, we get to the campground and they have concrete pads to park the camper on. That was a blessing because it made working on the camper a lot easier for Bruce. Then because Bruce comes to the camper to work on our camper, Jenny and I were not inconvenienced in the least. Also the campground we were in had to be willing to let someone work on sight. All that came together and all the parts were readily available. Thinking about all those details coming together is remarkable, and Jesus gets all the praise because He is the one looking out for Jenny and I!!!!

JANUARY 17TH, 2013

I received a phone call from Joe Coleman my best buddy form the navy. We had talked a couple times since mom died December 21st, but Joe had forgot to tell me about the Christmas card my mom sent him and Renee his wife. In the card mom sent she had hand written these words. "I hope you have a Merry Christmas Joe and Renee, I'm going to be with the Lord this year". Mom had sent the card about 5 days before she died. Isn't Jesus the most awesome God in the world; to have my mom so at piece with death and for Jesus to let me know of her piece through a Christmas card she sent to Joe and Renee? Jenny and I were there the day mom must have written Joe and Renee that card.

JANUARY 18TH

Jesus gave me the greatest gift. After showering and dressing Jenny I set her on the couch. I had a CD playing a Dan Mohler teaching. As I set Jenny on the couch Dan was saying God loves you, Jenny looked at me and said God loves you as best she could. I could not believe my ears. I just had to think for a minute, I hadn't heard Jenny speak a sentence in years, probably 8 or 9 years at least. I picked Jenny up and put her on my lap and she looked me right in the eyes. I started talking to her, saying Jenny I believe you just said God loves you to me and I believe that came right from your heart. Jesus in His word said from the heart a man speaketh. I believe I just heard from Jesus Holy Spirit, talking right through you, Jenny! Jenny responded by saying yea! I praised God and cried softly for a long time as Jenny fell asleep in my arms. You know I could almost say I live in what some people would call a fiancée world of love. The cool thing is it is not a fiancée it is reality!!!

As I sat there with Jenny I started to realize that Jenny might have something going on with her brain but her heart is still perfect! Jesus in his word tells us to write his word on the tablet of you heart. Jesus said out of your heart a man speaketh. I just heard from Jenny's heart and it was beautiful. Then Jesus confirmed the word with her saying yea. How much more beautiful can life be? I know for a fact that Jesus loves Jenny and I and His love for us goes beyond anything we can comprehend. Thank you Jesus.

January 29th, 2013

I took Jenny to swim in a heated pool at the campground. I mean Jenny was so relaxed in the water, I hold her in my arms while in the water so her little face is close to mine and we are touching all the time. I know Jenny cannot say that she loves swimming but it is obvious she loves being in the water. I sing to her so softly and Jenny responds as best she can. Today for some reason Jenny had a seizure while in the pool. On our way back to the camper Jenny had another one. We got back to the camper and I had to clean Jenny up, because she was soiled. After I got her on the couch, Jenny seemed to relax some but she was not coming back to base line. I did not panic, I just prayed in total faith that Jenny would be all right, but this time it took an unusual long time for her to come back to base line.

It is amazing to me how I can write and talk about how great God is and how much He loves me but this is where the rubber meets the road and I will see if the teaching from God have traction and is His love really in my heart?

I have talked about or ask the question; in an emergency do you call on God or call on Man (911). The answer for me in this situation is to call on God. Not necessarily because of great faith but because I know the doctors don't have any answers for Jenny's condition. So I just stayed alongside her and prayed, which is the best thing I could do. The problem this time was Jenny was not coming out of the seizure and getting back to base line. As I prayed I kept hearing the words of the doctor saying it will be a big seizure that will take Jenny away.

I ask God how does a doctor have the right to speak these curses over Jenny and then I have to stand in faith and break those words of death off her. I just know to lean not on my own understanding but to draw my strength form the one who made strength. I also know I was hearing form the voice of the devil saying she is dying and I was listening. At the same time I was hearing Mathew 7:11 that says;

> Mat 7:11 If you then, being evil, know how to give good gifts to your children, how much more will your Father who is in heaven give good things to those who ask Him!

In my mind I kept asking God, I know I have asked and I know I have asked in faith and I myself could not do this to a dog or cat so when am I going to see your love manifest in Jenny. I know Jenny is healed but what is taking so long for the healing to manifest in her? Father your word says, how much more shall your Father in heaven give good things to them that ask. I am asking for Jenny's healing to manifest in her now. Jenny condition seemed to be getting worse so I propped her back and head up to help her breath. I finally when to bed with Jenny on the couch, trying to sleep was horrible without Jenny next to me. I kept getting up to check on her.

January 30th, 2013

The next morning I made Jesus and I some coffee. I asked Jesus what was going on with that scripture? Mathew 7:11 seems very clear to me but I could not figure out the timing of it. It seemed as though I was losing faith over it instead of building my faith with it. Jesus asked me, how did the devil tempt me in the desert? I said by misquoting the scriptures when you were very weak from fasting for 40 days. Jesus said you didn't hear that scripture from me yesterday. Here I was upset all day yesterday because I could not figure what Jesus was trying to tell me in Mathew 7:11 and now I find out the voice I was listening to was not the Holy Spirit.

Discerning voices can sometimes be difficult. I usually discern by telling if the voice I am hearing is taking me to new heights of Gods love or away from God's love. Yesterday I didn't discern very well because I was dwelling on Jenny's problem. If I had stopped questioning God yesterday and started listening to God like I did today I could have walked in the Joy of the Lord and been rejoicing knowing Jenny was just fine and in the hands of the greatest doctor in the world.

> Mat 16:19 And I will give you the keys of the kingdom of heaven, and whatever you bind on earth will be bound in heaven, and whatever you loose on earth will be loosed in heaven."

I believe the keys of the kingdom of heaven are Joy, Peace and Love of Jesus in your heart and knowing that Jesus is the rock we build our believe on! I separated myself from those believes for couple hours but thank you Jesus for my safe return. I will bind your truth in my heart and in heaven and here on earth my soul shall rejoice with You and I will lose all the earth or fleshly desires to free myself so I am free to do your will here on earth. Jesus you are so special to me and I want to be just like you here on the earth. I pray for your wisdom not to display smartness to others but to pray for others and to have your wisdom and together for us to set others free! I thank you Jesus for setting Jenny and I free of the bondage of the world. My life is your life Father and in You, Jenny and I will live forever.

FEBRUARY 1ST, 2013

Today while walking Jenny in the wheelchair I met some people who were so upset about a Senate bill that president Obama was trying to pass and they felt helpless to stop the bill, they said Obama is going to ram this down our throats.

As they walked away I was upset because they didn't want to hear anything about God's plan. I thought, I wish they could stop for a moment and think back to what was there biggest concern four years ago, two years ago or even two days ago. If they would think back on the concerns of their past, they would realize they had no power to change them either.

Really all we need to concern ourselves with is being in the will of God. Jesus and the disciples never seemed to be concerned about what the government was doing back then. Their concern was saving souls from the devil's eternal damnation. They are the example we are to follow. Jesus said my burden is light and my yoke is easy. If we pray to have God change things our government is doing and stand in faith that it will be done, then you can rest that it will be done.

The disciple John tells us "he that doeth the will of God abides forever" The will of God is so simple, it is to love as Jesus loved, to forgive as Jesus forgave, read your Bible to see the example Jesus was for us; don't study it to show how many scriptures you can memorize. Just be Jesus while you are here on the earth. If they had any faith in God they would be praying for President Obama to hear the word of God and let it into his heart, they would pray for Obama to become who God created him to be. We should all pray for obama to hear the word of God and recognize it for the truth it is. It is the truth of God that sets us free from the snares of the devil. Let us pray for Obama and not just complain about Obama.

The best form of worship is to become who we are worshiping, worship Jesus by being Christ like!!!!

Let us be Christ like by emulating Jesus. Jesus never sat around and complained about anything because complaining does not change things. Jesus taught the truth and the truth is we need to pray for our nation. If we spent our time praying and talking to the one who can change things in America, we would have hope instead of hopelessness. We would have faith in our God to change our leaders hearts and God would hear our prayers coming up instead of hearing our complaining that changes nothing.

Jesus warned the apostles about the antichrist in the world. When Jesus spoke this warning He was also warning us. The antichrist are here today and Jesus made it real clear how to recognize them.

1Jn 2:19 **¹⁹** They went out from us, but they were not of us; for if they had been of us, they would have continued with us; but *they went out* that they might be made manifest, that none of them were of us.

1Jn 4:3 and every spirit that does not confess that Jesus Christ has come in the flesh is not of God. And this is the *spirit* of the Antichrist, which you have heard was coming, and is now already in the world.

I don't see how John or anyone can make it any clearer that the antichrist is in the world now and how to determine who the antichrist is. President Obama is an anti-Christ because he "confesses not that Jesus Christ is come in the flesh." That means that Obama has a spirit of antichrist. Please do not wish harm on him but rather pray for him. Our battle is not in the flesh but in the spirit and Obama is just listening to the wrong spirit, he is listening to the devil, he is manifesting the devil in everything he says and does, we need to pray for him to hear the voice of God. Nothing is going to change if you are not praying for him. Obama is an anti-Christ and we all need to pray for his life to be saved, I pray for the love of Jesus to touch his heart and transform it into a life of loving and serving Jesus Christ, amen!!

FEBRUARY 2ND, 2013

2 John 1:7 For many deceivers have gone out into the world who do not confess Jesus Christ *as* coming in the flesh. This is a deceiver and an antichrist.

Again I have heard people call president Obama an antichrist. He is antichrist because he will not acknowledge Jesus as the Christ Son of the living God! Obama is one of the antichrist! So pray for him to be transformed by the blood and truth of Jesus Christ. Jesus came for everyone, even the antichrists of the world. We can live in a great country again and we will manifest the love of Jesus Christ to the world. We shouldn't pray to have Obama to be impeached; impeachment would only change the flesh, we should pray for president Obama and his followers to become Christ like. We should pray for America to become Christ like.

FEBRUARY 3RD, 2013

So now we know how to discern who the antichrists are. Jesus also talks about discerning our thoughts. Discerning are thoughts is one of the most important things we will ever learn. The scriptures are very clear that we are to take every thought captive to the obedience of God's word. Let's bring the scriptures into modern day living.

I really do not see how anyone can watch television and discern their thoughts. The actions and words come at you so fast there is no way we can discern our thoughts. If what I am saying about television is not true then why would advertisers pay over a million dollars to advertise for 10 seconds during the game on super bowl Sunday. As we walk through life we have thousands of ten second intervals to demonstrate the love of Jesus and the difference between Christian living and living non-Christian. As Christians we have to make Godly decisions all the time and that can be really hard when we allow ourselves to be distracted by something that is so easily turned off.

I bet there are people reading this right now that will say television is not that bad, I bet they can tell me about commercials on television they saw as a little kid and yet they cannot tell me what the preacher talked about last Sunday at church service. Television has a lasting impact on our lives and it is not always a good impact.

Jesus was so in tune to discerning that He recognized the devil coming through Peter immediately. Peter had traveled with Jesus for three years and still did not discern who he let talk through himself. Remember Peter was not filled with the Holy Spirit yet for Jesus had not died and arouse again.

I found out January 29th I have a long way to go in discerning my thoughts. I have a great teacher and a best friend to guide me. Thank You Jesus for being my best friend and teacher. The examples Jesus just gave me in the Bible are good ones and I will learn from them. Jesus has revealed to me the best way to Hear His Voice is to listen. Yes listening to and for the voice of Jesus is the best way to have relationship with Him. Yes you still have to read your Bible to know Jesus because you need His truth to determine what a lie is and what is truth.

Pastor Dan Mohler once said "when you squeeze a Christian you should get a big squirt of Jesus out" those are probably not his exact words but they are close. Dan is saying when you are truly filled with the Holy Spirit and you are put to the test of life; when life doesn't go the way you want it to, don't let the circumstances of life take away your Joy of knowing God. When Jesus was squeezed, love and forgiveness came right out of His heart. We need to be Christ like in every way so I pray that when I am squeezed by life or by someone, I can demonstrate the love and forgiveness of Jesus in me. I thank you Jesus for forgiving me for not taking every thought captive and for not recognizing the voice of the devil, while Jenny was having the seizure. When I was squeezed I let some devil in the form of doubt come out but thank You Jesus you were right here to pick me up.

I hope I made that clear, here is another example of being squeezed. I have a friend who was complaining because life was very upsetting. He and his wife were both out of a job for a while. Finally she got a job and a week later he got a good job also. The day he was to start his job, his wife's car had a tire blow out in a bad neighborhood. He was still home getting ready to go to his new job when the call came in. He got so upset and was screaming at God; you finally get me a job and now I'm going to be late on my first day. I will probably get fired. He said he went on and on. He finally got her tire changed and on to work. When he explained to his new boss what happened; his boss said settle down, you made the right choice, I would not leave my wife stranded in that neighborhood either.

The point I am trying to make is we can take matters into our own hands or we can surrender to God. What if the man upon hearing his wife had a flat tire just stopped and prayed for God to send a Christian to change the tire for her. What if he prayed for his boss to understand? He could have been in peace knowing he asked the only one that can; to make good of this situation. Our problem is we just try to solve our own problems in our own strength and then when God makes your boss an understanding boss we don't even know to give the credit to God because we had never asked God into the situation. If we do see God's hand in our situation, we might even beat ourselves up saying how could I be so stupid not to trust you God!

God is so much more in our lives than we know. We can work our life through God and have peace and rest or we can be in panic mode all the time. When the storm came at sea Jesus was sleeping on the boat. The disciples were going crazy in fear. They woke Jesus up and said don't you care, we are going to drown and you are sleeping. Jesus got up and told the sea to be calm!

> Mar 4:35-37 On the same day, when evening had come, He said to them, "Let us cross over to the other side." Now when they had left

the multitude, they took Him along in the boat as He was. And other little boats were also with Him. And a great windstorm arose, and the waves beat into the boat, so that it was already filling.

What was our storm? "I have to be at work on time." Our circumstances? "the car had a flat tire and our wife is in a bad neighborhood." He screamed at God, "You finally get me a good job and now I will be late and I'll probably get fired." Our ship is filling up but we don't acknowledge God is even with us except to complain to him!

Mar 4:38   But He was in the stern, asleep on a pillow. And they awoke Him and said to Him, "Teacher, do You not care that we are perishing?"

The apostles were in fear just like the man in this story. The apostles even ask God "do You not care that we are perishing?" It almost sounds funny when they asked Jesus that. It sure isn't funny when we are going through the rough time. The man in our story was screaming at God! Almost like he thought God did not care.

Mar 4:39   Then He arose and rebuked the wind, and said to the sea, "Peace, be still!" And the wind ceased and there was a great calm.

(and his boss told him calm down you made the right choice.) Right there he should be thanking God and repenting to God for lack of faith.

Mar 4:40   But He said to them, "Why are you so fearful? How *is it* that you have no faith?"

(I believe the man when he settled, heard these same words from God) "why are you so fearful? Where is your faith?

Mar 4:41   And they feared exceedingly, and said to one another, "Who can this be, that even the wind and the sea obey Him!"

Hopefully we all recognize the voice of God because then we can receive the peace of God. Hopefully we will call on God to calm the storm and change the heart of Obama. I know God will calm the storms in our life if we believe Him and trust Him.

I ask my dear Jesus to bring those scriptures to my mind any time I start to panic about anything. If I have doubt or fear of anything I pray for a remembrance of the disciples in the boat. I also know we have the same power and authority Jesus has and He said we will do bigger miracles then Jesus did. So call on the Name above all names and watch Jesus love us also!

FEBRUARY 4TH, 2013

In my coffee time I started thinking about what Jesus said.

Look what Jesus said, "Why are you so fearful? Why is it that ye have no faith?" Jesus will ask us those same questions someday. I know you could say; but the apostles lived with Jesus and He was right there on the boat with them so why were they so fearful? Actually Jesus is right here with us also. We have His Holy Spirit living in us so why are we so fearful? Why are we without faith? Jesus dwells in us, we can be in continual communication 24/7. We have better commutation then the apostles did. Jesus is actually living in us! I believe this is the good news that sets us free of worry and unrest. Isn't Jesus the best?

Thank you Jesus for restoring our relationship to even better than it was before Adam ate of the tree of good and evil.

FEBRUARY 8TH, 2013

We are still in the same campground and it was 78 degrees in the shade today. I took Jenny to the pool again. She had a great time. I love when I see Jenny so full of joy, it does my heart good and makes taking care of Jenny a real pleasure. I thank you Jesus for these good times with Jenny, these good times bring great Joy to my heart also. Jenny and I are so blessed to be with Jesus 24/7 and that makes life sweet.

While at the pool, a group of older women came to exercise in the water. When they were finished a couple of the women came over to talk to Jenny and I. One woman said this must really feel good to Jenny and I agreed. I mentioned to her that getting Jenny in the pool is really the only time she is off her backside. Another woman asks, "Does she sleep on her stomach?" I said no because her neck is stiff and her head does not turn, if I lay her on her stomach, her face would be planted in the pillow.

Last night while trying to go to sleep Jenny made a noise and I turned on the light to see if she was all right. She looked like she was trying to smile and I hugged her so tight. Then I started to cry because I realized Jenny's only communication skills left are noises and some eye expressions where she can make her eyes move.

Her arms move some time but not too much, mostly they just stay crossed across her chest. I really seem to get the best responses out of her in the pool. When I said she was smiling I mean with her eyes not her mouth. I know a couple weeks ago when I kissed her and she botched her lips for more kisses and it was great for two reasons, one was to see her face muscles move and two Jenny was able to show me, her longing to be loved. I love how she just loves being loved because I love giving her loving. Jenny's sweet loving personality is so beautiful to witness and I just want to thank you Jesus for letting Jenny still share her love with me.

Jesus your love is so strong in my Jenny and I. I know Jenny is not able to communicate like she would if she did not have this condition but you make me know what is going on in Jenny and that is love to the maximum. Thank You Jesus!!!!

Hope for the Future

While at church the other day a woman came over and while praying for Jenny she put her hand on me and said don't give up hope. She ask God to renew my hope in Him for Jenny's life. I didn't get a chance to talk to her but I knew she was hearing from the Lord because I had been asking God what was changing in my life. I mean I know God loves Jenny and I, and Jenny and I love Him but for the last couple weeks I knew something was missing in my life and I could not figure out what it was.

Thanks to the women in church that spoke out loud the words "don't give up hope" I have my answer from Jesus. Now I know the answer was I was losing hope for Jenny's recovery. I guess I was losing hope for my recovery also. The spider eruptions were on my backside and leg again. They made my bottom hurt to just sit down and the eruptions were on my knee so it was hard to kneel down to put Jenny's shoes on her and my knee was hurting just to walk. There really is no comfortable position when these eruptions act up.

I believe the combination of that and watching Jenny condition declining was becoming over whelming. I believe my hope was fading. This loss of hope was declining so slowly that I didn't see it happening. I knew something was changing but I needed Jesus to help me pin point the problem. I believe the thief that comes to steal, kill and destroy our life is so sneaky that even though I have a great relationship with Jesus I can be deceived by the circumstances of life. I thank God for your messenger and for her hearing form God and then for her to have the courage to speak the truth over Jenny and I.

1Cor 13:13 And now abide faith, hope, love, these three; but the greatest of these is love.

You see the top three are Faith Hope and Love. Jesus said without faith it is impossible to please Him and faith is the substance of things hoped for. The last couple weeks I felt like something in me was dying, when the women at church ask the Lord to restore hope in me I knew she was on the right track. I knew Jesus was commutating to me the answer of my prayer through her. Thank You Jesus for the answer to my prayer and THANK YOU JESUS FOR LOVING JENNY AND I SO MUCH!

Jesus answers every prayer concern we have. Sometimes the answer comes through someone that has not herd the question. God you are just so amazing to me and I love You and I love having Hope again. I love seeing another tactic of the enemy destroyed. Hope is one of the top three and so you know without it nothing will turn out right

FEBRUARY 11ᵀᴴ, 2013

We arrived at Alliance Coach, a repair center for campers and motor homes. They are going to replace a leveling jack on the motor home. Alliance has their own campground facility so you just stay there until the repair is complete. You can even go out for the day and they will come get your motor home, work on it and put it back on your site, so you can sleep in it again that night.

Lately there seems to be a lot of people who ask me "what do you do all day?" I decided to write down what a day in the life of Jenny and Ron is like.

3:00 AM this morning I was having coffee with my beloved Jesus. We talked for over an hour when I got tired again and went to bed. I woke back up around six thirty and talked to Jesus some more. Jenny woke up at seven, what a blessing Jesus had for me today. Jenny was actually trying to smile at me and her eyes were open wide. I laid alongside her and just hugged her for a while. I am in a little bit of a hurry because we are in a campground where they are going to work on the motor home. One of the leveling jacks is not retracting and the company HWH is replacing it free even though it is out of warranty over three months. This is a big deal to me, you see the jack and labor is around $562.00.

I said we are in a bit of hurry because the repair men can come at any time to work on the motor home. I know they would be courteous but I want to be ready.

Jenny's kidneys had let loose, I mean loose, so I put her on the toilet and striped the bed. Her urine soaked through her Depends and through both throw away pads and the bath towel I have under her. Today it went into the top sheet and the cover; also into the fitted sheet and mattress pad. I opened the windows to let in fresh air and get rid of the smell.

Before I showered Jenny I set her on the toilet and give her some orange juice. Jenny can drink a whole glass of orange juice before she is showered but some mornings she doesn't seem to remember what the straw is. I have to remind her by squirting some orange juice in her mouth. It works every day and I Thank You Jesus for her drinking and swallowing. I know your word says nothing is impossible for us that believe and I believe and thank you for your word.

I thank you Jesus for talking to me this morning and every morning, it truly is the most awesome time of the day for me.

I showered Jenny and today is a bowel day so I sported some rubber gloves and cleaned her bowel cavity. It must feel really good to Jenny to get the pressure off. Today she had a lot of gas and seemed somewhat relieved to be done with that. I know I was. I know I Thank Jesus for a lot of things you would take for granted but these are really big blessings from God and I don't want to miss thanking God for them. I like thanking God when I think about it, and thanking Jesus for the easy clean ups.

It is now 8:48am and I'm going to feed Jenny, then off to the laundry. Every day I start Jenny with some Greek yogurt. She loves it and so do I. The texture seems to be good for starting her eating. Before, I talked about blending all of Jenny's food but that requirement has gone away again. We can eat out again, especially soft foods like French fries. Lately Jenny has liked cucumbers and melon.

It is 10:09 and I'm off to the laundry which is only a short walk. Two batches today, I usually can get by with one batch if the urine doesn't get into the covers. The blessing here is the machines are big and do a great job. They only cost $1.25 a load to wash and the same to dry. I love the old top loaders that use a lot of water. I mean the water all gets recycled anyway and I believe the bigger top loaders do the best job. While I was outside I also took the garbage to the dumpster.

Now I'm going to look up some campgrounds to see where we might go tomorrow, if they get our new Jack on today. It is kind of amazing to watch people in these million dollar motor homes, that is to watch how some of them think they should be the first priority here because they have such important places to be and deadlines to meet. I just feel so blessed by Jesus to not be in a hurry and I'm not sure but I seem to be at more peace then they are. I just pray for them to come to know the Lord Jesus Christ in their busy life and then for them to enjoy what they have. Peace is a precious commodity and is a real gift from God. Nothing else in life can give you peace like knowing God loves you!

10:39 and I am off to put the clothes in the dryer. Upon returning from the laundry I can do what Jenny likes best. I can hold her on my lap and speak life and blessings of walking and talking and the Mind of Jesus into her. I usually hold her until my legs go to sleep. It is so good to see this alertness in her eyes and face. Thank you Jesus for the alertness in Jenny. I love you Jesus.

Jenny and I sat for only a little while when I wanted to go up to the office to see if Will, our service rep here at the campground repair shop, could tell me how things were going. After situating Jenny in the wheelchair we went to the office, only to find Will was on his lunch break. Jenny and I went to the laundry and got our clothes out of the dryer. Then back to the camper to change Jenny and fold the laundry and put it away.

12:20pm I got Jenny back into the wheelchair and we went back to the office. Talked to Will, and he thought they would get the part on this afternoon. This time while in the office I recognized the receptionist as the one we had talked to last year. We started talking about Jenny and when I told her about the book Jesus and I wrote about Jenny, she wanted one. She complimented me on the cover and said she could not wait to read it. I was excited to see her again because she is going to marry a guy named Ron Johnson. How cool is that?

We stayed in the waiting room for about an hour and a half. It started raining like cats and dogs outside. I had opened the car windows to let the heat out on the way up here. I did not try to run back to close the windows on the car, I just figured it was too late.

In the waiting room, we met a young girl that was born with Williams disease. It seemed to me to be some kind of autism. I prayed for her and she was so cute, she then said her eyes were bad also, so I prayed for her eyes and she added her walking was not that good. It seemed the list could go on and on when her mother said you don't have to tell him everything. But he is praying for me mom she replied, to which I said we will just command everything that is not of God to go in the name of Jesus. Then she took her glasses off and started looking around and said she could see better. Her mom just rolled her eyes and smiled. We talked to her for over an hour with her telling me all kinds of stuff as she held Jenny's hand. I had to get Jenny back to the camper to change her. As we said good by she got up and hugged Jenny for a long hug. She looked at me and said Jenny loves me I can tell and I agreed with her.

When we got back to our camper I checked the car. Remember I said I had opened the windows to let the heat out. While in the office it started raining really hard. When I checked the car there was not a drop of water in the car. Even though I didn't ask God to keep the rain out Jesus kept it out somehow. I truly love you Jesus and the way you look out for Jenny and I. Dry car seats are a big deal and a big blessing for us both. Thank You Jesus for loving us so much as to provide dry seats in the storm.

Around 3:00pm after cleaning Jenny up we ate and then went to look at a campground that is only 10 miles from here. It was a nice ride and Jenny seemed to enjoy it. When we got back to our camper it looked like it might rain again. The woman next to me was having trouble with her gasket on her slide out. I was able to get it water tight with some duct tape, so they could leave their slide out while in the rain and not worry.

I changed Jenny again and then we sat on the couch for a while just holding her on my lap and loving her. I truly love when Jenny is in my arms and she is alert, eyes open and looking at me. Praise you Jesus.

4:30PM and time for coffee. I have some hamburgers thawed to cook on the grill later but I want to get the sweet potatoes in the oven. Coffee tastes great but it is starting to rain again so it might be a pizza night. It is really easy for Jenny to eat pizza and there is one that delivers to this campground. Yes I ask Ron and he said pizza sounds great and he doesn't have to cook. Don't you just love when you can agree with yourself?

4:42pm called the office and they said it will be tomorrow before they can work on our camper.

6:30pm the pizza should be here any time.

6:36pm the pizza is here and Jenny is hungry and so am I. It has been a long time since we had pizza and it really hit the spot. We will have three meals out of this one pizza. Thank you Jesus and for letting it be on sale for $11.00 dollars.

Around 7:00pm and I just got Jenny off the pot, it was a successful trip and another blessing from Jesus. The other day while over at Joe and Erin's camper, Erin was painting the fingernails of their daughter Regan, soon to be five years old. She was so excited to have her nails done. Every finger nail was a different color. When I went to the grocery the next day I bought pink finger nail polish for Jenny, I don't know if she will let me do her finger nails but after watching Regan with hers I'm hoping it will bring a little happiness to Jenny. It could be all in my mind but Jenny seems to like when I cut her hair or shave her legs. I know when we were at Kim and Jim's house last year their daughter Kara did Jenny's nails. Having Jenny's nails done looks a little dumb to me but like I said it was so cute watching Regan when Erin did her nails. I thought I would see if Jenny responds like Regan did.

8:30pm and I have been on the phone for a while. Jenny fell asleep on the couch and I did some dishes while talking to Jason on the phone. His hot water heater was not working and we figured out what it was and Jason has hot water again.

9:40pm. It is time to give Jenny her shower and scrub her teeth again.

10:38pm; I just got Jenny in bed and as usual she looks so special at night time. I love having pink sheets and pillow case for her. I love the way Jenny looks at me when I tuck her in. I mist her face and wipe her face a couple times a day but when I do it at night and sing to her Jenny just seems to relax and she realizes it is bed time.

3:01am; I'm having coffee and looking at my notes from yesterday. I finished typing this up and I'm going to have coffee with my best friend and brother Jesus. I'm thinking about the conversation I had with Jason last night and think it is one of the best conversations about God we ever had. Thank you Jesus so much for letting me talk to Jason about my love for You.

4:28am; still typing and listening to my brother. For some reason I feel tired like I might go back to bed. Jenny is asleep and I just want to spend some time hugging her. I cannot begin to tell how much I miss Jenny. For some odd reason every time someone touches me, I have an aware ness of how much I miss being touched. The other day in church some people came over to pray for Jenny, some of them were behind us and as they prayed I felt someone's hand on my shoulder. Their hand was warm and it just felt good to be touched, not in any kind of sexy way, not really in a loving physical way just a comforting comfortable way.

I don't know if that makes sense to you but it has been so many years since Jenny and I have talked, or touched. I know someday soon Jenny will wake up out of this condition she is in and we will have real conversation and Jenny will hold my hand as we walk down the path of life again together. That day will not come soon enough for me. I close my eyes and see us walking and talking and touching, I see us holding hands and singing to Jesus about how much we know He loves us. Jesus is real, so real I cannot imagine a day without Him. I can imagine Jenny and I holding hands and talking about all the life still to come.

I remember as a kid being told time and time again "don't get your hopes up to high, you are setting yourself up for disappointment." Now I know the word of Jesus and He says have your hopes sky high for in Him all things are possible. So you might think I am dreaming and not routed in reality but I am routed in the reality of possibilities of Jesus! The word of Jesus is reality to those that believe, so I know just as sure as the sun will come up tomorrow Jenny is healed because the word of Jesus says so. Jesus is my hero and best friend, my brother and the truth that sets us free to be who He created us to be.

5:08am and I'm going to bed to rest in the arms of my best friend Jesus. His word says we can have sweet sleep and I thank you Jesus for it. Amen

Faith, Hope, and Love

Around 2:00pm a mechanic came by to install the new jack. Greg started talking to us and instantly I knew he was a Christian and on a wonderful walk with the Lord. His first comment was, "I like your sticker on the back of your camper, COFFEE TIME WITH JESUS." I gave him a tract on how that got started.

He seemed really interested in Jenny's condition so I gave Greg the book about her life. Greg got the new jack on our camper in a very short time and had it working perfect, it was truly amazing. He then drove the camper back to our camping site and asked to pray for Jenny; of course I said yes. His prayer was awesome. He talked about where two or three are gathered in His name Jesus will be there, and I believe Jesus lives in us and dwells among us so Jesus was here and is here and listening and performing on His word.

Greg also said that we are the church of Jesus, and Greg is so right. Jesus is not in a building we call church but Jesus is in us and we are His church wherever we go. I know Greg prayed with sincerity, he prayed with great faith and full expedience! Jenny's healing is a done deal, Greg's prayer is not going unheard, and I will return to Alliance Coach someday with Jenny so he can see the result of his prayer also.

Sunday while attending a church the pastor and his congregation came back to pray for Jenny. One girl put her hand on my shoulder and said I have a word for you from Jesus, Jesus said don't give up hope. I thought to myself this is the second time Jesus told me not to give up hope. I really thought I handled this the first time. I prayed and asked God, where I am missing hope. Hope is precious; your word said faith is the substance of things hoped for. Hope is like faith and faith works through love.

> Gal 5:6 For in Christ Jesus neither circumcision nor uncircumcision avails anything, but faith working through love.

I think my love was faltering which meant my faith was faltering, which means I was not walking in hope. I repented for my loss of hope which ultimately means I was listening to the devil and I was letting the signs of Jenny's decline rob me of faith, love, and Hope.

If we lose our hope we lose everything. This is the second time God has spoken to me about Hope. The fact I am getting the same message from two different people must mean I need more one on one time with Jesus my source. Jesus and I talked about hope, faith, and love for the next couple days and I believe Jesus restored my hope. Thank you Jesus for showing me where I was missing You and listening to the devil. I love you Jesus and I always will!!!

You cannot have faith without hope. To me hope is the dream part of faith. I dream of walking with Jenny and holding hands, I dream of having coffee with Jesus and Jenny. Our friend Erin called the other day and said she dreamed we were in a van going somewhere and she ask Jenny a question, Jenny looked up and started talking and answered the question. Erin said I just started crying and held Jenny even closer. In a way you could say faith is the substance of things dreamed for. I know we have all had dreams we hope never come true so I'll stick with the words of Jesus and say Hoped for.

I do want to thank you Jesus for the dreams of encouragement! What a delight to even have dreams of Jenny walking and talking and what a delight to have Jesus as your best friend that looks out for you! How do you thank Jesus for blessings like these? I believe you thank Jesus by being like Him!

What is the ultimate way to show you think someone is great? For example, if a young boy likes a certain baseball player, he will want that baseball player's number on his shirt, he will want the same kind of mitt, and the young man will watch his favorite player every chance he can so he can emulate the player. I think we call it hero worship.

Our worship of Jesus is like that also. I mean we are to emulate Jesus by being like Jesus! We should study the life of Jesus and do as Jesus did and by doing so we are worshiping Jesus. It is so simple to me. Yes I sing in church and I go to church but to me that is not worshipping Jesus. That is fellowshipping with likeminded people and I love it also. You see in my mind I know I am the church and I am to be like Jesus 24/7 not just an hour every Sunday. I want to walk like Jesus, talk like Jesus, and most of all I want to love like Jesus. I am blessed to have Jesus as my best friend and Jesus said don't give up hope and I want to honor my best friend with my life. So hopelessness is never going to be part of my life again.

Unlike like the young child emulating the baseball player that doesn't know him, my Jesus does know me and thank you Jesus for even correcting me! Actually My Jesus lives in me and I just let Him love and have His being through me. Thank you Jesus for giving us all a chance to be who you created us to be. I give my life to you Jesus and I thank you for renewing my mind every day. No guilt, no shame, and no condemnation, just love and life more abundantly! Jesus you are the best friend anyone could possibly have.

I remember when Jenny's condition first started. I took Jenny to the doctor and hoped they had some good news, a good report. When the doctors finally came up with the diagnosis of Pick's decease and they told me there is no medicine for it, I started praying for a miracle. At the same time I went to the health food stores and bought all kinds of health foods, vitamins, minerals, drinks etc. Jenny and I had taken vitamins for years, and while in the Navy I was diagnosed with sugar diabetes. My best friend Joe Coleman's dad told me about vitamins and how helpful they are. I started taking vitamins and shortly after taking them, after about a year, I was able to eat everything I wanted again. Jenny and I also had a juicer machine. Jenny had read a ton of books on vitamins and health. We even made our own formula for our children when they were babies.

I know there are good effects from taking vitamins. I praised vitamins for getting rid of my diabetes and praised God for vitamins. Yet I didn't praise God for healing me. Now I just put all my faith where it should have been in the first place, in God. Back then I was Catholic and only thought of God for the big things like helping me not sin and keeping me from going to hell. I knew every Sunday at church we said the words, "only say the word and I shall be healed." I said it every Sunday but I never saw anyone healed. I don't remember anyone even thinking they would be healed. As a Catholic I had faith in doctors and medicine, not God. So I took vitamins and didn't realize it but I put my faith in vitamins, doctors and science not God. When scientist said margarine is better for you then butter, guess what; my mom and every mom I knew fixed everything with margarine.

Then the very first conference we went to, they said how vitamins and health food could rob you of your faith in God because you were putting your faith in the vitamins. I realized my faith was in vitamins, so I got rid of every vitamin and put my faith, my hope and my trust in God. The funny thing is the very same people that taught me to put my faith in God are now selling vitamins for a living. It is a good thing my belief about faith in God is rooted in scripture and not what others say and believe.

To this very day I have stuck with my decision to put my faith in God. I believe my faith and hope in God is rooted in scripture and in the truth of His Word! I am glad to have made that decision because almost every day I meet someone that says have you tried this or that. I tell them, I believe in God! I believe God!!! If I try everything else along the way, where is my faith and what is it in? I don't want to sound like I am against doctors or science, I just believe they are limited by their own minds and understanding. I believe in God who is unlimited, totally unlimited. I have my faith in God who has no boundaries, who literally can say the word and I am healed!!!!!

Yes I hear the great stories about people that were healed by taking vitamins and I wonder if they are in bondage to vitamins now. Do they believe without their vitamins they will get sick and die? If they miss a day or go somewhere and forget their vitamins what will happen to them? I believe it is a form of bondage. I know people who have their belief in vitamins and think the vitamins have given them a lot better quality of life here on earth. Like I said, I believed that for years.

Suppose I started giving Jenny vitamins and supplements etc., and then Jenny was suddenly healed. Where should I put or to whom shall I give the praise to? I have heard of people with cancer talk about a doctor in New York who said to do this and to eat that, and then when they followed his advice they were healed of cancer. Then they praised him for their healing, not God, and I wonder what God thinks? What if the doctor in New York told everyone to drink ten glasses of carrot juice every day and make sure the carrots are organic? The world would run out of organic carrots in no time at all and then what would we do? Maybe pray for God to send more organic carrots?

Are we to live in our own strength or let the joy of the Lord be our strength? I will not change my faith in God and that is where I will be the rest of my life. I know when I stand before Jesus for judgment I can say all my faith is in you Jesus and you alone. I do pray for Jesus to bless the decisions I make and I know He does when my decisions line up with His teachings. Jesus turned water into fine wine instantly, He did miracle after miracle instantly. My faith, my Hope, my Love and my TRUST are in Jesus the creator of us all, not in organic carrots. Why would anyone put their faith in scientists and their findings when you can put your faith in the One who created us all and knows all?

Jesus in His word talked about rest.

Mat 11:28-30 Come to Me, all *you* who labor and are heavy laden, and I will give you rest. Take My yoke upon you and learn from Me, for I am gentle and lowly in heart, and you will find rest for your souls. For My yoke *is* easy and My burden is light."

Are we resting in God if we have to take four glasses of carrot juice every day? Are we resting in God if we have to read every ingredient in everything we eat? Jesus said not to worry so are we going against His commandment when we worry about what we eat? Just ask Jesus to bless everything you put in your mouth and ask Jesus to help you make healthy decisions. Jesus really wants to be that personal with you. So let Him! Jesus turned the water into wine and He will do the same thing for us. Ask Jesus to bless your food and He will bless it with what you need.

Diligently seek Jesus with all your heart.

Heb 11:6 But without faith *it is* impossible to please *Him,* for he who comes to God must believe that He is, and *that* He is a rewarder of those who diligently seek Him.

When we stand before Jesus for judgment I believe Jesus will be more concerned about how much we trusted Him than anything else. I see trust in the Bible to be all inclusive, that is Faith Hope and Charity all in one word. In Hebrews 11:6 you see without faith it is impossible to please Jesus. God said we must believe Him, that is not a suggestion, it is a commandment! Jesus is a rewarder of them that diligently seek Him. You diligently seek Jesus by getting the world out of the way. I mean when we put the things of the world in front of Jesus "like I did for 50 some years" yes for 50 some years I thought I needed to work to provide for Jenny and our children. I only talked to Jesus when I needed Him and only about what I needed from Him. I never talked to Him about why I was here and if Jesus needed me to do anything for Him. Thank You Jesus that has all changed!

To diligently seek anything you must set your mind on achieving the thing you seek. No one can learn anything without wanting to learn it. You must have the desire to know God, if you are going to become friends with Him. When you fell in love with your wife you were diligently seeking to know her, to please her and give of yourself to make her happy. A relationship with Jesus is the same way; He wants us to fall in love with Him, to seek Him, to desire to please Him and to desire to spend time to know Him intimately. Jesus will be your best friend if you let Him. Please let Jesus be your best friend, I did and I will never regret it!

FEBRUARY 18TH, 2013

We went to Spring Hill Florida to see Tony and Cal our neighbors from Pond Run Rd. It was nice to see them and catch up on how they are doing. They also paid for half our camping fee, which helped us a lot. Jenny and I went to a church service that was close to our campground on Sunday morning. We were a couple minutes late so I had to park close to the church door, and because I was late I chose to carry Jenny into the church rather then put her in the wheel chair. One of the ushers moved our car for us, when he came back in he handed me my car keys and said don't leave until you talk to me after church.

The service was really nice and the people were friendly, we even got to talk to the preacher for a couple minutes. Then Tyrone the man that parked our car for us came over and said all through the service he kept hearing God tell him to give us a newer car. I was elated, surprised and overcome at the same time. Tyrone had never met us before; he told me he owns a car lot in Tampa. I ask how he could just give away a car and he said the cars were never mine in the first place. They belong to my Father in heaven and He says to give you one. When we left the church I was in heaven because a couple days before that I had tried the air-conditioning in our car and it did not work.

While at the campground we met another couple and became friends. Mary and Reed Alison. What a friend ship this is turning into. They invited Jenny and I to Brookside church where they were going on Sunday morning. We went and Mary and Reed were right.

The church is great and the worshiping of Jesus was super. It is a satellite church of the Andrew Womack churches and schools. From Pastor Wade, to the entire congregation the people were on fire for the Lord and the Truth of the gospel message. It is always a blessing to be part of a worship service but here the worshiping was so real and right from the heart. Jesus said from the heart a man speaks and when a congregation speaks from their heart in union with God; look out big things are going to happen.

The only thing better then fellowshipping with likeminded people is actually doing the word of God and seeing miracles.

Doctor Jesus

After observing Jenny and I a fellow camper asked how do you do doctors while traveling full time? I said I only have one doctor and He makes camper calls. She looked at me like I'm nuts. Then I said Jenny is healed and she knew I was nuts.

I guess I need to talk about Jenny's condition for a few minutes so you will know what is going on in our life that is what the fellow camper was seeing in the physical. Jenny's physical condition seems to be getting worse. I am not pronouncing that on her, I am just trying to convey what is going on physically. Smiling takes a lot of effort for Jenny; her face muscles do not cooperate with her desire to smile. Swallowing is a big effort also for Jenny; it seems to be a really big decision. Jenny falls asleep even while chewing her food.

Most of the time it is very hard to tell if Jenny can see. She will have her eyes open and looking at me but when I touch her she jumps. I used to be able to get her to drink from a straw. Now she doesn't seem to recognize what it is in her mouth. Feeding her can take an hour and a half. For a while Jenny seemed to like eating out where there was a lot going on to stimulate her. Now that doesn't seem to make a difference. Foods that used to bring a smile on her face and a little excitement in her life, just doesn't work anymore. I guess the worst part is how Jenny seems to get so frustrated and the blood veins in her face and arms look like they are going to pop out of her skin. It is really ugly to see.

Jenny's body is starting to bend like the letter C. When I hold her on my lap she is bent in a C and now her body is staying in the C shape. Her arms are crossed on her chest. Her hands are fisted all the time and her legs are crossed all the time. Showering her is a little difficult in the position she is in. I can see why people who don't know God and only look at the physical would think I am nuts for saying Jenny is healed. Please read on and you will see I am not nuts! Jenny is healed; I have the word of Jesus Himself to believe in.

Traveling has become more difficult. I mean it is more difficult for me not Jenny. It is more difficult for me because I miss her so much. When Jenny is awake she seems to get fidgety and the only way to settle her down is to hold her on my lap and talk to her. When Jenny is sitting on my lap, she looks at me as I talk to her and she relaxes to where she falls asleep. I usually hold her until my legs go to sleep and start to hurt. As soon as I move her she wakes up and starts getting fidgety again.

You might be thinking that I am spoiling her and I am, but I love it when I can just stop what I am doing and hold her on my lap. She relaxes in my arms to the point where she is like a wet washrag. I can move her arms and open her little fist, I can uncross her legs and I believe these are good things. I know it is difficult to dress her with her legs crossed and her arms crossed on her chest. When I do travel I do not set goals I just go as far as I can and let that be good enough.

Now for the good news about Jenny! Jenny and I are blessed to have a relationship with Jesus and Father God and through the Holy Spirit have the same life giving power, the healing power, the salvation power and power over the devil and his works. I have the same power and authority as Jesus gave the apostles, thank you Jesus.

Sometimes I wonder what people who don't know Jesus as their savior do in times like these. Jesus says to walk by faith and not by sight. Jesus is life and life more abundantly. Jesus called the apostles, trained them and then sent them out to teach the kingdom of God has come upon you, Jesus also sent the apostles out to train others to heal the sick, raise the dead and cast out demons. The apostles preached the kingdom of God and then they passed their relationship to God on to the church. We are His church; we are Gods chosen people if we chose to be. We are ambassadors for Jesus! I'm a son of the living God and because I know God loves me, I can look at Jenny and know she is healed! If you think I am a nut or crazy for saying Jenny is healed, go ahead think I'm a nut, that is okay; God calls me his SON!!!

I would rather be walking with faith in my Jesus and be thought of as nuts than to be smart in your eyes! You say, I need to look at reality; Jenny is getting worse, you say don't get your hopes up to high Ron you will only be disappointed. Why would I believe you or men that tell me "protect your heart Ron; don't be a fool Jenny is dying right in front of you." People think I am living in denial; people say I'm living in some kind of fantasy world because I believe in God. In God there is no such thing as having your hopes to High! "All things are possible" In God there is no disappointment! "All of God's promises are true" The people that say I am crazy or a nut case need to know God is real, God is truth, God loves me and those people need to experience the love of God! I'm not nuts, I'm just peculiar and I love it!

Deu 14:2 For you *are* a holy people to the Lord your God, and the Lord has chosen you to be a people for Himself, a special treasure above all the peoples who *are* on the face of the earth.

Yes I am a peculiar person to you but I am beautiful to my Father in heaven and He has chosen me to take unto himself. If I am nuts I want to stay that way for eternity.

The people that say I'm nuts, need to have a relationship with Jesus. I remember when I went to mass every Sunday and Holiday and received Jesus into my heart through communion. It was so wonderful to know Jesus was in me until the host dissolved. I could talk to Him for a few seconds. Yes I had the body and blood of Jesus Christ in me for a few seconds.

When you really start to seek a relationship with Jesus and you put Him first in your life, you will come to the truth that Jesus wants to be in us and with us, to talk to us and His plan is for us is to manifest Jesus 24/7. Communion was not just at the last supper and every time you reenact the last supper. Communion is for every second of your life! Along with that revelation I realized Jesus loves me and the two of us can talk, laugh, walk and cry together. In fact we live together as one, I am one with Jesus and I know the life giving power of Jesus flows through me as it did the life giving power of God the Father flowed through Jesus the man while He was on the earth.

I want to put to rest the words I used in the last paragraph (reenact the last supper) reenact is a poor choice of words, it sounds like we are acting; Jesus said

Luk 22:19   And He took bread, gave thanks and broke *it,* and gave *it* to them, saying,"This is My body which is given for you; do this in remembrance of Me."

THIS DO IN REMEMBRANCE OF ME! Jesus said this is my body and blood as he took bread and wine and blessed it in to His body and blood. I think people have been arguing ever since weather or not this is symbolism or did Jesus really change bread and wine in to the body and blood of Jesus?

To me the answer is so simple because Jesus came to show us life is really in your spirit. In the beginning Jesus breathed Spirit life into dust to make mankind in his image.

Gen 2:7   And the Lord God formed man *of* the dust of the ground, and breathed into his nostrils the breath of life; and man became a living being.

Isn't that cool, Jesus breathed life into the dust. I believe it because God said it! I don't need any other proof. Life is in your spirit. Jesus loves us all, He proves His love by dying for us all. I believe it! Do you?

I believe the whole Bible is true and I cannot figure out why is it so hard for some people who claim to be believers to believe Jesus changed bread and wine into the body and blood of Himself? Again Jesus said it, so I believe it. For me it is easy to say Jenny is healed because Jesus said so in His word. If you cut your finger, you expect it to heal. It is easy to believe the little cut will heal because you have seen it so many times. I ask you who made the blood that has to flow through your body to sustain life and then suddenly become a clogging agent when you cut yourself. If you said only a genius could make such a thing your right. God is my God, and God is my genius, God is my healer and God is best friend. You can say I'm crazy but God says I'm His Son!

I just believe what Jesus said in His word, there is really no arguing the point in my mind, Jesus said He created the world and I believe it! What is there to argue about? Jesus came and changed keeping the law from physical to spiritual. Jesus said to renew your mind, to be baptized into the Spirit, to live in the spirit and your battles are spiritual, Jesus said without faith it is impossible to please Him. Faith is your heart belief or better put it is your spiritual belief.

I can tell you this by FAITH I receive Jesus in to my heart 24/7 and by FAITH I live with Jesus in me renewing my mind to live the word of God made flesh by turning my fleshly desires into Spiritual desires of being like Jesus. THANK YOU JESUS!!!!!

I also believe in God all things are possible so why would I not believe Jesus when He said THIS IS my body and my blood, to me that settles it, there should be no argument! It is His body and blood. Jesus did not say this symbolizes my body and blood. Jesus said THIS IS!!!!!

> Mat 26:26-28 And as they were eating, Jesus took bread, blessed and broke *it,* and gave *it* to the disciples and said, "Take, eat; this is My body."Then He took the cup, and gave thanks, and gave *it* to them, saying,"Drink from it, all of you. For this is My blood of the new covenant, which is shed for many for the remission of sins.

I have the word of God to believe in! The words THIS IS are so simple for me to believe, what I don't understand is where all the unbelief comes from. Jesus is in my heart 24/7, we will live together forever! When people tell me I need to protect my heart I tell them Jesus is my protector. You see my heart is protected by the love of Jesus! Jesus said to bring heaven to earth, to do that, ask Jesus into your heart and start living in heaven now, heaven is not the destination, heaven is Jesus living in you NOW!!!!

Doctors study for years and years to become a doctor and then they have to read updated material all their life to stay up with the changes in medicine. My doctor wrote one book and it has stood the test of time for thousands of years, with no updates. I believe my doctor and when I go to my doctor I don't have waiting lines to see Him, I don't have deductibles, I don't have insurance contracts, I have FAITH, I have TRUST, and that gives me HOPE and most of all I have God's word for life more abundantly.

If you listen to people talking about doctors long enough you will hear stories about doctor's mistakes and doctors not caring! I'm tired of hearing about side effects of man-made medicine! I'm tired of hearing these words "sometimes you have to get worse before you get better or what alternative do you have?" Where is that in the Bible? I don't watch television but I hear people talk about all the new diseases that are being promoted on television. I really don't understand how people can think I'm the one that is nuts.

I don't have any of their diseases and I thank God for His word that says disease is captivity from the devil, the devil said he came to steel, kill and destroy our life. I cannot think of a better way to describe sickness then killing, steeling and destroying your life. You don't have to be sick too long to realize the truth, your sickness is (steeling) your life, sickness can (kill) you and sickness is (destroying) your life. Jesus was very clear about who came to kill steel and destroy you. Jesus said I am life and the truth that sets us free!!! THANK YOU JESUS FOR TRUTH, LIFE AND LOVE!!!!!

How can people put their faith in doctors that advertise on television? For example, Doctors advertise, "If you have these signs, you have restless leg syndrome" and we have a pill for you. The day before they started advertising almost no one had even heard of restless leg syndrome. Then they tell you the side effects of the medicine will probably kill you but your legs won't hurt and we will be rich so come see us now. Now that is a side effect your doctors can live with. It is really hard to understand how people can say "I'm the one that is nuts."

I don't want to put all your doctors down because there are some really good ones out there. Truthfully I might not be here if not for doctors. Before my faith was this strong for God; doctors were all I had to keep me alive and I thank God for them.

Now I thank God for faith; through God's truth my faith in Jesus has grown over the years to let me be so in love with Jesus and trust in Jesus that I put my life in His hands. If your faith in God is not that strong then by all means go to the doctor so you can live to have another day to seek Jesus and trust in Jesus. Jesus will meet you where your faith is!! Actually that is another way God shows He loves us; God is extremely patient and will work through doctors if we ask him too until our faith grows to be in Him alone. Thank you Jesus for truth and faith and grace and letting us live until we understand your love for us enough to TRUST IN YOU ALONE!!!!

Is a person a nut if they love and trust Jesus? I live to hear from Jesus. I live to be with Jesus and walk with Jesus, and talk to Jesus. I live to be like Jesus, that is to preach His word boldly, to heal the sick, to raise the dead and to cast out devils. To set the captives free is my desire and with Jesus living in me; nothing is impossible for me. Trusting in God is like breathing to me, knowing God is all powerful is wonderful to me, but knowing the creator of the universe loves me, is life and life more abundantly to me. He knows me personally, He hears me, and Jesus is so real I can talk to Him like you talk to your doctors, the difference is with Jesus there are no evil side effects! The best knowledge you can gain in life is, God wants to call you His son; yes God wants you to be so close to Him that He knows you by name!

With Jesus I get love! Real love, not sympathy that creates a desire for more sympathy. I do not have bills that add to the stress and I don't live in captivity of medicine and doctor appointments. I live in freedom of asking God what are WE going to do today? I love my Jesus and His freedom from all sickness; Jesus is freedom form disease and freedom from death! I'm not nuts; the way you think of nuts but I am free and I don't live in fear or in need of sanitizer to keep germs away. I'm in love with Jesus and the side effect for loving Jesus is everlasting life! I believe in Jesus and the side effect of believing Jesus is Joy, Peace, Faith, Hope, freedom from fear, perfect health and knowing the perfect love of Jesus is for us 24/7!!!! Don't forget you can be a Son of God too!

I see people healed instantly; when they hear the word of God preached! I see the lame walk; I see the Joy in the hearts of people that hear the word of hope from Jesus and that is what Jesus came to do, give us Hope! Trusting in Jesus is SETTING THE CAPTIVES FREE. Forgiveness is freedom, health is freedom, a life of Joy is freedom and life starts with an intimate relationship with Jesus. I simply put my trust in God and his words of truth! The word of God has not changed for thousands of years and I believe God is the final word! I know God's love is all I Need and I know God loves me so I am being purified daily. Ask God for truth and Seek God for relationship and I guarantee Jesus will hear your prayer and answer your prayer with truth that sets you free!

Joh 8:32 And ye shall know the truth, and the truth shall make you free.

The truth in the Bible is setting Jenny and I free from all sickness and all infirmities! Jesus is purifying us, watching over us and most of all JESUS IS LOVING US. I no longer pray for the sick and down trotted because nowhere in the Bible did Jesus say I will pray for you. Jesus just commanded sickness to go, Jesus is our example; I follow Jesus and I just command the sickness to go and it has to go! If your faith is not their then go to the elders and their prayer of faith will save the sick. Notice it is the prayer of faith, not the prayer of fear! THANK YOU JESUS for making your love so clear! Yes thank you Jesus for making Jenny and I peculiar!!! We are so blessed to know your love for us!! I could write a book a thousand pages long and still not thank God for everything He has done. I love being peculiar!!!

Jesus and Jenny and I love you and we pray for you to be peculiar too! Are you a Son of God? Does God know your name? Is your name written in the book of life? The answers to these questions can all be YES if you just ask God for intimacy with Him and trust Him for a real relationship. Speaking about is your name written in heaven's book of life; I believe all our names our written in the book of life. Jesus called it the book of life so if we have life, all our names are in it. The question should be "is your name crossed out of the book of life?" Yes we have the power to remove our name from the book of life by the choices WE make!!! Choose well eternity can be heaven or hell.

It is my desire for everyone to know God so well that you will proclaim His word boldly and bask in the perfect love of God that frees us from all fear and sends the devil packing back to Hell! Life is easy when you trust God!!!

On the way to Carrabelle I started writing a little teaching to read to pastor Don's congregation. Here it is!

Sickness and Faith

First I want to thank Pastor Don for being such a good friend and a very good Pastor! Coming back to Carrabelle and the good people of his congregation is like coming home to a good home for Jenny and I. The warm hearts of everyone here has given us light and warmth. It is true the special people of Don's congregation are good people and a true blessing to be around.

You might wonder why I used the word good to describe Pastor Don and all of you. I could have very easily used the word great or greatest or excellent or superior to describe all of you. I chose the word good because when Jesus spoke the world into existence He said "it is good" and when Jesus was finished He called His creation "very good". In my pursuit to be like Jesus I am trying to use His words in my vocabulary. Plus I think when we try to describe people in better terms then good it is like putting down good and maybe elevating us to a higher standard. I remember in

> Mar 10:18 So Jesus said to him, "Why do you call Me good? No one *is* good but One, that is, God.

So calling you good is putting you in some very good company! Most of the people here know Jenny and I have been coming to Carrabelle Beach for four years now. Probably everyone here has lost a loved one. Most people would say losing a loved one is never easy. I lost my mom December 21, 2012; she was 93 years old and really she was ready to go. In my heart I felt as though Jesus sent her an angel and ask her if she wanted to spend Christmas on earth or in heaven. Mom chose heaven. I can tell you this 5 days before mom died, Jenny and I were setting with her having coffee, mom talked and walked to the bathroom. She was alert and her only complaint was, she said her body hurt. Two days later I received a phone call from my sister saying mom had taken a turn for the worse. Mom died two days later in her own bed with her loved ones being around her and we were all in peace knowing it was the right timing of the

Lord Jesus Christ calling her home. I don't feel as though I lost my mom I feel like she decided to go home to her final reward.

I believe that is how death should be. I can tell from watching people's reactions that most people for the last eight or nine months have looked at Jenny like she should be in a home or better yet I should release her spirit to go be with the Lord. I believe sickness is from the devil. The devil's mission is to kill, steel and destroy our lives. One look at Jenny and most people would say the devil is succeeding in his mission.

If you go by the outward signs, or the circumstances you would be right. I guess that is why Jesus told us not to look with our eyes or think cardinally minded. As soon as you look at the problem, you will take your mind off Jesus and the fact you have His Holy Spirit living in you and you will start feeling weak and helpless to solve the problem. You run to the doctor who only has the knowledge to practice medicine. You are falling right into the hands of the devil.

Jesus said it is the prayer of faith that will heal the sick, not the prayer of fear. We are to have the mind of Christ and eyes of Christ and the love of Christ in us and flowing through us. We are to be like Jesus looking down on our problems not like helpless humans looking up through our problems. From God's vantage point, which is our vantage point when we have the eyes of Jesus, even mountains seem small. We are to speak to the problem and command it to change, don't talk to God about the problem; He already gave us the answer. Jesus gave us the same power over the devil that He has. Just believe and use your power!

A lot of people who pray for someone will talk to God about the person they are praying for. Almost as though God does not know the sick person. They talk to God about the problem or when we talk to God about our self's, we talk to God about our problem. Don't pray the problem, it takes no faith to pray the problem or to ask God for help, but Jesus said it takes a prayer of faith to save the sick. A prayer of faith is praying the answer God gave us for the problems. Jesus showed us compassion by commanding devils to leave, Jesus commanded sickness to leave, Jesus forgave us all our sins and Jesus showed compassion by raising the dead for us the living.

Jesus did all these things by having relationship to His Father, a loving spiritual relationship! Jesus said our battle is spiritual and our armor is spiritual! We accept the fight physically and we do an exceptional job physically and physically we are very compassionate. Jesus commands us to be compassionate physically, so taking care of the physical needs of others is very God like and is very pleasing to God. God just wants us to be that compassionate in the spiritual battle also. Jesus wants us to have relationship with Him so when the battle comes we are ready spiritually and physically to do His will on earth. Jesus would never command us to do something; without giving us the tools to do it with. So we have the command and the tools, let us put them to use and have some fun. Just believe in God's word!

Jesus said when He comes back we should have the devil under our feet. Jesus gave us the same Holy Spirit that raised Him from the dead. I have the Holy Spirit of Father God and Jesus living in me! There is nothing that can get in His way except my unbelief. Fear is of the devil and fear is faith in the devil, fear is unbelief and fear will rob you of faith. Don't give way to it. Just believe in God!

We are to know the will of the Father and to do His will! To know His will look to the words of Jesus who said He came to reveal the Father to us. Jesus was perfect love so the Father is perfect love and we can be perfect love if we are surrendered to the Father and have relationship 24/7. Jesus is perfect love; Jesus is the perfect love that cast out fear (devil). Look to the Bible and read how Jesus took charge over every situation. Don't read the Bible and try to figure out if this is true, just believe the one who said "He cannot lie" and accept the Bible as truth. Accepting the Bible as true is the childlike faith Jesus talks about. The more you believe the more you are set free. Jesus said my truth will set you free. I know the more of the truth of Jesus you have in your heart the harder it will be for the devil to talk you into sinning. Just believe in the word of Jesus and you are set free of the devil and you are free of his sinning nature! We do not have a sinning nature; we are made in the image of God; so we have to except a sinning nature from the devil to have one. Just cast it off.

Jesus was a man while on the earth and was as human as we are. Yet I never read anything about fear being in Him. He is our example to follow and look up to. Let the love of Jesus in your heart and watch fear flee. Just believe and let Jesus in your heart and be free.

Circumstances do not dictate the outcome of sickness, YOU DO!!! With Jesus and Father God dwelling in you, you BETTER dictate the outcome. Jesus did not die just to be the atonement for sin! Jesus came to show us we have power over DEATH and so death does not exist, we just leave here for judgment, and we should only leave when Jesus calls us home, not from sickness that we have God's power over. Jesus describes sickness as captivity and bondage, which is how we should describe sickness. Sickness is not Pick's disease; sickness is not cancer or any other name we give it! Sickness is captivity and bondage. Jesus said He came to set the captives free and He did and so can we!!!! Just believe!!

Jesus also told us to take every thought captive to the obedience of His word. If you're watching television, I can guarantee; you are not taking every thought captive and I can guarantee you; the Lord that sent His only Son to teach us and be our example in life, will not talk over the noise of the television. Be sill and hear His voice. You want the truth that sets you free just be still and Hear His Voice! Get up in the morning and ask yourself what does Jesus want to do today? For some reason we think life in God is all about God helping us have a nice day. Again that is the reverse of what our life should be. We are here to do the work of the kingdom! Ask the Lord every morning "what are we going to do today." Ask Jesus who do you want set free today and He will lead you to someone that He wants set free! Watching someone set free is Joy beyond our understanding!!! I want that every day!!!

Kingdom work is listening for our marching orders and then doing them. Jesus said over and over I only do what I seen My Father do. What did Jesus do? He healed, forgave, cast out devils (set people free) raised people from the dead and preached the word boldly. So we can say I only do what I have seen my Father do! Jesus gave you and I the same set of orders and by faith we can complete them. Just believe! Jesus would not ask you to do anything, without giving you the power to do it. Jesus said you were given the measure of faith so what is holding you back?? Maybe you don't believe Him. That would be a tragedy. Jesus died for me and I will not waste my time trying not to sin when I can spend my time glorifying God by believing Jesus lives in me. That is taking the tragedy of nonbelief and turning it into the MAGESTY OF BELIEF!! I'm set free and I thank you Jesus!!!!

Don't wait for someone else to do it, you will be missing out on all the fun! You will miss the Joy and the love of Jesus. You only have one life to give so make the best of it for Jesus. You are the best Jesus has and Jesus is okay with that. The devil is the one that makes you feel insignificant!!! I hear Christians say "oh Lord bring the rapture, I want out of here" I think to myself that sounds REALLY self-centered. Not all my loved ones are saved so I know I need more time. I pray for God to put off the rapture! Please don't think for one second you don't have a mission to accomplish because you do! Please don't say I can't because with Jesus in you failure doesn't exist. Just believe and nothing will hold you back!

Don't read the Bible to see if it is true, don't argue with it!!! JUST BELIEVE IT!!!! CHILDLIKE FAITH IS NOT AN OPTION!!! Childlike faith is praise worthy! Power and authority are yours for just believing!!! If you need proof or have an argument in your mind about anything you read in the Bible you are in doubt and listening to the devil! Just believe what you read in God's word. When I read the Bible I put myself in the place of Jesus. If the Bible says Jesus raised Lazarus from the dead then I read Ron raised Lazarus from the dead. It is simple Jesus said for us to raise people from the dead and so we can. Just believe.

If I look at the circumstances of my life; I see the deter ration of Jenny's condition. The circumstances will make me think death is coming real soon. The circumstances make me look like I'm crazy for saying I believe the word of God. Am I crazy to declare Jenny is not going to die of this disease? Am I crazy to declare Jenny will live, Jenny will walk, Jenny will talk and Jenny will be totally normal again right now? You see I have the word of Jesus that Jenny will be totally normal! I have the word of Jesus that says by His strips Jenny was healed. I believe and I declare it to be and so it is, I have the word of Jesus on it!

Two different women over the years have delivered two words of knowledge from God to me. The first came about three years ago when I came across the scriptures about a sin unto death.

1Jn 5:16 If any man see his brother sin a sin which is not unto death, he shall ask, and he shall give him life for them that sin not unto death. There is a sin unto death: I do not say that he shall pray for it.

After reading this scripture I ask God to reveal the sin I needed to repent for. I waited and when I never heard from the Lord, I pleaded please God you know I choose You; only You have life! I knew God knew I would change and turn away from all wickedness if I just knew what I was doing wrong. After a couple days of asking the Lord about this scripture Jesus sent me a messenger.

The next morning a girl came to my camper and said I have never done this before but I believe I have a word from the Lord for you. She said I have known idea what this means to you but the word I keep hearing to tell you is "not unto death" I thanked her for being obedient to Jesus and for telling me the word God had for me. I immediately had the peace that surpasses all understanding in my heart. I continue to this day to speak those words over Jenny "Jesus said not unto death". Now I pray in thanks giving for I know that Jenny is healed and I know that Jenny will not die of this disease. Thank you Jesus for coming into my life and renewing my mind!

About a year and a half later Jenny and I were in a campground in Tennessee. They had a little church service in the campground so Jenny I went there for the service. It was a bright sunny morning and the service was under a pavilion with no walls. Jenny and I were late arriving, and as we approached the pavilion we were very quiet because we were in grass, (the wheel chair made no noise) but still somehow a lot of people turned around to see who came up behind them. I was kind of startled by them turning around because we made no noise and the preacher did not say anything or even look at us. Any way after the service I was walking Jenny back to our camper and some women stopped me to say why they turned around in the church service. They said even though it was a sunny day they felt the whole pavilion light up when we came. One woman said you glow with the love of Jesus in you. Then they walked away.

As Jenny and I continued to walk to our camper I had tears running down my face, I was crying so hard because I ask God to let me manifest His presents everywhere I go. I had my head down because I didn't want everyone to see me crying. There was another younger girl walking in front of us that suddenly turned around and ask if she could pray for Jenny. I replied sure, but before she started to pray, her two sons and husband that were behind us came walking up. As we talked for a moment I had reached my hand down and picked up Jenny's hand to hold it and with my other hand I was rubbing Jenny's face. This girl, the mother of the two boys said to her sons; "do you see why I said every time I see this man with his wife, I tell you boys I see Jesus". She continued to tell them, you see when you don't feel good Jesus is there with you holding your hand, Jesus will rub your head to comfort you and if you cannot walk Jesus will pick you up and carry you into your camper.

Then she started to pray for Jenny. In the middle of her prayer she stopped and said wow I just received a word for you. She went on to say "this one is to manifest the glory of God" after she finished her prayer I went to the camper and looked it up.

> Joh 9:5 And as Jesus passed by, he saw a man which was blind from his birth. And his disciples asked him, saying, Master, who did sin, this man, or his parents, that he was born blind? Jesus answered, Neither hath this man sinned, nor his parents: but that the works of God should be made manifest in him. I must work the works of him that sent me, while it is day: the night cometh, when no man can work. As long as I am in the world, I am the light of the world.

As I read these scriptures I knew God was talking to me through His messengers again. Isn't it amazing that the creator of the universe has time to talk to me? We are all this special to God and if you're going through anything tough right now ask the creator to talk to you and He will comfort you also. This is why I tell everyone Jenny and I are so blessed. Jesus wants a relationship!!!

So when people look at me like I am crazy, I let them look because I know the truth of Jesus sets us free and the truth is God loves me and I will stand on these scriptures and I will see Jenny walking, talking, I know Jenny and I will have coffee with my brother Jesus! What a glorious day that will be! I command it to happen and it will happen because Jesus gave me His word on it. Jesus said anything I ask in faith I will receive that the Son may bring glory to the Father. Do you know the meaning of the words Father God? Father means to come forth from and God means the source of life. So when I go to MY FATHER GOD, I am going to the one from which we all come forth from and is the source of life. I mean I might as well go right to the source and I go to Him through my brother Jesus. I call that being blessed!

I know Jesus loves Jenny and I so much, He came to restore the relationship Adam lost by eating the fruit of the tree of Good and evil. Jesus came and restored that relationship so we walk and talk together 24/7. I have relationship with Jesus and my Father 24/7 and there is no better place to be then in the company of my Jesus and Father. If people want to say I am crazy I don't care, I know who I am and I know who loves me. Jesus said we will be peculiar and I love being what Jesus said I would be! I know Jesus said we can bring heaven to earth and I know I am already in Heaven because I know Jesus and my Father love me! Father God calls me His Son! Believing as a child in the word of God is rest and it is the only blessing I need! So to be blessed, I rest in God!

Yes I want Jenny healed and yes I am seeking her healing like I should because Jesus said by His strips we were healed, done deal! I also know that some people have said look how much closer you are to God because of this sickness in Jenny. I do not and will not ever believe that God puts sickness on people to bring them closer to Him. If you believe it is the will of God to put sickness on people to bring you closer to Him, you should never go to a doctor because you are asking the doctor to sin by going against the will of God!!! Also if sickness is the will of God then we should never fight it; we should just accept it, we should pray for more sickness so we can be in His will! You see how contrary to the Word of God sickness is!!!! JESUS SAID HEAL SICKNESS, DON'T ACCEPT SICKNESS!!!!! Especially don't except it!!!

No one comes to God unless He calls us first. I don't see anywhere in the Bible where Jesus called anyone and said if you do not come I will make you or your wife sick to get your attention. He might let a donkey talk to you but He never put sickness on anyone. Sickness is the work of the devil, not God. If you believe God put sickness on you, you will not or should not fight to get better, I mean after all, you think it is the will of God, right? Look at what Jesus calls sickness. Captivity, spirit of infirmity, bondage, and Jesus said He came to set the captives free, to free us from the bondage of sin and the spirit of infirmity. We in America have doctors that have a name for every kind of sickness, but I believe all sickness is a spirit of infirmity and if you cast out an evil spirit of infirmity the sickness is gone, the pain is gone and health with life is back. Your health is renewed like the eagles. We can and should live in divine health every day. Devine health is ours for just believing.

I believe the first line of defense in sickness and disease is the church and not a hospital. If your faith is in doctors then by all means go to the doctor and live another day to have time to learn what a relationship with Jesus looks like. Learn what divine health is all about. The love of Jesus is so strong and it is His will to heal all!!!! Jesus will meet you at your faith level and even heal you through a doctor but when you get to heaven; wouldn't it be cool for Jesus to honor your faith like He did the men in Hebrews 11. I know when I get there I want to hear the words "well done my GOOD AND FAITHFUL SON; RON YOU BELIEVED ME!"

Faith is a substance like Jesus said but I believe the substance of faith is how much of your life did you live by the spirit of faith, the spirit of love, the spirit of truth, and how much did you believe in Jesus. Yes sin will be an issue for some but only for those that did not believe enough to repent. I really believe when you are standing before Jesus for judgment; how much you believed in his coming and dieing for us to have relationship with Him is going to be a bigger factor then how much you repented for sin. I mean when you have relationship with Jesus the devil flees and takes sin with him. Then if you do fall short of the glory of God you have an advocate and your advocate is JESUS AND JESUS LOVES YOU AND WILL FIGHT FOR YOU!!! When I sin I go to Jesus and thank Him for removing it and thank Him for restoring me back to Himself right away. I do not dwell on that failure I dwell on Jesus and His forgiveness for it is the truth of God that sets us free form sin. Just believe and watch the word of Jesus come true for you too! It is the truth that sets us free and Jesus is the truth!

Sin is so over ratted in church today. I know it is a big deal; sin can put me in hell for eternity so sin is a big deal! I said it is over ratted because they tell us we have to fight the devil all the time. Jesus said stand firm in His word and He does the battle. In other words I don't get up trying not to sin every day. Being Sin concusses is setting yourself up to sin because that is where your mind is. Trying not to sin every day brings us to a place where that is all you think about and after a while you will give in. If all you think about is sin, you will grow tired of fighting sin and you will back slide.

I don't get up and try not to sin, I get up to do the work of the kingdom by keeping my mind on Jesus, so I don't have to fight the devil because he is already defeated by Jesus. Jesus never fought the devil, he just ran over the devil because Jesus is like a speeding freight train on its way to Heaven. Jesus laid down some big tracks for us to follow! Let us all be a speeding freight train; destroying the works of the devil and full of the love of Jesus and by manifesting the Love of Jesus we will fill all our passenger cars to overflowing! Kingdom work is rewarding and uplifting, it is Joy beyond our understanding. Kingdom work is full of purpose so you don't grow weary and you won't back slide; in fact Jesus said I will give you rest. You will front slide right into the loving arms of Jesus for the biggest bear hug possible. It is a bear hug with a big well done my faithful Son who serves. Jesus is alive and well and He wants to flow through you and for you to manifest Him 24/7! MANIFESTING JESUS IS HOW NOT TO SIN!!! JESUS LOVES ME AND I KNOW IT SO I WIN!!!!

Remember when you fell in love with your girlfriend. You hoped with all your hope that she would fall in love with you. Your mind was on her 24/7. When she did fall in love with you, you relaxed and her love gave you peace in your heart to where your Joy was so full, you say I will marry you and take care of you the rest of your life. When you seek a relationship with Jesus as diligently as you seek a spouse, you will have the love of Jesus that surpasses all understanding and it adds new meaning to the words "take care of you." The Joy of God's love surpasses all our understanding! I believe in the loving joy of Jesus so I receive the loving joy of Jesus and I know Jesus loves me! That is truly the everlasting Joy of the Lord! I don't understand it but I sure in Joy it!!!

Most people are taught that receiving Jesus in to your heart and being saved is a bus ticket to heaven. I hear preachers say if you died tonight where would you spend eternity? They are selling your life insurance but instead of paying the premium with money you pay with good deeds. Then after a while you get tired of paying the premium because the policy is just words on paper and maybe you hear about the joy of the Lord but wonder what is that? Being Christian becomes a bunch of works. They hear of a life more abundant here on earth but wonder where is that? We really need to teach relationship with Jesus comes first. When you were seeking a wife, did you go to all her friends and do nice things for them hoping that somehow that would win her heart? No! You went right to her and pursued her, to win her heart.

A relationship with Jesus is pursuing Jesus first. You cannot have the Joy of the Lord without knowing Him. Jesus said bring heaven to earth, I tell you living with Jesus in you is bringing heaven to earth and then you can spread heaven around. Freely you received the Joy of knowing Jesus so freely you can spread the heavenly Joy of knowing Jesus around. Jesus is the ultimate motivator. His call to action was given to the 12 and then to the 70 and then the 120 and now to you!!! Turn off the television and the computer and anything that distracts you form Jesus. Jesus told me to get the world out of the way and then you will hear what I have to say! Remember Jesus will not talk over the noise of the world, you have to set time a side to listen and just believe.

The world says "don't get your hopes to high", you will be disappointed. Yet my Bible tells me nothing is impossible for me with Jesus Christ living in me. I believe the word of God! My hopes are Jesus high!!

The world says to a new Christian, "you're on fire now but don't worry you will cool down" or some call it backsliding. To some degree in church today, it is almost expected for a new Christian to backslide. In the church today we pray to have new converts and yet Paul prayed unceasingly for the established church. The real attacks from the devil come after you are baptized and on fire. The devil wants to steel those new seeds before they root into your heart, and by us saying don't worry he will cool down is like pronouncing that on them. Encourage as Jesus encouraged, be light as Jesus was light, love as Jesus loved, live as Jesus lived, do the things you see your Father do and you to will have the Joy of the Lord. You will have converts that come to you because they will see the Jesus in you, the Joy in you, the Love in you and you will be contagious. People will want what you have! Just give them Jesus and be contagiously contagious! It's a good thing!

The world tells us to do this or to buy that and you will be happy. Jesus told me that happiness is the opposite of Joy. Happiness always comes from getting something for yourself or having something done for yourself and happiness is always momentary. Happiness is always about yourself! Joy is doing for others and Joy is sustainable forever!

The world says for us to do nice things for others and God will love you. That is backwards! Jesus didn't come to reap servants that are trying to please Him by works. Jesus came to reap Sons and Daughters who are in a faith relationship with Him! You serve others because of your intimate relationship with God! You do not serve others to have relationship with God! When you truly have relationship with Jesus and Father God the Joy of the Lord glows in you and flows out from you and people will want what you have. You bring people to God because of your relationship to God, you don't bring people to God to have a relationship with God! God is the light that people always go to! Let your relationship shine the love of Jesus to everyone you meet. Jesus told us to preach the gospel to the entire world so it must be possible for each one of us. You are in this world so preach right where you are. Jesus will use your light to be His light, right where you are. Just believe with God all things are possible and they are! You to can be a light because you have Jesus in you!

Life and light are called the Joy of the Lord! Read the life of Jesus and you will see the ultimate giver! Read His life and you will see Jesus gave of Himself to show people the love of His Father but you cannot give the love of the Father until you have relationship with Your Father! It is really hard to give away something you do not have. Life more abundant; life full of Joy; life of peace; life of rest; is impossible without knowing the one that makes all things possible. Please read about the possibilities and start a relationship with the one that makes all things possible! You cannot earn one and you cannot deserve one but I can guarantee you Jesus wants you to receive His relationship free of charge. Then Jesus said freely you received and freely you give. Give His love, give His peace, give His hope, give His trust, and you will light up the world. Most of all tell people how to have a relationship with Jesus.

Get the worldly out of the way and then you will hear what I have to say. Thank You from God! It is worth repeating! Get the impossible out of the way, by having relationship with the one that makes all things possible! Imagine the possibilities, imagine the Joy when you walk through life knowing Jesus the Son of God is your brother and Father God is your FATHER!!! Yes being a Christian is more than a bus ticket to heaven!

I'm going to close with this story form Jesus. Suppose your married and you have a young son and he was being bullied in school. Every night he asks his dad to talk to the teacher and so his dad does. The teacher said he will look out for Billy but he cannot be everywhere Billy is. So the three bullies knock Billy's books out of his hands while in the hallway. They still kick him around on the playground. So you decide to enroll Billy in carroty classes and boxing classes and a martial arts class. You want Billy to defend himself. In 6 months Billy has won all kinds of awards and is great in every class. In the fall when school starts again you are excited and you tell your wife this year will be different, Billy will show those three bullies a thing or two.

But Billy still comes home every night and complains about the bullies beating him up. Dad asks "son why don't you kick their tails, you know you can"

Billy says dad; I don't want to make them made at me, they might go and get more bullies.

In our new covenant with Jesus we have all the weapons we need to kick the devil back to hell. Jesus came and demonstrated these weapons; Jesus wrote down the instructions for us to pass on too future generations so the bullies will know they cannot mess with us who are in the Lord. We have the best defense system mankind has ever seen. Jesus is more than a bus ticket to heaven, He gives us power and authority and life without fear of bullies. Kicking out bullies in the name of Jesus is bringing heaven to earth.

Jesus said the only two requirements are to believe you received the power and authority and then use them. "I will show you my faith by my works" We should walk in power and authority! So when a bully called cancer comes on you and you are walking in power and authority; you will just command it to leave in the name of Jesus and believe by faith it is dead and gone. We give the bullies names like cancer or the flue; but there is really only three big bullies 1) kill 2) steel 3) destroy! Jesus called them devils and spirits of infirmity and He ran right over them. He put them under His feet. Are you getting the picture! We have power and authority and we are commanded to put the devil under our feet. So power up and use that God given authority. Give the devil some hell because he will give you a big dose of it if you let him!

This is the short version of sickness. Jesus and I are writing a longer one where we back up every statement we made with scripture. I know Jesus lives in me and so I can say we and I mean we, Jesus and me!

Jesus, Jenny and I love all of you!!!

Return to Carrabelle Beach

We arrived at Carrabelle Beach and from the minute we pulled in people were greeting us. Jenny seemed to enjoy being there also. I got our camper set up and Jenny and I went for a walk around the campground. We were only here for one week last year; so this year people wanted to say hello and see how Jenny was doing right away in case we were only here for one week again. There seemed to be a joy in the air and the joy picked Jenny up also. Jenny ate really good Saturday and I was sure glad to see her eating. I walked Jenny into the office and the girls greeted her with such love. I mean it was awesome being here again.

I cannot wait to go to church and see everyone there also. Being here is like coming home. I think Jenny knows where she is, we are camped right across from where we were the very first time we came here four years ago. I know from looking at Jenny and being with Jenny, she is excited and I believe the miracle of Jenny's health will happen real soon!

APRIL 7TH, 2013

I thought the love from fellow campers flowing at the campground was great but when we went to church today the love was truly overflowing. The joy at church Sunday seemed like heaven to us and really we are in heaven here. I received so many hugs and words of encouragement at church that I feel like a hero. Even the children were hugging and praying for us. I'm not sure what it will be like to go to heaven but I am pretty sure the people of Christian Carrabelle Center are role models. Thank you Jesus for getting us here and for making everyone so warm and wonderful!

The only down side on Sunday was Jenny seemed overly tired and did not eat much. I assumed Jenny was tired from all the excitement Saturday. I took her back to the camper and held her on my lap. I truly love holding her on my lap, Jenny seems so comfortable and so restful. I have to thank my Jesus for this comfort and the enjoyment of holding Jenny on my lap. In just a short time she woke up and ate pretty good but still not as much as I would have liked. After feeding her I set her on my lap again and Jenny slept some more. As Jenny was sleeping I started thinking about her eating habits and trying to figure out when she started slowing down on her eating.

I looked on the calendar to see when Jenny's last seizure was? On January 29th Jenny had a long seizure and it took her about two days to return to base line. It came to me that Jenny has not been eating regularly since January 29th. Some days she would eat everything I gave her and other days she would hardly eat at all. Another difference I was noticing in Jenny was her drinking. She was not drinking as much either. For a long time Jenny did not seem to recognize a straw until I put some of her drink in her mouth. Now she doesn't seem to recognize the fact I want her to drink. When I put the straw in her mouth she was trying to chew it instead drinking through it. I really miss Jenny's excitement about the food I prepare for her. I know my Jesus will make the food she is getting everything she needs so I just praise Him for this miracle also!!!

APRIL 8ᵀᴴ, 2013

Monday the 8th Jenny and I were sitting under our awning when a man came up and said Hi Bill, now is Jenny doing? She is doing great but my name is Ron, he started laughing and said no wonder I couldn't find anyone who remembered you two. His name was Don and his wife was Val. They had camped here four years ago for one night. Their big motor home was brand-new and had a broken drawer so I fixed it. They have been coming every year since and hoped they would see us again and find out how Jenny was doing. Now we all ended up here at the same time, how cool is that? They are from Canada. Their daughter and five month old granddaughter who are also from Canada flew down to spend a ten-day holiday here with them. Jenny and I are blessed to see them again and then Jesus put some icing on the cake with letting us meet their daughter Leah and her baby girl.

I gave Don a copy of Jenny's book to read and he read it in two nights, I really loved hearing Don's opinion on things because he has such a neat way of expressing himself. Together Don and Val have traveled around the United States four times in four years. They have also traveled to different countries and in their travels they have helped many, many people.

They are like missionaries but without organized church backing them up or as Don put it holding them back. Don talked about their journey and shared how they sought out the back roads in the countries they visited. They would find needy families and fulfill their needs. Don's special way of expressing himself carries over to the special way his big heart expresses his love for mankind and the people that most people would overlook. Jenny and I hold a special place in our heart for them and I know Jesus does too! Jesus I love you and love the good people you put in our path.

In the Bible Jesus refers to life as a vapor of time. Our vapors will be gone like the wind, as Jesus said you don't know from where it came or where it shall go. The cool thing about us vapors is when we get out from behind the television or computer and let the Lord led our wind, no one will know from where we came or where we go but they will know we have been there. Make your vapor count by letting your love of the Lord show. To let your love of Jesus show, simply let your love go to all you met along your journey.

April 11th, 2013

On Thursday I called our three children and told them about the down turn in Jenny. I also called Jenny's birth mom (Rosemary) to give her a little heads up about Jenny. Rosemary lives with her sister and two nieces, Carolyn one of the nieces, answered the phone and immediately upon hearing about Jenny ask me if Jenny was in the camper with me. I said yes. She told me Jenny needed to be in a hospital. I ask her how she could make a judgment call like that in a thirty second conversation. She started screaming so I just hung up the phone. She left me four or five nasty messages, then she left one saying she called adult protection services to report that I was not taking care of my wife.

For the past six or seven years I have visited Jenny's mother Rosemary once a year usually around Christmas so Rosemary could at least see and spend some time with one of her daughters. Rosemary had 9 children and all were in foster homes or adopted. In my heart I felt no connection to Rosemary and I know Jenny never did either.

I did feel as though it was the right thing to do and I considered it an act of kindness to visit her. Rosemary seemed to enjoy these visits with us and I really think Jenny did also. I looked forward to them because there is a joy that comes from doing the will of my Father. The worst part of visiting them was there are five people living together in a small house and they all smoke and there was no ventilation at all. The smoke would get to my throat really quick and I figured it was getting to Jenny's also, so we only stayed about a half hour, and then we would leave. I will say out of a courtesy they did not smoke while Jenny and I were there.

The message from adult protection services was very upsetting. To think after all these years of taking care of my Jenny, I would be under investigation and to think the investigation was triggered by a 45 second phone call is just beyond belief to me. Just the thought of someone taking Jenny away made me sick to my stomach.

April 12th, 2013

On Friday morning I did call Carolyn and ask her not to call anymore. I told her I would call again if there were any changes in Jenny but I did not want her calling me anymore. I said anyone that would try to take my wife away from me doesn't need to call me anymore. She knows Jenny and I have been married for 40 years and she knows I have loved Jenny and for the past 9 to 10 years taken care of Jenny 24/7.

Friday afternoon I did receive a message from the police department in Pierce Township, wanting to know where Jenny and I were because they had been to our old address and no one was home. When I called back they said the investigating officer had gone home for the day and would not be back until Wednesday the 17th.

Upon hearing about his mom, Ronnie left home that night to come see Jenny. He had to work around his work schedule so he drove 14 hours, stayed 5 hours and drove 14 hours back home. It was the best 5 hours I have ever spent with Ronnie. Our time together went so fast. We talked about faith, Jenny's healing, God's will, and living a God centered life. I cried when he left the camper because our time was so short and the camper seemed so empty. Just seeing him here and seeing the love for his mom and I; seeing his concern and knowing he is alright with the decisions I'm making was a wonderful reassurance. Naturally I love our children but it is an awesome thing to have mutual respect.

After Ronnie left I started pondering this journey I'm on and how my children never said a word when I spent literally every bit of money I had trying to pay the house payment and pay the medical bills. They never second-guessed me when I borrowed against the house time and time again to pay the medical bills. They never voiced an opinion when I sold the business and when that money ran out they let me sell the house without any opposition.

When I told them I was buying a $10,000 camper to live in, I know they were questioning my judgment but kept their questions to their selves. Now looking back at those decisions I realize what a blessing it was not to have any interference from them. Even after the first motor home I bought caught on fire and was totaled they didn't voice opposition to me buying another one. They really have held their tongues and just let me be in control of their mother's life. I mean taking Jenny on the road in an old camper probably didn't look like the best decision to them. One big repair bill on the camper or a medical bill could have wiped out my finances and then I could have been a burden to them. I thank my Jesus that didn't happen and I thank my Jesus for their understanding and for their quiet tongues.

On Friday afternoon our friends John and Patty came down from Crawfordsville to spend a long weekend with us. They are so nice and told me not to plan any meals because they had them for us. I know they were shocked that Jenny had changed so much in the last year, but they were so helpful and so loving. I thank God for them being here and for their loving, caring way of helping in any way they could. Jenny and I were so blessed to be with them.

April 13th, 2013

Patty and John and Jenny and I spent a lot of time together and even went to the beach on Saturday. Jenny really enjoyed hearing the waves and feeling the sun. You could tell Jenny loved being by the gulf, because she actually tried to smile. I liked being by the gulf because she was so calm and content. It was good to see Jenny so happy and content listening to the waves. I was hoping Jenny's appetite would pick up after being on the beach that afternoon but it did not.

Jason arrived Saturday night and we had a great visit also. Jason had a hard time looking at his mom. Her face is drawing in and she is so skinny. You can see all her bones; she really is hard to look at. While talking Jason ask me what would I say to someone that has earnestly prayed for over a year to find a better job and has not found one. I was not prepared for his question so I said out loud "Holy spirit how should I answer" immediately I heard the answer. I told Jason the Bible teaches me it is possible for you to pray amiss.

Jas 4:3 Ye ask, and receive not, because ye ask amiss, that ye may consume it upon your lusts.

You see Jesus sees the whole picture and if the things you are asking for do not line up with the word of God or His will, He might not answer that prayer. Then Jesus gave me this example.

Let's say Jason you are super rich and you have a son who asks you for a new corvette on his 16th birthday next month. You have the means to just write a check and your son knows it. You start thinking to yourself; a corvette is way too much car for a 16year old. You desire to make him happy but you realize if he had this powerful car, he might have an accident and hurt someone or worse he could end up dead. You think this car he wants could take him away from me and so in your wisdom you tell him you will not buy him a corvette for his 16th birthday, but when you turn 25 years old if you are mature enough I will buy it for you then.

I believe God is like the wise man that did not buy his son the corvette. You see God sees the big picture also, when we pray amiss we are asking God for something that might take us further from God or we might hurt ourselves with it or we might kill ourselves with it. I believe it is the desire of God to have a personal relationship with us, toys like campers, motor cycles, boats etc. can take our mind off Jesus and become a lust or sought after items that take us away from Jesus instead of bring us closer to Jesus.

When we pray I believe God answers all prayers but maybe the answer is not what we believe Him for so we say our prayers are not answered; when in reality we are just not listening. The boy that wanted a corvette might even be mad at his dad for not letting him have a corvette, but we can see the wisdom in the dad's decision. If we just give God some quite time we will see His wisdom also! To give God quite time is one of the biggest gifts you can give your

Father and in that quite time you will hear form the creator and you will be astonished at what Jesus wants to talk about!!!

The boy Jason knows prayed for a job for over a year. Then when he didn't get a new job he said I'm going to stop praying. That also reveals his heart. You see he was not looking for a relationship; he was just trying on God. If he gets what he wants from God then God is good, but if he doesn't then he said I will stop praying. The only reason he prayed was to get what he wanted. He was not seeking a lasting relationship with God; he just wanted what he wanted form God. Jesus doesn't really ask for much except a little of your time here on earth. Please give God your time and have a relationship that will last for eternity.

When Jason left the camper again I felt emptiness in my spirit and in the camper again. I haven't had time to think about it but I think I had wanted our children to experience the love of the people of Carrabelle and for my friends to meet them. Like the vapor of life, you cannot hold in your hand or capture in a physical place. You can put it in your heart and like the word of Jesus; there you can recall it any time. Seeing both our boys here was a real treat for Jenny and I and having someone on one time with them has blessed my Spirit forever!

I talked to Heidi and she said she made her peace with mom when we were in California in 2010. So she did not come. I know Heidi is really okay with the decisions I am making for her mom and I think she has a peace about that!

April 14th, 2013

Jenny and I went to church; Pastor Don had another great message. Our friends loved on Jenny and prayed for her. A guy named Kim and his grandson (Tyler) earnestly prayed for a long time. In my heart I know Jenny is healed and I know all these prayers are going to be answered real soon.

Jenny's breathing seemed labored and a couple people said the oak pollens were really bad this year. I was able to suction Jenny's nose and that seemed to help her breathing a lot.

Jenny's eating is getting worse. This happened about a month ago also! All I did then was blend her food in a food processor and I was still able to get food in her. It only lasted a couple days and praise God Jenny started eating again. This time I'm doing the same thing but Jenny is not eating much. I have tried her favorite foods and nothing is working. Kim from church brought over some protein powder and Pediatric drink. I'm getting some in Jenny and she seems to like them both. I continue to pray, I ask the Lord to bless our food and to make the amount or the quantity that Jenny is getting the right amount for her. Thank you Jesus for making every little bit I get in Jenny the right amount to sustain Jenny's life until the healing manifests which has to happen real soon.

Hospice

Monday morning we hung out with Patty and John. They took us to a restaurant for lunch and although the food was very good Jenny didn't eat much. Monday afternoon Patty and John went to the gulf to fish so Jenny and I went for a walk in the roadside park across form the campground. We met a really nice lady and talked to her about Jesus for about an hour. She seemed to be very receptive and wanted a book about Jenny. When she left she seemed to have a little more zip in her step, I know I did! I think she said she was 80 years old but very spry.

Jenny and I went back to the camper and I did get Jenny to eat a little and she drank a lot which was very good. The bad news is by about nine o'clock Jenny's discharge from her nose turned green. It made feeding her even harder. That evening I called pastor Don's wife Lisa, who is a nurse, to ask her about Jenny. I told Lisa about the discharge from her nose being green and Lisa said Jenny has an infection and should be on antibiotics. So on her recommendation I took Jenny to the emergency room. Lisa also recommended I think about calling hospice. I told her I would.

On the way to the emergency room Jenny fell asleep and her arms relaxed, they had been folded across her chest for months now. When I got to the hospital which was only about 18miles with no traffic lights, in other words an easy drive. I carried Jenny into the emergency room and the nurses were not busy thank you Jesus. The nurse checked Jenny and reported to the Doctor.

When Dr. Conrad came in he asks Jenny to lean forward and take a deep breath. Naturally Jenny did not respond and I ask the doctor if he knew what Pick's disease was. He looked at me and very true fully said "when the nurse told me I had a patient with Pick's disease, I remembered a couple questions about Pick's disease on an exam I took a 30 years ago." He said I did stop and look it up on the computer before I came in, I just didn't know what stage she was in. Dr. Conrad ordered an x-ray of Jenny's lungs. After checking them he said Jenny has the start of pneumonia and added her lungs are still working at 100% on room air and that was a very good sign. He ordered a shot and gave me a prescription.

When the nurse came in she ask me to roll Jenny on her side so she could give Jenny the shot in the muscle mass, I told her there is no muscle there. After examining Jenny's bottom she said I will ask the doctor if I can give her the antibiotics in her vein.

A little while later Dr. Conrad came back into the room and asked me how long have you been taking care of Jenny? I told him. He said he could admit Jenny for a couple days to give me a break. I said thank you doctor but I want Jenny to be with me in the camper and I really do not need a break.

Pastor Don whom had come to the hospital to be with Jenny and I said Doctor I have known Ron for four years; no one knows how he does it but I can tell you he does not want or need a break. Doctor Conrad then wrote his personal phone number on a piece of paper and said I could call any time day or night and he would do everything possible to help Jenny and I. What a blessing; God never ceases to amaze me. Thank You Jesus for the nice people you put in our path.

The good news was Jenny and I were on our way home and the hospital visit was less than two hours. Thank you Jesus! Dr. Conrad did recommend Hospice be called and so we set up for them to come Tuesday morning.

APRIL 16TH, 2013

Patty and John left on Tuesday morning to go back to Crawfordsville. It sure was nice having them here and it was really nice not to cook all weekend. They have been good friends since we met four years ago. Thank you both for being here and helping so much. I know Jenny enjoyed the beach last Saturday and that would not have been possible if Patty and John didn't help get Jenny there.

Also on Tuesday I had time to think about how nice it was for Doctor Conrad to give me his personal cell phone number. I tell everyone Jenny and I are so blessed and God keeps blessing us with nice people in our lives. It was totally above the call of duty for Pastor Don to come to the hospital that late and it was above the call of duty for Dr. Conrad to give me his personal Cell phone number. Again THANK YOU JESUS FOR THESE BLESSINGS.

Hospice started coming Tuesday morning. Lisa was right, they are a big help and I am glad they are here. They all know I believe Jenny is healed and they also know how God has guided my footsteps all the way along this Journey. If they think I am crazy they respectfully and professionally have kept those comments to themselves.

The antibiotics worked and Jenny is breathing better. Hospice ordered oxygen just in case we would need it. As it turns I put Jenny on oxygen that night for a couple hours. . I really did not know if Jenny needed oxygen but it seemed to relax her and she slept better. I started having her on oxygen part of every day. When nurse Diane came she would check Jenny's lungs and said they were at 96%. Her eating picked up after she started breathing better. And I was able to get three 8oz bottles of pediatric solution and 8oz of insure in Jenny. Jenny ate about half a can of red beets.

That night I unpacked Jenny's bowels and she had a good one. These are big blessings from My Jesus and I love Him for being so good to Jenny and I. Even though Jenny ate well today I am excited because I know Jenny's miracle has to be close. She is very very skinny and bony. It really is hard to look at her so thin and frail looking. I truly cannot wait to see her healed. God has blessed me a million times and more with every kind of blessing possible, I thank you Jesus and Father God for these blessings!!! I am getting really excited to see the miracle of Jenny's healing.

I believe I had to call hospice in for a reason. They checked Jenny for bed sores and could not find any. They were totally amazed. I told them it has to be a gift from Jesus because I cannot stop bed sores form coming no matter what I do here on earth except I do pray against them. Another blessing form my Jesus. Thank You Jesus!!!!

April 17th, 2013

Nurse Diane came and saw me scrubbing Jenny's teeth.

I have to put the sealed end of a sharpie felt marker in between Jenny's teeth to hold her mouth open to allow me to scrub the inside of her teeth. The sharpie pen is soft enough that it does not hurt her teeth and yet hard enough to keep her mouth open to allow me to clean her teeth. I use the sharpie felt marker while cleaning the roof of her mouth. If God did not tell me these tricks I don't know what I would do. Nurse Diane said that was really a cool way to keep Jenny's mouth open while cleaning her teeth.

I totally give all the credit to God for these tips on how to take care of Jenny because I don't think of them on my own. I simply ask God I need to clean Jenny's teeth and the next thing I know I have an answer. I ask the nurse how do people that don't believe in God handle something like this. She said that is easy, they put the sick person in a home and they go on with their lives. To me that is so sad because God has blessed with everything I need and more to take care of Jenny. I know not everyone has the desire to take care of their loved one so I thank you Jesus for the desire to take care of Jenny and for making it so easy.

A bright side to the nurses coming is they check Jenny from head to toe and found no bed sores. Nurse Diane estimated Jenny's weight to be around 60 pounds. She said you must be taking really good care of Jenny for her not to have bed sores. I said I give the credit to God because I cannot stop bed sores form being on Jenny. Nurse Diane said you and Jesus are a team aren't you? I said we are a team and the cool thing is Jesus loves us like no one else can love us!!! Without my Jesus there is no team.

I told Nurse Diane, I have noticed Jenny's feet swell a little during the day but come back to normal at night when they are elevated. She said that is fairly normal and that we should keep checking them, but as long as they come back to normal at night that is good. Again thank you Jesus.

In the afternoon I received a phone call from adult protective agency in Cincinnati. The investigating officer asked about Jenny and where we were. I told her, we have lived in the motor home for over four years. I gave her the names of Jenny's doctors and how long we have been seeing them. She ask me a couple questions, then I told her hospice was coming to the camper every day and she ask for their phone number. I believe when the investigating officer heard that hospice was involved, she was satisfied that all was well and Jenny was getting proper care. I thank you Jesus for telling Lisa to have me call in hospice and for giving Lisa the wisdom to see I needed them.

April 18th, 2013

Linda the human resource lady came and gave me a list of papers I need to have on hand, like power of attorney, medical power attorney, birth certificate, living will and our marriage certificate. I called Jason, gave him the list, told him these papers are all in the fireproof safe and he faxed them to me.

Linda also wanted to know what funeral arrangements have I made. I said none because Jenny is going to be healed by Jesus. I knew what she wanted, so I told her Jenny and I have been organ donors for about thirty-five years now. I showed her Jenny's state ID card with the little mark that designates this. Linda said Jenny does not weigh enough to be an organ donor. Linda said she would find out if the science labs would take her for research?

Linda asks if I wanted Jenny resuscitated, I told her no! She said that was easy. I told her I don't want man to resuscitate her because if they were successful Jenny would still be the same. I said I want Jesus to resuscitate Jenny so she will be healed. Later while talking to Nurse Diane; she said that was a good decision because Jenny is so small the procedure for resuscitating Jenny would really hurt her.

After Linda left I noticed there was some white stuff in the roof of Jenny's mouth, so I called Nurse Diane and she came over and gave me some special sponges on a stick called Den Tips. I cleaned that white stuff out of Jenny's mouth but there was more the next day. I never noticed it before so I guess it is just something to be cleaned every day. I don't know where it comes from.

April 19th, 2013

Jenny seems really tired to day, I have been trying to get her to eat but there doesn't seem to be any interest. Jenny's tongue isn't moving her food to the back of her mouth. I know I have prayed about this before and Jesus has always made it work but this time it seems worse. I am literally watching Jenny shrink. She keeps losing weight. I have blended everything I can think of and Jenny is just not eating. Dearest Jesus please show me what to do. Jesus, You always come through and so I am just going to rest knowing Jenny and I are in your hands. I know for sure Jenny's condition is going to be healed because you say so in your word and that is all I need. Thank You Jesus for your encouragement from years ago when you said "this one is for the glory of God" I believe your word and Jenny's going to be healed for the glory of my Jesus!!!

Nurse Diane came by so I told her, Jenny's tongue will not move food from the front of her mouth to the back so feeding her food is not happening. Nurse Diane said I should probably start using thickener for her drinks to keep Jenny from choking and aspirating. I told her I can get liquids down Jenny without her choking. The problem is food doesn't move to the back of her mouth, how will thickened drinks move back? So I have been giving her liquids and praying they go down the right path and guess what they are. I thank my Jesus they are and Jenny is not chocking and I continue to pray for her tong to start working again, and thank you Jesus it will!

Today while nurse Diane was here Jenny got real fidgety, Diane asked if I thought Jenny was in pain. I said I don't think so; I was at our table doing some paper work for hospice. I stopped what I was doing and went over to pick Jenny up and put her on my lap so we could snuggle up together. Jenny melted into me as usual and went to sleep. Diane smiled and said that is wonderful, it is better than any drug we could give her. Some times while holding Jenny I have a CD playing the word of God. I forget to talk to her because I am listening to the word of God. Jenny will wake up, try to look around and if I don't start talking she gets upset. As soon as I start talking or singing to her, Jenny relaxes and goes back to sleep. God is still blessing me with Jenny recognizing my voice and my touch. How do you thank Jesus enough for all these blessings?

When I have Jenny on my lap I know for a fact I am in heaven! Jenny is the sweetest most delightfully precious present God can give me and He does so every day. Thank You Jesus for these precious moments, I only hope when Jenny is healed that we don't get so busy that we miss this special time with you! Thank you Jesus for these special times with You and for my Jenny too!!! Jesus you always go exceedingly beyond anything I ask for and I thank You!

I know I am blessed to have this awesome relationship with Jesus and I thank You Jesus for every day with you also. Our relationship is so awesome; I believe in you and you alone so I rest even in my circumstances because You alone are the one who can make Jenny eat, drink, swallow, breath, and love! Thank you Jesus for your continual flow of blessings.

When I showed Nurse Diane how I was giving Jenny liquids she told me how to use a syringe to put liquids in the side of Jenny's mouth, she said this new way will help her swallow the liquids faster and better. I tried it and it is working. I can get Ensure and Pedialite down Jenny a lot faster. It is not food but it is something. Thank you Jesus for sending your help through Diane. Yes that is right I am hearing from my Jesus through Diane. I just have to recognize Jesus is talking through the people He is putting in my life right now. Thank You Jesus!!!!

Diane said she was going to Wal-Mart Saturday and asked if she could pick anything us for me while there. I said I need replacement toothbrush heads for our Sonicare tooth brush. I gave her an old brush head one to match the new ones up with. After Diane left I thanked my Jesus again for all the nice people He has put in my life.

When hospice asked me if I wanted someone to bathe Jenny, I told them to come and observe me bathing Jenny so the hospice person could tell me if she had any special helpful tips to make Jenny more comfortable while I bath her.

The girl from hospice came to observe me bathing Jenny, she said you seem to have a joy about you and I said I do because I have been praying for ten years for a miracle and it has to be very close! I mean Jenny has not had solid food or any food for days. To me that is already a miracle of life. Right now she is asleep, barely breathing but I am able to have her swallow liquid. The good news is Jenny is alive and loves to be held by me, if that is not a miracle then what is. What a blessing from my Jesus to be able to love Jenny and hold Jenny and feel her tiny little body get so comfortable by just being held and loved.

She observed and I have to tell you it was the worst shower I have ever given Jenny.

I stood Jenny up in the shower and started to bathe her when Jenny's legs started giving out. I tried to set Jenny on the little seat in the shower but she kept sliding off the seat. I stood her up again and held her up with one hand and at the same time I had to help hold Jenny up with my head against her body to steady her and I finished bathing her in this awkward position. It was truly upsetting to me because bathing can be a problem but this time bathing Jenny became a nightmare. Shortly after I dressed her the girl left and I settled down. Jenny was exhausted and slept for a long time on my lap. I have never had that much trouble bathing Jenny but her legs kept giving away, at least Jenny is clean and I love her clean. I love and praise my Jesus that again Jenny still has no bed sores.

APRIL 20TH, 2013

Jenny woke up kind of happy today. I don't really know how to explain that but Jenny just seems happy. It is such a good thing to see. I thank you Jesus and I praise you that Jenny will drink and eat today. As the day progressed I did manage to get liquids down Jenny and some of our laundry done. We have been in the camper for over a week and Jenny seems to be doing very good today so I took her outside and she set in our lawn chair while I grilled some hot dogs.

APRIL 21ST, 2013

I got Jenny up, gave her a shower, I was able to get some liquid in her and we went to church. Don's message was really great and I needed to hear it. Jenny didn't seem to want to stay in the wheel chair so I took her out and held her. For about a half hour or so Jenny was asleep in my arms and real content, and then she started stiffing out. I could not get her comfortable no matter what I did. I finally just took Jenny out of church and to the car, I just could not get her comfortable in church so we went home to our camper. I held Jenny on the couch and she looked like she found her long lost friend. I held her until she fell asleep.

The rest of the day I spent feeding Jenny liquids. Jenny slept a lot Sunday but when she was awake she did drink some. I prayed to Jesus and talked to Jesus about the decisions I was making about Jenny's body. I wanted her to know I was fully expecting her to live because I knew she could hear my conversations with hospice. I told her it was no different than when we made the decision to donate our bodies to be organ donors 35 years ago. We were not expecting to die right away but we were making future plans. Now because of our circumstances I was making more future plans.

I don't know how much of that Jenny understood but I felt if Jenny understood what my conversations with hospice were about I needed to make it clear these plans were all in the future. One thing I wanted to make crystal clear was my intensions were for her to be healed 100% by my Jesus! I believe Jesus let Jenny understand because Jesus in his word says in all your getting get understanding.

> Pro 4:7 Wisdom is the principal thing; therefore get wisdom: and with all thy getting get understanding.

I believe wisdom is the understanding of wisdom! I believe Jenny did understand all the paper work I had to do for hospice was necessary for their records but I was not making plans for Jenny to die, I was simply going through the formalities of their paper work. I rest in You Jesus to make that perfectly clear to my Jenny and I know since it is a desire of my heart to have her understand; Jenny does understand!!! Thank you Jesus for your perfect love that takes away our burdens. I have Your perfect love in my heart and I know Jenny does too so I rest in it. Praise you Jesus for coming and dying here on earth to restore our ability to have an awesome relationship with you.

As I set here with my little Jenny on my lap, I really want to cry my eyes out. I want to scream my lungs out but I know these things are fleshly desires and would not accomplish anything. These fleshly things would upset Jenny and so I know they really would only make things worse. Again I am thankful that Jenny is here with me and the two of us can still enjoy each other's company. What a blessing form Jesus and what a Joy I have knowing Jesus is the best comforter and the only comforter that can make any sense of this!!!!

APRIL 22ND-24TH, 2013

Jenny spent a lot time sitting on my lap sleeping. I had scriptures playing 24/7, bathing Jenny and I in the word of God. I am so thankful for the word of God in my life. Some of the time while holding Jenny on my lap, as she slept my mind would drift back to the past and how we raised our children. I would think about the good times and want to cry. I thought about our vacations with our little family of three, and how all five of us slept in the tent together. I loved when all of us were together, the love we shared, the time we spent on vacations were some of the happiest times to think about. I talked to Jenny about those times because I didn't want her to forget them. Jenny seemed to listen even though she was asleep for most of those conversations. Jesus you are the greatest and I will never forget your love and how you let me be the recipient of your love flowing through my Jenny.

I admit that crying about old times is probably a sign of giving up. I know that hospice said if Jenny starts crying it is a sign of choking but I believe Jenny was thinking about our past life together and our happiest times, like I was. We have been and are so blessed, our children are all doing pretty well and they are blessing also. I believe Jenny cried during our talks because of the happiness we shared and are sharing right now. Thank You Jesus for all these happy memories and for the Joy they bring, I know Jenny enjoys them also!

On Tuesday I decided to take one of Jenny's books to Dr. Conrad. I loaded her in the car and off we went. Jenny seemed to know she was in the car and going somewhere. Jenny's little face seemed to show some excitement. We drove the 18 miles to the hospital and dropped off the book. There is an IGA store right there also so I took Jenny in the wheel chair and we went shopping. Jenny did great sitting up, I only needed a couple things so we were not in the store long. I set Jenny back in the car and we headed home. I didn't realize it then but this trip really exhausted Jenny, on the way home Jenny fell asleep, in about 25minutes we were home. I carried Jenny in the camper and sat her on the couch, she woke up for a couple minutes, long enough to get her to take a drink, and then she slept for two and a half hours.

All three days were spent feeding liquids to Jenny and she did really well but she continued to lose weight and that was very hard to look at. Her legs were becoming skin and bones, her arms also were skin and bones, actually her whole body was skin and bones. I could not seem to get enough liquid down Jenny to keep weight on her. I ask God to bless what I was getting down Jenny and for God to make it enough. My life, my time, my everything for the past ten years has been spent taking care of Jenny and getting to know Jesus in a personal way. I would not change one minute and I thank you Jesus for every one of those minutes because they are all precious to me also.

A while ago I was talking to a guy going through a divorce. It was an ugly divorce and the things they did to each other, I mean the hate, the hurtfulness, the tearing each other up right in front of the children and them both using the children to hurt each other. To me that was way worse than what I'm going through. I never suffered rejection and hate towards me from my loved one. In fact our love grew through our trial. We never doubted each other, in fact we prayed to stay together, our love stayed intact and in forty years of marriage we are more in love now than anyone I know. I have so much to be thankful for, I have really big blessings from my Jesus and the best part of knowing Jesus is knowing He will never leave us or forsake us. I bet anyone that has gone through a divorce would like a guarantee like that from the love of their life. The cool thing is they can have love like that if they just believe the one that said I cannot lie and if they can believe Jesus meant it!!!

Jenny and I are more blessed then anyone I know. Our love never faltered, we both have known the love of Jesus and there is nothing better than knowing Jesus loves you. Someday soon Jenny will be healed and we will talk about every day of this journey, we will walk, hold hands and know the best is yet to come. I believe Jenny will know everyone we have met along the way. I believe everyone will be totally surprised by what she remembers.

April 25th, 2013

Today Jesus had something special for me because I woke up and had my coffee with Jesus when I heard Jenny stir. That was really good news because the last couple days I have had to wake Jenny up. Today Jenny woke up on her own. Thank you Jesus! I changed her, bathed her and got Jenny something to drink. Jenny always liked orange juice in the morning so instead of her insure I gave Jenny some orange juice. She really did good drinking but fell asleep in between sips. I could gently move her and she came awake again to drink some more.

It is hard to believe it was over thirty years ago when Jenny and I decided to be organ donors. We have that indicated on our driver's license for years and it is on Jenny's state I D. Linda the hospice social worker said now Jenny does not weigh enough to be an organ donor. She checked and found a place called Science Care that might want Jenny's body to study because of the Pick's disease. I know Jenny has always been a giver of everything all her life and so now she will be one after death also. I enrolled Jenny in to the program today. There were some painful decisions to make, it really hurts to be talking about her death and planning her death when I know Jenny is healed. All this planning is not necessary because Jenny is healed and the hospice nurses will see that real soon. I know it is just a formality that we must go through so I do. Kind of like when they ask Jesus to pay taxes and he did to fulfill their formality.

About two o'clock this afternoon, Linda, came for her visit. She had the information about Science Care. We did the interview on the phone. I had three options to consider about Jenny's body.

1. They keep Jenny's body for six weeks and after they harvest what they need, they cremate the rest and send the ashes to me.
2. They keep Jenny's body for three years and then cremate the remains and send the ashes to me. The girl on the phone said they learn a lot more in the three years.
3. They keep the body indefinitely and learn even more.

I chose the third because Jenny was always a 100% giver and I did not want to change the way Jenny lived after her death, so I could have a bottle of ashes.

There were other decisions to be made and none of them were easy. It is hard to talk about these things while Jenny is sitting there, I know she can hear and I believe she understands.

After Linda left I sat with Jenny and told her again how we made the plans to be organ donors thirty years ago, now I am making plans for the future but that does not mean these plans will happen anytime soon.

Thursday was a good day for getting drinks down Jenny and scrubbing Jenny's teeth. Jenny's urine was not as strong and she filled three pampers. Now that was a miracle!

I ask Jesus when I was finished enrolling Jenny why I should even go through the enrolment, because Jenny is healed and it seemed so contradictory to Your word. Then Jesus asks me if you were thirsty would you get up and get a drink of water or would you sit and wait for me to get you one? I said I would get myself one.

Jesus said why would you get yourself a drink of water when you know I am your provider, why don't you just sit and wait for me to get you one? I said because you did provide me with water and you did provide all my needs but I must still use my free will and decide to get the water you provided for me. I said I think I understand Jesus. I am in the world and I understand I have to do things like get my own glass of water. I understand I have to pay taxes and live by the rules of my government. I guess I have to be understanding of the non-believers and play by the rules they set, even when they don't understand the healing power of my Jesus.

Any way Jenny is enrolled in the science care program and those hard decisions are finished. If Jesus decides to take her home to her final reward then her body will not just go in some hole in the ground and rot. The scientist can study it and maybe find a better way to help fight Pick's disease in the future. After 40 years of marriage I can say without a doubt that Jenny would have made the same decision for me and I know she would be right also!

As I sit and hold my Jenny on my lap, I sing to her and I talk to her about our victory we have in Jesus, I quote scriptures that prove Jenny is healed. I love this time Jesus has given me with Jenny. I know I have purpose and purpose gives me a reason to keep going. I know some people think I need a break from care giving but I don't need a break from care giving because my life as a care giver is filled with purpose and purpose gives me joy. Does anyone need a break from Joy? I know I don't!!!

When Nurse Diane came today she said I looked even more joyful than usual. I said guess what I have been doing today? She answered with "knowing you that could be anything" I told her I wrote the requirements. She looked puzzled and ask "requirements for what" Jenny's healing of course. Jesus said you have not because you ask not! So I decided to write the requirements now so when Jenny is healed everyone will know Jesus meet every one of the requirements. Nurse Diane looked at the list and smiled; she then said so you want Jenny to be 95 pound bomb shell and have her long hair back so she can put her hair up in a bun and you can tell her she looks bunderful, like you did when she was young!!!!

April 26th, 2013

Jenny and I had a really great day. Jenny was able to drink a lot of liquid again today. I spent the entire day feeding Jenny with the eye dropper. I got eight ounces of insure in Jenny and eight ounces of Pedialyte and some more cherry juice. Jenny filled her pamper with urine four times today. I was so happy to see her kidneys working so well. Nurse Diane came by to check on Jenny and I told her how hard it was to check Jenny's bowel, you see for years I have manually unpacked Jenny bowel in the shower. So any mess was easily rinsed down the drain. Nurse Diane said she had another call to go on but on her way back she would stop in and show me how to unpack Jenny while laying Jenny on her side in the bed.

A couple hours later nurse Diane came by and unpacked Jenny while on her side in the bed. It was so easy with two people working together. Jenny just held my hand and I talked to her while Nurse Diane worked. Jenny's stool was soft from the cherry juice and it came out real easy. Again I want to thank God for an easy bowel movement and an easy clean up. I also want to thank God for Nurse Diane and all her help. After Nurse Diane left I Gave Jenny a shower and Jenny stood up better then she has for over a week, another great sign that Jesus is bring Jenny back one day at a time. I really don't care if it takes nine more years or even twenty more years to bring Jenny back, I just love the fact that Jenny is coming back and I thank you Jesus.

Jenny seemed so strong today. I held her on my lap for hours and Jenny responds by relaxing so well. Holding Jenny close and seeing her so comfortable is so rewarding to me. I know if I could only find a way to sleep while holding her on my lap I would hold her all night. I love this time Jesus is giving me and when I say Jesus is my best friend I mean it.

Jesus has provided me with no worries about anything. Jesus gives me peace, so I can hold Jenny for hours and not need or want anything. The peace Jesus gives me is like being in a place I have never been in before. The comfort of this peace is unlike anything I have experienced. I believe Jenny is in this peace and comfort also because she falls asleep so easily. These are big blessings for both of us. I wish I could find a better way to describe my love of Jesus so anyone that reads this book could understand it. Jenny and I have been on an assume journey and you know Jesus is my best friend.

Jenny is With Me Now

I got up early with my Jesus today and wrote a lot of this book. I love my coffee time with my best friend and can't wait to see Jenny healed. I'm so anxious for the healing in Jenny. I hear her little sounds right now so I know she is waking up. Thank you Jesus for more improvement today!

I went back to her bed to hold her and talk to her before I got her up but Jenny's breathing seemed different, it was very faint. I hugged and kissed Jenny like every morning, I gently rubbed her face and caress her face like every morning, I took her covers off one at a time so she could acclimate to the temperature of the camper. Then I tried to pick Jenny up and set her on the toilet like I do every morning but this morning it was like nothing I had ever seen before. Picking up Jenny was like trying to pick up a five foot piece of Jell-O without breaking it. This has never happened before. Then I noticed that Jenny's arms were not crossed on her chest and her legs were straight.

I called out to God and asked what is going on Lord? I couldn't believe my eyes; I mean Jenny seemed so much stronger yesterday. I laid her right back in bed, I prayed, I called Don and Lisa the pastor and his wife of the church we attend. I called hospice and they are sending a nurse over. I held Jenny in my arms as I lay beside her in bed but her breathing was so faint. I ask God is the day the day of her healing? I know her healing has to be soon because I never seen Jenny like this before.

Don and Lisa came and we prayed, I continued to stay beside Jenny and hold Jenny; the hospice nurse came. She checked Jenny's pulse and said it was fine. She told me, she had seen patients last for months this way. She called the hospice doctor and he prescribed morphine and some drops to put in Jenny's throat, if she started choking. I apologized to Don and Lisa for getting panicky and I released them to go but thank you Jesus, they wanted to stay. I checked to see if Jenny was soiled and she was not, so I got Jenny up and carried her to the couch and propped her up. I used a den tip to clear Jenny's troth and she stopped gurgling. I tried to get some orange juice down her but she was not awake enough, that is when I realized Jenny's tongue was so small I could see beyond her tonsils. I had never been able to see that far down her throat before. I then rearranged her so I could set her on my lap. Jenny went to sleep and she was breathing better. Praise my Jesus!!!

Don and Lisa went to get Jenny's prescriptions. When they came back they stayed again which was great with me. Jenny was awake but still not able to drink. I was only putting a couple drops at a time in the side of her mouth but Jenny would still choke.

Around four in the afternoon I noticed the roof of Jenny's mouth had little white dots on it. I asked Lisa what that meant. She said it is an indication of Jenny's body shutting down. As I put Jenny back on my lap I noticed her foot was discolored; I thought I had bruised Jenny's foot somehow. Thank you Jesus, that Lisa was here; Lisa said it is another indication of the body shutting down. I kept telling myself the miracle must be really close. Jesus must be going to do it right soon. I had been talking about testimonies all day and I kept thinking Jenny's testimony is going to be the greatest testimony I have ever seen.

I told Don and Lisa about Jenny and I having a special song tilled "I will" by Chuck Girard, I explained how the I will song came to be our favorite song and how we should not even sing that song to each other because Jesus sings the "I will" song to us. The refrain is "I will love you forever, and I will need you forever and I will want you forever till the end of time" in the song Jesus also talks about thoughts He has that are elusive and how these words and thoughts escape him. This really resonates with me because every time Jenny and I go for a walk I sing to Jenny and sometimes the words I sign are so meaningful that I want to write them down, but when I get back to the camper I cannot remember them. Sometimes I would get frustrated at myself because I thought the lyrics where so cool and I wanted to share them. Now I know they were a gift from God and just for Jenny and I at that moment.

After hearing the story about the "I will" song Don said I would like to hear it Ron. I turned it on and because it was already in the

CD player, it came on right away. As soon as the music started Jenny's little face transformed in to a big smile, this was a big miracle because Jenny's face muscles had not worked for months. I was so happy to see her smile and then Jenny started crying at the same time. We all were crying so hard, hearing Jesus sing "I will love you forever, I will need you forever and I will want you forever until the end of time" these are the best words I could possibly hear. I just held Jenny and kissed Jenny and told Jenny I love you too. In just thirty or forty seconds Jenny's smile went away and she relaxed in my arms.

When the song was over, we were still crying when I asked Don to turn off the radio. Don and Lisa and I were totally amazed at this amazing blessing from God. It was truly a miracle, a miracle of love. Then I noticed Jenny was not breathing and Lisa got up and checked for Jenny's pulse and there was none. I wanted to scream "okay Lord I have waited long enough and now is the time" We called for the hospice nurse, she came and pronounced Jenny's death was 7:20 April 27th 2013. I thought to myself it is time Lord all the witness are here please just RAISE JENNY UP!!! The nurse called someone and gave them the time of death. Then she ask for the drugs and even though the drugs she had ordered just hours ago were never opened and they were still sealed she had to destroy them. She left and that was that.

I continued to hold my Jenny on my lap when Kim came from church. Don had let him know. Kim had prayed for one person to be raised from the dead and that person came back to life. So he started to pray his awesome prayer and I just believed. Then as he was praying I heard loud and clear from my loving Jesus; RON JENNY IS WITH ME NOW!!! I told Kim to stop praying and he did. My delightfully precious Jenny is now the bride of Jesus, but she will always be my delightfully precious Jenny too! I'm sure glad Jesus is into sharing!

I believe I was in shock. I knew all my life that I never ever had all of Jenny's love because her first love was always Jesus and anyone that needed a big dose of love from Jesus would receive it from Jenny! Jenny never held back her love just like Jesus never holds back His! Jenny was always there for me, always true to me, and will always love me. I told everyone that saw me with my delightfully precious Jenny, how much I am blessed. I don't understand how she could die, I mean I had so many scriptures that say Jenny will be healed. All I really need to know right now, Jesus has already told me "RON JENNY IS WITH ME NOW" what an awesome six words! I do not understand my Jenny is not healed physically or why Jenny is in heaven right now but I am thankful for the knowledge and faith to know Jesus loves me!

I was happy to hear the hearse was going to take a couple hours to get here. I held Jenny in my arms as we waited; it really felt as though she was just asleep, except her body was cooling down. I just held her closer to keep her warm, I wanted to scream as loud as I could but I knew God was hearing me, I knew God loves me, and I knew that his love will never leave me or forsake me. So I just sat quietly and held my Jenny while I could!!!

I asked Lisa if we should dress Jenny and do her hair. Lisa had told me earlier when her mom died they dressed her real nice and did her hair. Lisa said it was up to me, I selfishly decided to just hold Jenny in my arms. I just could not let Jenny go. Lisa did take Jenny's wedding rings off her finger and set them on the table. The Hearse arrived around 10:30 and at 10:50 I carried Jenny out of the motor home and put her on the stretcher, as they zipped her in the bag and strapped her in I told them not to cover her head and I said if she wakes up on your way to the Science Care place please bring her back!! I put the original book *"Jenny's Wheelchair: How Did We Get There"* inside the bag so they would know who they were studying.

We went back into the camper and Don asked if I wanted them to stay or go. I said I want to be alone with my Lord for a while and they left, but before they did Don hugged me and said "Ron you did nothing wrong," he said "so don't blame yourself." Those were really powerful words and they were really great advice because the devil was already telling me God did not heal Jenny because I didn't deserve a miracle. The devil said I told you, you are nothing. I just kept saying over and over I know you love me Jesus. I know you love me Jesus, I didn't understand how Jenny could die, I mean I had all these promises from my Jesus.

By His stripes we are healed done deal! These were not just words in a book we call the Bible. They are promises from the creator of us all. If you cannot trust His words then what can you trust? I could go on and on about how great my Jesus is and I could quote scriptures that say for sure we are healed. Right now what I need more than anything is time to be alone with my best friend Jesus.

I do know for a fact Jesus loves Jenny and I. I know His words are true and I know Jesus and the Father love Jenny and I and that is really all I need to know. Jesus sees the big picture and I have to trust Him like I say I do, or I will fall into unbelief! I believe Jesus and I will stay in love with Him and I will do His will here on earth. My little Jenny's body was in a hearse being hauled away. All I could do was cry and try to silence the thoughts I was hearing in my head. Jesus is my best friend, I have proclaimed that to all, I'm a son of God, I'm born again, I live with my brother Jesus' Holy Spirit living in me and Jenny and I have the victory. I know we do, but right now it doesn't seem like it!

Watching Jesus change people's lives is the most joyful, uplifting and fulfilling part of my life! Like I said right now I am hearing all kinds of things in my head, which are not of God and I thank you Jesus that someday I will understand. For now I will keep the faith and think on only those things that are of a good report. Jesus is my best friend and best friends don't leave each other when things don't seem to be right.

I love you Jesus is not just for the good times, it is for the times we don't understand. I sat on the couch where I had held Jenny all day. I was so joyful for my Jenny to be with Jesus and I thanked God for Him telling me. Then I saw her shoes on the floor where I kept them and I busted into tears and said Lord please help me! I just sat there and cried; but as soon as I cried the devil was right there knocking at the door to my heart.! I mean I knew Jenny was in heaven but the thought of not having her with me was unbearable. Jenny and I had been together 24/7 for the last ten years.

Then I started to think about Jenny being in heaven, I started to dwell on the fact I knew Jenny was in Heaven and with Jesus. You know the good report Jesus talks about thinking on and I realized the more I dwell on Jenny being in heaven the more thankful I could be! I knew I needed Jesus now more than ever!!! I knew Jesus was with me now more than ever. I could feel my strength coming back. I could feel Joy right here in my camper!!!

The good report is Jenny is in heaven. That is right Jenny is in heaven; the reality is Jenny is in heaven! I called Heidi, Ronnie and Jason, I told them about mom and Ronnie and Jason said dad we will be here in 14 hours. Heidi said she was going to fly into Tallahassee airport and drive down. A little while later I went to bed, but the only way to quiet the devil was to keep saying I love you Jesus and I know you love me and Jenny is in heaven. By dwelling on the good report, Jenny was with Jesus I could not be defeated. I went to sleep knowing Jesus loves me so much He told me where Jenny is!

Saturday, April 27, 2013 will be the end of our forty years, six months, sixteen days and three and a half hours of marriage. This is hard to believe our marriage came to an end and for the first time in over fifteen years I went to bed alone. Jenny and I loved to snuggle up at night but Jenny's body was always too hot for me and I would start to overheat, so every night after our snuggle we would separate but still have to be touching to fall asleep. In 14,799 nights of marriage I bet we weren't apart more than 60 nights. That is an awesome blessing also. I thank you Jesus for loving us so much!!! I thank You Jesus for being my best friend ever!!!

I went to bed by myself and continued to think about all the blessings my wonderful God has given me. Jenny out lived the doctors estimations by four to six years. Even with these extra years I cannot begin to tell you how short life is. Jesus calls life here on earth a vapor of time and He is right. I believe my Jenny is all tucked in and sleeping well in the loving arms of the ultimate, most delightfully precious Jesus, and you know that is where I'm going to sleep someday also. I sure am glad the devil knows his place is a long way from here as long as I believe, because he is doing some pretty loud knocking but I am not listening and I know I am worthy of a miracle, not because of anything I did or didn't do. I am worthy of a miracle because Jesus says so in his word. Take that devil, I'm going to sleep.

After She Left

APRIL 28TH, 2013

I'm up and heading to church but truthfully not without a lot of heart ache. I think again how blessed I am but somehow my little delightfully precious Jenny is not here with me and I think, oh dear God please bring her back, I mean you brought Lazarus back four days after he died. I will not give up hope! Nothing is impossible for my Jesus! I know if I let my guard down even for a moment I will start to cry but I also know Jenny is in heaven with her first love and that brings me great joy. It is almost like a little war going on in me, if I think about not having Jenny with me and make life all about me then I am very sad and want to cry. If I think about how great my Jesus is for giving Jenny her final reward then I have Joy beyond belief!

Church was good and Pastor Don prophesied over me, that this is a new beginning; it is a new awareness of seeing with the spiritual eyes of God. I needed to hear his prophesy and it gave me great comfort, I needed to know I will still have purpose. For years I have ask God for His spiritual eyes and for years I believe I have seen people's hearts but now to see as God sees us is not just a request of mine, it is prophesied! Thank You Jesus!!! THANK YOU JESUS!!!

After church Pastor Don and Lisa took me out for lunch, I hope I was not to quiet, we sure had some great food and I loved being with them. I know I have Jesus and his love will see me through but it is also wonderful to have real people to love on you also. I thank you Jesus for having Jenny and I here at Carrabelle Beach with so many nice people and for surrounding us with their love.

After lunch with Don and Lisa, I went back to the camper. I was only there a short time and Megan called from Canada. She said her sister who does not know Jenny and I except from Megan telling her about us heard a word from God for us. She was not sure what it meant but the word from Jesus was "Jenny had a choice also." As soon as I heard the word from Jesus everything and I mean everything fell into place. All the promises form God are true, God does heal all, God does raise people from the dead, God does answer prayers, God heard every request I have made for the past ten years and he fulfilled them all. Jenny had the right to use her will just like we all do. Jenny chose Jesus and being with Him in heaven is more comforting to me than having her here with me. I only want the best for my bride, even if giving Jenny the best hurts my heart, my heart rejoices for my Jenny. Heaven is such a fitting place for my Jenny to be, I know Jesus has prepared a special place for her!

As Megan and I talked Megan prophesied over me the same words Don said earlier in church. I almost dropped the phone. They were almost the same exact words. I guess Jesus is trying to tell me something. I still have purpose and Jesus will use me because I am available. Thank you Jesus.

About an hour after talking to Megan I received a phone call from Maylin, she is from North Carolina. I told her about Jenny and we both cried. As we continued talking Maylin prophesied the same words Don said. That is three times in one day. I am sure Jesus has work for me and I am sure I will be ready to do it.

Ronnie and Jason arrived Sunday evening and we talked to about 1;00 am. They went to a motel, the next morning we went to subway for breakfast on St George Island and sat at a picket table where Jenny and I had frequented quite often. It was so nice of them to come and visit me. We shared the love of Jenny and Jesus, which was so beautiful. I will admit I cried when they left but it was really nice to have their love and support. I thank you Jesus for their safe trip down here and back and I thank you boys for coming. 28 hours on the road with a small break in between is a long road trip but my boys made it with smiles on their faces, love in their hearts and that is all I needed. Thank you Jesus.

April 30th, 2013

Four days have passed and I realized Jesus waited four day until He raised Lazarus up! I thought Jesus raised Lazarus from the dead in four days so why not Jenny. The fourth day came and went without a phone call from my delightfully precious Jenny and no sighting either. I know all things are possible and just because Jenny's body is in the science lab doesn't mean Jesus won't raise her up. I love you Jesus and I know it was Jenny's will to be with you and I know Jenny made the right choice. I'm just holding on to a little hope that she might change her mind and you would grant her wish. I will say having the knowledge of Jenny being in heaven is the most comforting, peaceful wonderful thoughts I can have.

I thank you also for the knowledge and wisdom to know some big changes are coming for us here in America and it is a real comfort to know no one and I mean nothing and no one, can hurt my Jenny. I Thank You Jesus for the revelations and the wisdom but most of all to know your love will see me through the years ahead.

To sum things up, I am still the most blessed man in the world. I have the love of Jesus in my heart and I know Jenny is with our FIRST LOVE. Life really cannot get any better than that!!! I know that loving Jesus and knowing Jesus is the joy that surpasses all understanding. I know the Joy of knowing Jesus is more than a bus ticket to heaven. I know Jesus said we can bring Heaven to earth and having a relationship with Jesus is being in Heaven right now. Thank You Jesus for your love and for allowing me to be in heaven right now!

May 18th, 2013

Today while having coffee with my Jesus I noticed the original Jenny's Wheelchair book sitting on the couch. I said out loud I don't remember having her book out last night. I felt prompted so I picked up Jenny's book and opened it to page 48; it was not just a random pick. I started reading, the first paragraph says

"I remember in October of 07 Jenny and I were in the living room and Jenny said I want home. I said Jenny we are home. Jenny got frustrated and said I want home. I said Jenny we are home. Then Jenny said I want Jesus home go to. I said you want to go to heaven and see Jesus and Jenny smiled. I said you will but I want you here for a long time. Jenny looked like she understood and just put her head down and said ok."

Today I cried as I read about my Jenny wanting to go home and I realized that was almost six years ago, Jenny asked to go home. Jesus never ceases to bless me and amaze me. I mean Jesus gave me almost six extra years with My Jenny, and now realizing and knowing Jenny had ask to go home in October of 07. Thank you Jesus for all the time you gave me with my delightfully precious Jenny. Thank you my delightfully precious Jesus for making us in your image and likeness. Thank you for forty years six months sixteen days and three hours of marriage to your delightfully precious Jenny. JESUS I WILL LOVE YOU FOREVER UNTIL THE END OF TIME!!!!!

May 20th, 2013

It has already been three weeks since Jenny went to be with Jesus and looking back I have realized what a blessing I received from my Jesus, that is when Jesus said these six words "Ron, Jenny is with me now". How many people never know for sure where their loved one is and yet Jesus blessed me with this wisdom. Those are the most powerful, the most wonderful; the most blessed words anyone could hear form their creator and best friend Jesus. Jesus I love you with all my heart and Jesus I love you forever.

Also as I think back over the years I remember when Jenny and I first started dating and how I literally could not be with Jenny enough. I looked so forward to being with her. I don't remember ever asking God; is Jenny the right girl for me? I do remember asking God can I make Jenny happy the rest of her life? Can we be a joy to each other forever? I had doubts about providing a good home for Jenny but I never doubted our love!

I remember our honeymoon like it was yesterday. I remember when I went back to work after our honeymoon was over. I worked at Proctor and Gamble, the night shift from four in the afternoon until midnight. At midnight, I was always the first one out the door and the first car out of the parking lot every night. After a couple weeks of this some of my co-workers ask me during our lunch break if I thought my wife Jenny was cheating on me.

I was totally surprised by their question! They explained how I ran to the car every night and speed out of the parking lot, made them wonder if I thought Jenny might be having an affair on me. They thought I was trying to catch her in the act. I said guys; I just cannot wait to see my Jenny, she waits up every night to see me too! Those nights were really wonderful, the time we shared our hopes and dreams for the future. Jenny would always have something for me to eat and because it was midnight we didn't have a lot of distractions, like phone calls etc., so we really enjoyed that time together. The men looked surprised by my answer and I think there might have been a little envy also.

I don't think anyone realizes what we have until it is gone. My physical time with Jenny is over and that is so hard to believe, waking up without Jenny next to me is as lonely as life can get. Going to bed without Jenny is the hardest thing I think I have ever done. To live without her is like trying to live without my heart. The void in my heart can only be filled with love, nothing but love, nothing satisfies like the true love of Jesus, that is why I will continue to seek God with all my heart and He is rewarding me with His love!!! I believe I could of laid down my life for Jenny just as Jesus did for us. I believe Jesus made my Jenny's love so special to me and through her love I have tasted a small taste, yes I would say a vapor of the love Jesus has for us. I believe I am loved by Jesus and Father God and although their love is not physical, it satisfies my spirit and our spirit is truly the only place we can experience love.

THANK YOU JESUS FOR YOUR LOVE!!!!

MAY 28TH, 2013

It is really weird to think about Jenny being gone thirty days already. I know Jenny is in heaven and as you know that brings great peace to me. Now I have a different set of problems to contend with. While Jenny was alive no one ever ask how do you do a wheel chair in the camper, or where is your wheel chair lift? No one ever ask those questions because they saw me carry Jenny in and out of the camper all the time. Now without Jenny here those questions are coming up. I thought, most people that read this book would like to know also. My camper is a 1995 motor home without slide outs. The walkways inside are very narrow. This was never a problem for Jenny and I, because I could just carry her to the bathroom or to bed etc. I hope that explains how I got Jenny around in the camper.

I did modify the camper a little. The bathroom door was too small. I originally took it off the hinges and that gave me about another inch and a half of opening. This proved not to be enough so I took out a wall between the bath and bedroom. It was not that big of a deal except for the wiring in that wall. The section I took out had two light switches in it, one for the bedroom light and one for the bathroom light. There was a 12 volt plug for a television and an antenna connection for the television. Also in the wall was a 110 volt receptacle and a floor marker light that is a special light near the floor that you could turn on at night while driving, so some someone could walk around and see where they were going, without the light bothering the driver. Also there was lot of wiring going into the ceiling for lights and the air conditioning unit in the bedroom. If that was not enough there was also an accordion door that would shut for privacy from the bedroom while showering. We did not need that either so it went with the wall.

Jenny's First Love

I decided to write a letter called "Jenny's first love." I wrote it to give to my friends here and to send to friends and relatives. Jenny's last days are so precious and the miracles God performed are so above and beyond anything I could imagine. I can say Jesus loves me, because He proves it to me every day. I am going to insert a copy of the letter "Jenny's first love" here even though you have read some of it in this account.

I find it hard to believe it is already five days since Jenny went to be with Jesus April 27th 2013 at 7:20 pm. I'm in the camper and it seems so empty. I look around and know Jenny will never physically be here again. The camper seems so much bigger. I have given away Jenny's pampers and that freed up space in a cabinet. I looked at my grocery list and could erase about half of it. I know I will have more empty cabinets when I give her clothes away today. We have lived in this thirty-foot camper for four years and two months now and I still had empty drawers while Jenny was alive. I don't know what to do with the space but if I hang onto the memories that come from looking at Jenny's clothes, they bring sadness. So I think I will give Jenny's clothes away; so someone somewhere will have them on and they will bring joyfulness to that person and to all that see them.

I want to talk about Jenny for a moment. About fifteen years ago Jenny started doing some odd behaviors. Eventually Jenny was diagnosed with Pick's disease. How did my Jenny get Pick's disease and where does it come from, is still a mystery. Pick's disease steels your life one ounce at a time. It steels your ability to communicate; it steals your memory, it steals your dignity, in Jenny it stole her walking, her eyesight, her control over bowels and urine and it took the memory of her family!!! Eventually Pick's disease took her ability to smile, to swallow and to breathe. When Jenny left here to go on to her final reward Jenny weighted somewhere between 50 to 60 pounds.

For over nine years I have taken care of Jenny 24/7. A common comment from the beginning of this journey has been "you need to take a break" any book you read about care giving will tell you; "you need to take a break". Two weeks before Jenny died I took her to the emergency room because she had green discharge from her nose. I thank God, Don's wife Lisa recognized Jenny had an infection and told me to take Jenny to the hospital because it was an infection not sinus. The doctor told me, Jenny had the start of pneumonia. He said he could admit Jenny into the hospital for a couple days to give me a break. I told him I don't need a break I just want Jenny's infection cleared up. Pastor Don was there with me and he told the doctor "I have known Ron for four years now and he has never had a break." We were only in the hospital about two hours and Jenny and I were on our way home again. Thank you God for making this a short visit to the hospital. The next day Jenny's infection had cleared up and her breathing was back to normal.

When I called in hospice, the first service they told me about was they could give me a break. I don't know why but I don't need a break. Today I ask my Jesus why I never needed a break, I really didn't know what all this talk about taking breaks was all about. I just knew I didn't need or want one. I decided to go right to my source so I ask my Jesus and Jesus spoke to me and asked me "does anyone need a break from Joy or Love"? Then I understood; Jesus has made care giving to me a Joy and showed me that it is his love. Thank you Jesus and you are right; I don't need a break from YOUR JOY, or YOUR LOVE!!!

Everyone knows I fully expected God to miraculously heal Jenny and the two of us should be together here on earth right now. I thought the joy of Jenny's healing and the miracle of it would be a very strong testimony for the whole world to see and through it we could lead people to Jesus and give Him Glory. I took pictures and had doctor's records and home movies, in other words I had proof of how sick Jenny was, so with all this evidence Jenny's healing was going to be an undeniable miracle. I just stood in faith and didn't look at my circumstances. I know the word of God says He heals all! Even the hospice nurses new my faith was for Jenny's miracle. I professed it to all and never wavered. SO HOW COULD JENNY DIE? Then when Jenny did die I though okay Jesus is going to raise her from the dead, WOW! EVEN A BIGGER MIRACLE!!! As you know that didn't happen.

After the body was hauled away, Pastor Don hugged me and said "you did nothing wrong Ron, don't blame yourself." Those were the best and most powerful words anyone could have said to me because I was already hearing from the devil. The devil was already shouting in my ear, you are not deserving, you never were, I told you you're nothing. My child hood was flashing in front me and memories of sins were bombarding me. I started praying and praying and praying and praying some more!

I ask God to talk to me! Then I realized God had talked to me already. Yes God had used the voice of Don to talk over the devil and tell me I have done nothing wrong. Suddenly I could see how big My Jesus is and how big His forgiveness is! Isn't GOD GOOD! THANK YOU GOD FOR YOUR LOVE FOR JENNY AND I!!! THANK YOU JESUS FOR LOVING ME!!!!

After they left I kept saying I know you love me Jesus. I really don't understand any of this; but I know you love me Jesus. I bet I said it a thousand times, I know you love me and your love is all I need. I said it loud to get over the other voice in my head. I kept saying it until I fell asleep. I know you love me Jesus!!! I know it was the love of Jesus that got me through that night!! Thank you Jesus for loving me so much.

Today I was packaging up some of the "Jenny's Wheelchair" books to send to friends; when Jesus prompted me to send one of our friends a teaching Jesus and I wrote a while ago. I didn't know which teaching he needed so I went to the car; looked into my file and said, "Okay Lord which one?" Jesus said, "FRUITS." Before I put the Fruits teaching in the envelope; Jesus said, "Read it." So I did! It is all about recognizing the Fruits from God and discerning our thoughts. As I read it God was reminding me of the Heroes teaching also. Both talk about motive and how motive affects the outcome of your prayers and actions.

I was reading the Fruits teaching when Jesus spoke to me again! Jesus asked, "What was your motive for marrying Jenny?" I said, "To bring her joy, to provide for her and together for us to build a love so strong it would hold us together no matter what life brings.

We wanted a love that will last the rest of our lives, and as you know Jesus heard our prayers and answered them.

When I met Jenny, she was in a foster home and I wanted to give her security and a place to live. I wanted to watch us grow together, love together, be together, to have children and watch them grow. I wanted to protect Jenny from all harm and be with her always!

Then Jesus asked me, "What was your motive for the last ten years while you took care of your Jenny." I said, "To bring her to a place of your healing and to make her as comfortable and joyful as possible until her healing manifest, here on earth." I said, "You know Jesus I wanted her to see how you changed me from flesh that should need a break, to spiritual that never grows weary. I wanted Jenny to see how your love for us transformed us into the image and likeness of YOU! I wanted her to see the new me, you made me into. I wanted Jenny to have coffee with you and me, Jesus! I wanted Jenny to be free of Pick's disease. To smile, to love, to laugh, to run, to have and know her family again, and most of all for us together to share you Jesus and Your love to the world!"

Then Jesus said, "Did you succeed in your goals?"

Just then I realized all the goals and more are met and Jenny is more joyful than I could have made her here on earth, Jesus showed me Jenny is safe in His arms now and no harm can come to her ever. If Jenny was healed 100% here on earth she could not be as joyful as she is right now. Nothing we could ever do here on earth could even come close to the joy of being face to face with my Jesus. Jesus showed me all my goals are achieved! We, that is Jesus, Jenny and I have the VICTORY! Yes Jesus made all the goals and more come true. THANK YOU JESUS FOR SHOWING ME ALL YOUR PROMISES ARE TRUE!! I LOVE YOU TOO!!!

The night Jenny went to be with Jesus, Kim Allen came over and was praying for Jenny to come back from the dead. As He prayed I heard Jesus say, "Ron, Jenny is with me now" I told Kim to stop praying. The next day I heard from Megan (a friend in Canada) that God told her sister during the night to tell Ron "Jenny had the right to choose also". As soon as I heard those words I remembered Pastor Don telling me about his mother and how he released her to be with Jesus. His mother cried and said, "You know Don I will always love you, but I love Jesus more than anyone on earth." I know Jenny loves me and I know Jenny's first love was and always will be Jesus. Jenny very intelligently and with full mental capacity chose Jesus and I know she made the right choice!

At some point that night I started telling Don and Lisa about the "I will" song by Chuck Girard. This song was our favorite song. The refrain is "I will love you forever, I will need you forever and I will want you forever until the end of time!" I know now it was the Holy Spirit talking through Don when he ask me to play the song. The CD was already in the radio so I turned it on and when the music started Jenny's face lit up. Jenny suddenly smiled at me and started crying, she was able to hold her smile for at least thirty seconds and we all started crying, I told Jenny I love you over and over. When the song was over I had Jenny on my lap, in my arms, and holding her as close as I could! Then I noticed Jenny was not breathing and Lisa checked and there was no pulse. Jenny went home to be with Jesus, her first love! Pastor Don and Lisa where there with me and I thank God for them being there! They witnessed Jenny's last act of kindness and Jesus blessed me with knowing even Pick's disease could not steal Jenny's love for me!!! I know Jenny is with Jesus and that is as sweet as life can get!!!

Everything I prayed for came true and all though my hopes were for a physical healing and for us to be together I know Jenny's choice should be and was Jesus and I know Jesus has always been; Jenny's first love!

A lot of people have said Jenny was healed in heaven and I want you to know I don't agree with that. I mean I don't think there are any hospitals in heaven. Jenny's spirit was never sick and so Jenny's spirit never needed healing.

I thank you Jesus for the "I Will" song and the miracle of Jenny's smile; that came forth so big and bright, to let me know how much Jenny loved me! I thank you Jesus for the tears form Jenny's eyes that showed me how much her heart wanted to stay! I want to thank you Jesus for letting me hold Jenny on my lap and letting her know how much she was loved right up to the last second. Jesus you are so beautiful to me!!!

I thank you Jesus for telling me that Jenny was with you and putting to rest any doubt. I thank you Jesus for telling me that Jenny chose You and for showing me how all my dreams for her have come true. I thank You Jesus for teaching me; the most important relationship anyone can have is with You. I thank You Jesus that Jenny did not need any narcotics, or drugs of any kind. Jesus; you are Jenny's first love and You will be forever; my first love too!!!

Jesus gave Jenny the most beautiful transition anyone could ask for! Jesus showed me all His promises are true and being true to his word Jesus allowed Jenny her desire to be with Him. Today I am so secure knowing Jenny is in His arms and He is telling Jenny how much she is loved and I can rest knowing I have this awesome relationship with My Jesus too! I know the word father means to come forth from and the word God means the source of life. I know Jenny is with her Father whom we all came forth from and is the source of life! That is the peace Jesus promised that surpasses all understanding and it is the Joy that will propel me to continue on; until Jesus calls me home.

Being with Jesus is heaven and heaven is knowing Jenny is in the loving arms of My Jesus!!! "JENNY'S FIRST LOVE" thank you Jesus, I love you too!!!

My delightfully precious Jenny went to be with our precious Lord April 27 2013 at 7: 20pm! Jenny's leaving was her choice not the work of Pick's disease! Praise you Jesus for such a special and fitting transition! Jenny never showed any pain, had no shortness of breath and was in my arms until the last second!!! These are really big gifts from my delightfully precious Jesus!!!!

A couple years ago while having coffee with my best friend Jesus; I ask Him "Jesus I always call my Jenny precious but I would like to know how you refer to Jenny?" Immediately I heard the words "delightfully precious" I thought I agree, Jenny is totally delightfully precious to me too!!!!

Thank You Jesus for this awesome Journey, for wisdom to know how to tend to Jenny, for understanding and grace you flowed through Jenny to me and for the faith to be in your presents continually!!! Thank you for the hope that I too will come home to see you and be with you someday. I guess you get the picture, I am thankful for my forty years, six months, sixteen days, and three hours of marriage to my most delightfully precious Jenny! It just was not enough, but then I guess it was!! My delightfully precious Jenny is with My delightfully precious Jesus!! I will remain forever thankful to you Jesus and to all that helped us along the way!!!

To sum things up Jesus talked to me six times, in less than 24 hours.

- First, was with the "I will song to show how much Jenny loved me and wanted to express that love!"
- Second, when Jesus said "Jenny is with me now"! So I knew not to keep trying to raise Jenny from the dead.
- Third, when he had Pastor Don say "you did nothing wrong." The devil is knocking every day with what I could perceive as something I didn't do right but I put Jesus in my mind and don't give those thoughts time to raise any doubt.
- Fourth, when Megan called to say "Jenny had a choice also"! That is right, Jenny had a choice and she rightfully chose Jesus!
- Fifth, was when three different people prophesied, on Sunday. Pastor Don prophesied in church; then Maylin form North Carolina called me right after church and said almost the exact words Don used and then Megan called form Canada with the exact prophesy Don had!
- Sixth was going on all my life and continues still today! Jesus told me how much He loves us and He is still telling me How Much He Loves Me today. Because of His love I have Purpose and peace knowing I did nothing wrong! Jesus gave the desire to take care of Jenny right to the end and then Jesus fulfilled that desire and allowed Jenny to be in my arms smiling and crying right up to the last second of her life!!! I am the most blessed man on earth; I have relationship with my Jesus and life cannot get any better than that!!!! Jesus is my best friend and He proves it every day!!!

To me love is the most powerful force on earth. I can say that without any reservations because Jesus said He came to show us the Father and all Jesus did was show us love every second of His life. Jesus forgave all and loved all through that forgiveness. So I know without a doubt that His love will see me through and carry me on to new days filled with His kingdom work! Jesus is our example and I will follow Him no matter what the cross looks like.

Ron's First Love

Jesus and I wrote another paper about my thoughts thirty two days after Jenny passed. Wow it has been 32 days already, Jenny is in heaven with my Jesus and I am so Joyful for her! I have been trying to figure out what the proper response is to Jenny's death. I mean people that knew Jenny and my relationship will never question my love for Jenny. Now with Jenny at home with you Jesus, people I meet do not get to witness our love flowing through and between us. I don't know if this is imagined or not but some people seem to question my love for Jenny when they see me Joyful so soon after her death.

Right after Jenny passed I tried to stay busy and found that was not the answer. I slept more those first couple weeks, than I ever have slept. Sleep was not the answer. I went across the street to the park where Jenny and I have walked and prayed for people to be healed for four years now. I wanted to see if I could find someone to pray for, there was one person in the park so I approached her and we did have some good conversation about Jesus. She even came to church that Sunday. I just knew in my heart I was not quite ready to pray for others just yet. So I went to my source and ask God "where am I missing it?" Jesus said "seek you first the Kingdom of God!" I thought you're right as usual Lord I haven't been seeking you the way I should be. I started seeking God, not for sympathy or answers but for our relationship again.

I thank God I have a relationship with Him. When I started really seeking God full time again I really started receiving healing to my heart and I am Joyfully announcing to all; I have the Joy of the Lord back!! It might be 30 years before I see Jesus and Father face to face but it will happen and it will be even a bigger party because I know they will wait until their timing of my going home is their perfect timing, like they did my Jenny. That is correct; I believe Jenny's going home to be with Jesus was the right perfect timing of my Jesus!!! Thank You Jesus for your perfect love and for letting me see your perfect love that protects Jenny forever!

When you seek Jesus first in your life you will have the Spirit of Joy dwelling in you. Jesus said the Joy of the Lord will be our strength. I have Joy because Jesus gave me confirmation as to where Jenny is spending eternity, not that there was any doubt, but because Jesus loves me so much He removed all the temptations from the devil to have me think differently! I am joyful because I know Jenny is in the loving, safety of my Father and Jesus. I am Joyful because I know absolutely no harm can ever hurt my Jenny again. I am Joyful and I give thanks to my Jesus for taking Jenny home to be with Him. That's right I am giving thanks to my Jesus for taking Jenny home, I realize nothing and no one can even come close to the Love Jenny is experiencing right now. With the knowledge of knowing Jenny is home with Jesus "Her first love", how can I not be joyful?

Even if I live here on earth another 30 years it is just a blink of an eye to eternity. I obviously have more work to do here on earth and with the Holy Spirit dwelling in me, I am up for the challenge, whatever that challenge is! I have the Holy Spirit living in me, dwelling in me, and I hear the voice of my God guiding me every day. If that doesn't bring Joy in your life you must be clueless.

I have purpose and Kingdom work to do, I have the power to heal the sick flowing through me, I have the power to raise the dead working in me, and the power to cast out devils and power to set people free. These are real powers and in the name of Jesus I will watch the Holy Spirit perform these miracles.

Jesus is more real now after Jenny's passing then before her passing. Dan Mohler once said in one of his talks, trials to our faith will come our way, but the trial the devil is using to try to break you with; (destroying your faith) he (the devil) runs the risk of that trial making you (building your faith).

For example; after praying and believing and standing in faith, that Jesus would physically heal Jenny, I believe the devil thought he could use Jenny's death to break my faith in Jesus. I'm not saying the devil killed Jenny, I don't believe the devil has that power, unless we give him the power. I'm saying the devil is an opportunist and being an opportunist he saw an open door when Jenny went to heaven and he jumped at the chance to tell me Jesus did not heal Jenny because of some unworthiness on my part.

It has been 32 days since Jenny went to be with Jesus and the devil is still trying to tell me it was my fault Jenny was not healed. When I was young I used to listen to the devil when he told me I was a slow learner, and so I thought I was a slow learner. I used to listen when the devil would tell me I was too stupid to get good grades in school. Do you get the picture I'm trying to paint? The devil will tear you down and make you feel worthless, if you let him. The devil will destroy you if you listen to him.

I was reading this letter to Pastor Don and he gave me this verse, I think it is so appropriate to show or explain the meaning I am trying to convey. Thank you Don and thank you Jesus for the friends like Don in my life.

1Pe 5:8 Be sober, be vigilant; because your adversary the devil, as a roaring lion, walketh about, seeking whom he may devour:

Pastor Don was very quick to point out that the devil is not a roaring lion, the scripture says as AS, as in as, so do not give the devil any power, the devil has no power over your life except the power you give Him, when you start listening to him. The scripture says the devil walketh about seeking whom he may devour. See the words may devour, the devil cannot devour you unless you listen to him and give him the power or permission to devour you. That is why I will focus on Jesus and keep my mind on Jesus and the perfect love of Jesus that cast out all fear. Like I said the devil was talking to me and the devil will talk to you, that is why we must learn to DISCERN our thoughts.

I mentioned Jesus talked through Pastor Don to me a couple times. Even though I trust Don to be a great friend and know his heart is to hear from God and to flow God's word on to me, I still have to use discernment. I believe discernment is one of the biggest and best gifts the Holy Spirit can give you. Lord I thank You for the gift of discernment.

The perfect love of Jesus is knowing the truth that I am a child of God, I am loved by God, yes Jesus loves me, Jesus never created a slow learner or anyone useless! I am born again, so I am born into the image and likeness of God. I am no longer restrained by the original sin of Adam, I am free to be who God created me to be and

I am free to love Jesus with all my heart. We all have purpose and if we really get the understanding that Jesus died to show us how much He loves us and Jesus died to restore our relationship to Him, we will all be in a better place and the world will not be able to hurt us ever.

Just as when I was younger and heard the voice of the devil talking to me, destroying me ever so slowly, I now hear the words of Jesus saying I created you in my image and likeness. The image of God is love and the likeness of God is to share the love of Jesus to all you meet. I get up in the morning and I'm excited, I'm ready to share the love of Jesus, I am ready to be the love of Jesus to all. That makes me Joyful no matter what my circumstances are.

When Father God Took Lazarus Home

Can you imagine Jesus saying and praying and asking His Father "why did you let Lazarus die? Why did this happen? Why was I not there? Why why why?" Come on now those why words would sound stupid coming out of the mouth of Jesus and they should sound just as stupid coming out of the mouths of believers. Jesus the man was just a believer like us, tempted just like us, and at times heartbroken just like us.

Yes the devil will be right there from time to time to try to talk you out of sharing God's love, but you and I do not have to listen to him. We simply have a choice to make! I do not have to fight the devil I just simply trust in the love of God, you too can trust in God who sent His Son to show us His love. Any time you hear a voice in your head that belittles you, tears you down or says you are not worthy, check your source, Jesus said He will never leave you or forsake you, and I believe Jesus.

Believe in Jesus and trust in Jesus and watch the devil run to find greener pastures, who are the greener pastures for the devil, anyone that doesn't know the love of Jesus: that is someone that has not meet YOU yet. YOU are alive to Show the love of Jesus and to BE the Love of Jesus to the world and with the love of Jesus YOU can make the devil find a completely different world to do his dirty work in. When you show people love and when you are the walking, talking love of Jesus I know people will notice and they will want what you have.

We are to be the representative of the love of Jesus; Jesus will flow through you to others. When people see the love of Jesus in you they will want what you have and you can freely give your love and not worry about rejection because yourself worth comes from God who will never reject you. Can you even imagine Jesus worried about rejection; Jesus knew the love of our Father so He never worried about rejection and neither should you. I know I am loved, do you?? Jesus NEVER made life about himself.

Yes Jenny died and for a week or two I was very sad, yes I have been sad to the point of crying, I realized every time I cried, I was making life about me and life is not about me. When life becomes all about me the devil can get his foot in the door to my heart and it is very hard to shut a door when someone's foot is in it. Never make life about you or yourself because selfishness has nothing to do with God. Selfishness is sinfulness to the max, selfishness is totally ungodly because God is love and in the Bible love is actually translated as Charity. Jesus said "but the greatest of these is charity"

1Cor 13:13 And now abide faith, hope, Charity, these three; but the greatest of these *is* Charity.

Charity (love) has nothing to do with selfishness. Thanks to Jesus there is so much of God's grace to see us through and the love of God is stronger than any grief.

When I decided to give Jenny's clothes away, I folded each piece and I cried as I remembered her wearing each outfit. There was real pain in my heart and there was a voice in me that said hold on to the clothes, it's all you have left. I placed them in the bags and carried them to the car and I cried the whole time. I actually wanted to hold onto the pain for some reason, (who was I listening to?) I wanted to feel the loss so bad, I wanted the hurt to explode my heart. I wanted to be with my Jenny!!!! Do you hear all the I's in that paragraph? This paragraph is all about me and that is sadness to the max.

I drove to the church that would find needy people and give them Jenny's clothes. As I pulled away from the church I felt as though a big burden was lifted. I realized all the pain from looking at Jenny's clothes was gone and wanting my heart to explode was gone also. I realized I was no longer making this all about me and I realized I had no need for sympathy. I realized when life is all about yourself, pain can be your friend because people will feed that pain by saying "oh look he is so hurting, or his pain is the worst I ever seen!" I can tell you sympathy is nothing but a big zero and zero times anything is still zero! That is why anyone who needs sympathy will always need more sympathy!

Please don't get me wrong, Jesus showed compassion toward others and Jesus sent us a comforter (the Holy Spirit). The difference between the good compassion of Jesus and the devils counterfeit sympathy is the compassion form God lifts you up and makes you sore on the wings of angles. The compassion from God moves you past the hurt and pain of the problem or loss of the loved one. Where the counterfeit (the devils sympathy) just brings more sadness and attention to your own selfish needs. I will not go there; instead I will dwell on the fact that Jenny is in the loving arms of my Jesus! I do not need sympathy when I think of Jenny being with Jesus! I will dwell on being like Jesus and doing whatever he has for me to do today. I do not need sympathy because I have purpose! Thank You Jesus!!!!

Jesus gave me an example of compassion verses sympathy! If your mom went into the hospital and the doctor said, to save her life we must cut off your legs. A minute later, In walks someone from a church and says can I pray for you, he prays; Lord let the doctor do a good job, let the recovery be swift and help her find the resources to buy a great wheelchair. You thank Jim for the beautiful prayer. An hour latter another guy form a different church walks in and ask to pray for your mom. He prays Lord in the name of Jesus I command this spirit of infirmity to go! I command this woman to get up and walk! Then he grabs her hand and says get up and walk now! I bet everyone would say the sympathy of the first prayer would be received just like the doctors report. The second prayer, the prayer of compassion would be rejected and people would ask who does he think he is. They would probably say if he comes back don't let him in he just upset mom.

I ask who is more Christ like the first or the second person to pray. I tell you the devil has turned the action of compassion into sympathy and if your mother has her legs cut off and she lives, you will give the credit to the doctors. I don't see anywhere in the Bible where Jesus ever prayed for the doctors to do a good job.

Read these verses from Peter and see real Hope Faith and Charity can be and how Hope, Faith and Charity replace the need for sympathy

> 1Pe 1:3 Blessed be the God and Father of our Lord Jesus Christ, which according to his abundant mercy hath begotten us again unto a lively hope by the resurrection of Jesus Christ from the dead,

We should bless God all the time because of His abundant mercy. It is His mercy on us His creation that gives us a lively hope for eternal life through the resurrection of my loving Jesus Christ. I have a lively Hope and trust that Jesus will dwell in me forever. I have a lively Hope that the same Spirit that raised Jesus from the dead (defeated death) lives inside me. With blessings of a lively hope who needs money or earthly junk. I am the most blessed man I know. Jesus is alive and well, dwelling inside me and I love our relationship.

> 1Pe 1:4 To an inheritance incorruptible, and undefiled, and that fadeth not away, reserved in heaven for you,

You see how that makes giving Jenny's clothes away the right thing to do. We have an inheritance that is incorruptible and undefiled, my inheritance is knowing Jenny is in the loving arms of Jesus. Knowing Jenny is in heaven is incorruptible and undefilable and that is true Joy now! That is heaven now! Our inheritance is reserved in heaven if we give up the earthly desires now. So why should I hold on to the sympathy that comes from looking at her clothes and the sad memories they bring.

I have a treasure chest of great promises God gave me to hold on to and they bring great Joy, they bring great hope and they bring the love of my Jesus home to me now! I have the inheritance of the love of my Father and the love of my Jesus and most of all I have it right now through the Holy Spirit that dwells in me now! Jesus said to bring heaven to earth and I have heaven right now! If I hold on to earthy junk I will miss my heaven now! I will miss my comfort now! I will miss God's plan for my life and that would be a big tragedy! I will never trade God's love for the momentary satisfaction of someone's sympathy or earthy junk!

> 1Pe 1:5 Who are kept by the power of God through faith unto salvation ready to be revealed in the last time.

We are the kept and by the power of belief in God through faith we will receive our salvation and Jesus can reveal it to our loved ones here on earth. Thank You Jesus for revealing Jenny is in heaven!! There is nothing on earth that can come close to the freedom and peace that comes from a heart to heart relationship with God. I will not let anything come between my heart and the heart of my Jesus, I have His Holy Spirit in me and I love it!

1Pe 1:6 Wherein ye greatly rejoice, though now for a season, if need be, ye are in heaviness through manifold temptations:

Yes I do rejoice, yes I am rejoicing and yes I am in a season of heaviness from the loss of My Jenny but I will resist the temptations to be depressed (in need of sympathy) for I am useless to everyone when I only think of myself. I can guarantee you anyone that is depressed is only thinking of what they want in life and even if they got 99% of everything they wanted they would still be depressed. I refuse to let the loss on my Jenny dictate my feelings! I refuse to let my circumstances dictate my Joy or lack of it. I will rejoice knowing I have a loving brother who is my best friend!!! I am rejoicing in the love of my Jesus and I rejoice in our personal heart to heart relationship.

1Pe 1:7 That the trial of your faith, being much more precious than of gold that perishes, though it be tried with fire, might be found unto praise and honor and glory at the appearing of Jesus Christ:

Life is a trial of Faith, but thank you Jesus I am more precious than gold and I will be found to be praise worthy and like gold, I will not smell like the fire that purifies me; I will give honor and glory to God who gave me the faith to use in times like these. Faith is like love, it is to flow through us not just to us. So you go God, I am a believer and signs and wonders will follow me wherever the Two of us go! Praise you my Jesus and my Father God for all your sacrifices and for giving your Holy Spirit to anyone that asks for Him!!!! That is right the Holy Spirit is there for anyone that seeks a relationship with Jesus. Notice I did not say He is there because you went to church, the Holy Spirit is there for anyone that spends time seeking Him. Talk to God about what God needs done today and He will tell you, I have the Joy of my Jesus not the momentary happiness of the world.

Jesus, Your word says you are no respecter of persons and believing in your word, I believe you will give your Holy Spirit to anyone that asks for it. What a gift to give away, your word says freely you receive and free you give. I know everyone can have Him, if they just believe, the problem is most people want to use your gift to just have a better day for themselves. Their faith is for a blessing daily, I hear people pray for momentary things, like money, a better car, a bigger house and their children are watching television all day while both their parents are out working two jobs. Our prayer should be what we can do for you Jesus, Yes our prayer should be to do the work of the kingdom, and forget the junk of this world and let's spend time with our children. I mean if you do not show your children who Jesus is; then who will? I know television will not!!!! I know Jesus trusted you with temporary guardianship of His children and it is up to you to show them Jesus in word and deed!

Dearest Jesus I pray for more selflessness in my life. I pray that I never get in your way. That is I pray that whatever you want done today I will give you the time you need to do it. I pray to be an example of your love; actually, I pray to be your love! Thank You Jesus for being love and showing that love is the supernatural force that moves mountains. Thank you Jesus that we can and will move some mountains today and together we will cast them in to the sea like your word says. Thank you Jesus I have compassion and not sympathy to give to others. Thank You Jesus for Your good example for all to see! Thank You Jesus, You love me!!! Thank You Jesus that your love is purifying me and renewing my mind daily, so I can walk boldly knowing You are who I want to be!

I know you know by now but I'm going to say it any way, Thank You Jesus for being my best friend and forever you will be MY FIRST LOVE.

Everyone that knows me knows I have my coffee with Jesus every morning and they know I communion with Jesus all day through. The other morning a friend, Maylin was telling her little boy, who ask her what she was doing, at five o clock in the morning? I'm having coffee with Jesus and then she ask her little boy if he wanted to join her in conversation with Jesus? The little boy excitedly said yes but I think Jesus would like some scrambled eggs. I honestly love the honesty of little children.

Jenny, Ron and Jesus will love you forever until the end of time, so be blessed and seek the Lord with all your heart.

I pray for you to have your best day ever by having some heart to heart time with Your best friend and mine, Jesus.

P.S. I think Maylin's little boy is right! Jesus would like some scrambled eggs with His coffee; so I'm going to make Him some.

A Closing Thought

I believe it is time to close this book on Jenny's life. I know Jenny's little life has made an impact on others because Jenny is a 100% giver of love, just like Jesus. I hope and pray that after reading this book you are inspired to know Jesus on deeper level and have a real relationship with Him! Truly life has no meaning without Jesus. Closing this book is really hard for me; it is like ending Jenny's life again!

The good news is Jesus has inspirited me to write another book about Jenny. This one will start with the beginning of Jenny's life. Over the years I have collected information about the younger years of Jenny's life in the foster homes. This was not easy because Jenny never talked much about those years. I think what I do have will be worth sharing and hopefully help others to be overcomers like Jenny was. I do know Jenny was more than a wife to me; Jenny was an inspiration and I thank God for these wonderful years together. Yes thank You Jesus for this time with your delightful precious Jenny!!!! I love you Jenny and look forward to coffee time in heaven with you and Jesus and Father God!!!! Thank You Jesus for making Jenny your bride!!!! Thank You Jesus for these precious years with YOUR JENNY!!!!

Jesus and I love you forever, until the end of time!
Like I tell everyone, for a little bit of heaven call
(513)377-1727
www.CoffeeTimeWithJesus.com